CATHOLICISM IN A PROTESTANT KINGDOM

STUDIES IN MODERN HISTORY

The recent proliferation of controversy in many areas of modern history has had common causes. The revision of assumptions and orthodoxies, always professed as the role of scholarship in each generation but seldom really attempted, has increasingly become a reality. Historians previously unused to debating their major premises have been confronted by fundamental challenges to their subjects – the reconceptualisation of familiar issues and the revision of accepted chronological, geographical and cultural frameworks have characterised much of the best recent research. Increasingly, too, areas of scholarship have passed through this phase of conflict and recasting, and works of synthesis are now emerging in idioms which incorporate new perspectives on old areas of study. This series is designed to accommodate, encourage and promote books which embody the latest thinking in this idiom. The series aims to publish bold, innovative statements in British, European and American history since the Reformation and it will pay particular attention to the writings and insights of younger scholars on both sides of the Atlantic.

Catholicism in a Protestant Kingdom

A Study of the Irish *Ancien Régime*

C. D. A. Leighton

St. Martin's Press

DA
948
.A2
L38
1993

First published in Great Britain 1994 by
THE MACMILLAN PRESS LTD
Houndmills, Basingstoke, Hampshire RG21 2XS
and London
Companies and representatives
throughout the world

A catalogue record for this book is available
from the British Library.

ISBN 0–333–58666–2

Printed in Hong Kong

First published in the United States of America 1994 by
Scholarly and Reference Division,
ST. MARTIN'S PRESS, INC.,
175 Fifth Avenue,
New York, N.Y. 10010

ISBN 0–312–10301–8

Library of Congress Cataloging-in-Publication Data
Leighton, C. D. A.
Catholicism in a Protestant kingdom : a study of the Irish *Ancien
Régime* / C. D. A. Leighton.
p.   cm.
Includes bibliographical references (p. xxx–xxx) and index.
ISBN 0–312–10301–8
1. Catholics—Ireland—History—18th century.   2. Church and
state—Ireland—History—18th century.   3. Ireland—Church history.
I. Title.
DA948.A2L38   1994
941.507' 08822—dc20   93–5866
                                                              CIP

And a' the names in History mean nocht
To maist folk but 'ideas o' their ain',
The vera opposite o' onything
The Deid 'ud awn gin they cam' back again.

Hugh MacDiarmid, 'A drunk man looks at the thistle'

Contents

Acknowledgements

My thanks are due, in the first place, to the master and fellows of Corpus Christi College, Cambridge, the abbot and community of Holy Trinity Abbey, Kilnacrott and the fathers and brothers of the Province of SS Peter and Paul of the Congregation of the Most Blessed Sacrament. Were it not for the generosity of these bodies, the present work could not have been completed. My thanks are also offered to the University of Chicago, the Maryvale Institute, Birmingham and the Cambridge community of the Institute of the Blessed Virgin Mary.

The individuals who have assisted me in various ways – by reading drafts, with discussions, references and simple kindness – are too numerous to list. Some, however, should be mentioned. First among these is Dr Brendan Bradshaw of Queens' College, Cambridge, a scholar who displayed rigour and thoroughness and a man who displayed patience and kindness. I must also mention Professor R. Vincent Comerford, Professor Donal Kerr and Dr Jacqueline Hill of St Patrick's College, Maynooth, Dr T. J. Hochstrasser of Downing College, Cambridge and Dr T. C. W. Blanning of Sidney Sussex College, Cambridge.

Introduction

This study is not much concerned with events – those mere 'ephemera of history', as Fernand Braudel calls them. It began with an intention to read and comment on the tracts which dealt with the Catholic question in Ireland in the years from around 1750 when the dominant figures among Catholic and pro-Catholic writers were Charles O'Conor of Belanagare and John Curry. This body of texts, however, was hardly to be well understood without reference to the apparent Catholic quiescence in the first half of the eighteenth century and the Catholic question as it was agitated in the decades after the first two important relief acts, in 1778 and 1782. Concern was primarily with the ideas the literature contained, rather than the political or social circumstances that provoked its composition. The work as completed remains more anxious to offer explanations of how eighteenth-century Ireland thought than to produce commentary on its history.

Nevertheless, something of the latter has emerged. It is hoped that this commentary is not, at heart, the author's own, but rather that of the writers of the tracts. For those who are concerned to understand the course of political events or of social change, pamphlet literature is of restricted, but still not inconsiderable value. Pamphleteers are frequently ill-informed, nearly always tendentious, and uniformly lacking in the sense of proportion which only temporal distance gives. In consequence, their contribution to a detailed historical narrative is usually slight. But then, a detailed historical narrative is not, at least in the first place, what is sought by most. A general understanding of the period is preferred and commentaries are turned to. Among these, the contemporary commentary of the pamphleteer holds a privileged position. The assumptions and beliefs it discloses incidentally are likely to be at least close to those of the actors in the events commented on. More importantly, it sees those events free from the distortions imposed by knowing which gained approval in declarations of significance from a later period and knowing what consequences actually flowed from them. It leaves the events of the past unobliterated by the moral sensibilities of the present – or the more recent past – and with the range of potential outcomes they once possessed.

Still, pamphlet literature's own distortions remain. Corrections and interpolations will be necessary. There must also be translation into terms derived from modern historiography. Perhaps this process has exceeded proper bounds and rendered this work more an essay in reinterpretation based on that historiography than a research piece. Even so, it may not be without interest. For the modern writings are used to focus on Europe as a whole as the context for interpretation and this focus has been more persistently held (because the primary sources used suggest its appropriateness) than is usual in the composition of Irish history. The unusual focus may provoke thought.

Whether it is that of the author or that of contemporaries, the reader will wish to know quickly what the general understanding of the period being put forward is. Thus, after a chapter which introduces the Catholic question in the eighteenth century, the context proposed for the understanding of it is at once stated. This is further explicated in the second part of the work. It is only in the third and fourth parts that almost undivided attention is devoted to the writings that were the initial focus of research. The third part is concerned chiefly with the writings of O'Conor and Curry, while the fourth comments on the debates of the last decades of the century.

Note

Dates given according to the Julian calendar have been left unmodernised. The spelling and punctuation of quotations in the text are also unaltered.

Part 1

1 Unimportance and Importance

R. B. McDowell, the distinguished historian of eighteenth-century Ireland, once recorded what struck him as a curious fact about the Irish Protestants of the period he studied. 'It is remarkable how the members of this proud community were able to ignore the existence of their helots. Furious controversies on Irish politics could be carried on without reference to the Catholic question.'[1] It is a statement well worth examining for the assumptions which underlie it.

McDowell, in fact, mistook the nature of the Catholic question in its earlier stages. Then a concern with helots was by no means at the heart of the matter, though some, on occasion, tended to make it appear so. It was Daniel O'Connell to whom the 'hereditary bondsmen', to use the phrase to which he was so attached, were of central importance. They became so to him, because he perceived that the entry of the mass of the Catholic population into the political arena was the only means by which the Catholic cause could be advanced. When they did enter, they inevitably brought with them their grievances. Nothing else could have sufficiently motivated them. In any case, their grievances constituted better propaganda than anything that had been used before. Thus, for the first time, Ireland's peasantry were consistently and, in some degree, realistically depicted as the major beneficiaries of Catholic relief.[2]

In contrast, in the early stages of the Catholic debate the peasantry entered it only in the mass and only as a topic for discussion, a topic that was by no means central in the eyes of all who participated. Among those hostile to the Catholic claims, the peasantry was of course frequently seen as a threat. No doubt Irish Protestants shared the fear of peasant revolt common to many eighteenth-century Europeans. Commonly, however, the fear was not, as it was in the 1820s, of the peasants themselves; it was rather a fear of the pretender or the king of France, who might use them to advance his designs.[3] Neither a French invasion nor the ensuing Jacobite restoration was likely to bring about a social revolution.[4]

On the other side of the debate, the peasantry received more sympathetic attention. Reference to them was fairly frequent. For the early Catholic relief argumentation was, to a considerable extent, preoccupied with economic matters and Ireland was an overwhelmingly agrarian economy.

3

The subject of peasants could hardly be avoided. Nevertheless, it was incidental. The wealthier sections of the peasantry might, it was argued, be of considerable importance in the improvement in the economic life of the nation, if the constraints under which they were placed by the penal legislation were removed. Such economic improvement was likely to benefit those threatened with destitution and hunger especially. The point could be emphasised if the occasion required.[5] Generally, however, it did not and arguments which spoke of economic betterment were more commonly addressed to Protestant self-interest than to Protestant altruism.

Between opponents and proponents of relief were those they sought to convince. The most important part of that body of movable opinion was, of course, to be found on the benches of the then still quite new house in College Green. These landowners and their representatives were less than likely to be convinced by the economic arguments of the Catholics and their allies. They were aware that the penal laws did not, in fact, place the restraints on the wealthier peasantry that they were said to.[6] This, however, did not necessarily render them hostile to Catholic relief, which had arguments other than economic ones to recommend it. In any case, some, if not the peasantry, might benefit.

In the end, the points made about the peasantry in the argumentation against the penal laws were probably of no great importance to those whom it was most important to convince. For they were aware that peasants were not the ones whom the code disadvantaged, in any more than indirect and peripheral ways. As one pro-Catholic writer, while no longer acting specifically in the role of an apologist for the Catholics, casually remarked, 'a few only' felt the restraints which the Irish constitution placed on Roman Catholics.[7] It was those few, the nobility and gentry, the middlemen and well-to-do farmers in the countryside, and the merchants and proto-industrialists in the towns, who were the real objects of the eighteenth-century relief legislation. They were the only ones likely to be in a position to reap substantial benefits from it.[8]

It would probably be but little misleading to sum the matter up by stating that the objects of relief legislation were not Catholic peasants, but Catholic gentlemen. This term may seem an odd one to use when speaking of the members of some of the groups just mentioned. More commonly they have been designated 'middle-class'. However, the former description does a good deal to explain the support which the Catholic cause could obtain among Protestants and is not unwarranted.

It is frequently acknowledged of the middlemen at least, that 'their ethos and outlook was that of the gentry'.[9] Many of the more prosperous farmers seem to have shared that ethos and outlook. Even if they might have had difficulty in furnishing an attested genealogy for a son entering a foreign service for example, yet they remained anxious to assert their gentility. So it was with the family of the mid-eighteenth-century bishop of Cloyne and Ross, John O'Brien. They were, according to the bishop's biographer, strong farmers. Their reduced state, they claimed, however, was due to their fidelity to the Catholic faith. At any rate, it was added, they had never merited *dérogeance* 'by following any vile or mechanical profession', but had 'lived in a decent and credible manner, in the farming way, as all other Roman Catholic Gentlemen in this Kingdom are generally obliged to do'.[10] In fact, an Irish gentleman had to fall low to merit *dérogeance*. There was certainly no stigma attached to following the profession of the merchant. The younger sons of landed proprietors constituted an important element in the Catholic merchant community. More importantly, the ethos of gentility they inherited quickly came to be shared by their fellow merchants and manufacturers, men of similar wealth, if humbler origins.[11] It may well be that the Irish category of 'gentleman' was rather more flexible than its English equivalent.

In any case, however one may categorise those who were likely to be in a position to take advantage of the early Catholic relief measures, it will not be possible to include among them anyone who might have been described as a helot; nor was any very serious attention devoted to such people in the debate about the affairs of their betters. At its lowest level the eighteenth-century Catholic question was of concern to urban artisans and tradesmen, who used it, in the form of the quarterage dispute, to escape from guild control.[12] Such men, living in an English-speaking, literate and often politicised environment, continued to take an interest in the Catholic cause, even after it had served their immediate purpose. When, in the 1780s, the matters raised in the Catholic debate extended beyond the purchase of land and security for loans to include access to the professions and political power, they may have felt that they had good reason to do so.[13]

Leaving aside the juxtaposition of his two statements – about helots and the Catholic question – one may go on to question whether McDowell need have expressed surprise at the facts he recorded. As to the capacity of Irish Protestants to ignore the existence of the Catholic masses in day-to-day life, it was, no doubt, no greater or less than the capacity of other privileged elites in Europe to conduct their affairs without reference to the interests of the population at large. As to Protestant lack of interest in the Catholic question, a partial explanation has already been given. The Catholic question at this time, as it did not relate to the Catholic population as a whole, brought forward no very serious threat of social change, as it did in the 1820s. Some Protestants were indeed deeply disturbed by its emergence; but by no means all saw that there was reason to be.

Further explanation of Protestant lack of concern with the Catholic question in its early stages can be found in those studies of the effects of the penal legislation that have appeared since McDowell made his observation. Reflecting the divergent nature of the laws themselves, this topic has been investigated in part by ecclesiastical historians, in part by social and economic historians. Their conclusions have tended in the same direction. They have warned against any assumption that more than parts of the code were consistently applied and against any exaggeration of the consequences for the Catholic community of what application there was.

Disagreement among historians about the intentions of the framers of the penal laws has been marked. In truth, intentions varied and a true judgement on the matter will be a synthetic one, though placing emphasis on a desire for military and political security. This is not necessarily to disagree with those writers who have been willing to suggest that the primary purpose of the legislation was the destruction of the Catholic religion.[14] The Irish Jacobite threat which they faced was, in the view of seventeenth- and eighteenth-century Protestants, merely a particular manifestation of the universal Catholic threat. This view seems, at first, to place at the centre of the penal code the Banishment Act of 1697, which sought to eject from the kingdom both bishops and the regular clergy; the Act of 1703, which sought to exclude any priest from entering the kingdom; the Registration Act, which came soon after and sought to record the presence of those already in Ireland; and the Act of 1709, which tried to complete an edifice of law which would, if adequately enforced, have destroyed the Catholic cultus by starving it of priests.[15] Of course, it was not adequately enforced. Central to this failure, though by no means its sole cause, was the excess of whiggish zeal which the legislators displayed in 1709, when they insisted that registered priests, as a condition of continued toleration, deny on oath the rights of the Stuarts. This was unenforceable and, in effect, destroyed the principle of registration which gave the entire system some hope of effectiveness. Even when enforcement of the system was most zealous, in the period when enactment was taking place and in the following decade, basic Catholic practice was generally possible, except for limited periods or in limited areas. Indeed, something more than basic practice was generally in evidence in these years. For example, the community life of the friars seems never to have totally disappeared. By about 1720 it existed even in the capital. By the same time, Dublin also had two convents of female religious.[16]

Certainly at mid-century, the Catholic Church in Ireland showed every sign of having made a good recovery from the blows delivered to it during the reigns of the last *de facto* Stuart monarchs. Its worship was uninterrupted, its hierarchy was intact and it was provided with an adequate supply of priests. The friars by now had less to fear from the Irish legislature and government than they had from Benedict XIV; for at the beginning of the 1750s he acted to regulate their activities and brought about a sharp decline in their numbers.[17] Fear and harassment there still was. In addition, there were decided regional and local differences in the physical and organisational manifestations of Catholicism. This was in part due to varying degrees of hostility on the part of authority. A hostile landlord could still ensure that the Catholics used a mass rock instead of a mass house. However, differences from place to place were due also to other factors, such as the difference between urban and rural conditions.[18]

The failure of the penal code seriously to restrict the Catholic cultus has been taken as evidence that this was not the central objective. An auxiliary argument points out the lack of a sustained effort on the part of the established church to proselytise. Was the conversion of the Catholics truly sought? In the first place, it should be noted that its failure to sustain any substantial campaign of proselytisation was due at least as much to the Church of Ireland's lack of plant and personnel as to its lack of will.[19] A similar lack of material resources might be adduced in part-explanation of the secular arm's failure to enforce the laws for the suppression of the priesthood.[20] But, in this case, the lack of will was more important. This is to be understood chiefly in the light of the conviction of the period that the lower ranks of society would not for long act independently of their superiors in matters of religion or that, if they did, it was, in most respects, of little consequence. While this was accepted, the key role in the obliteration of Catholicism could be assigned to the laws which assailed the existence of a Catholic social elite, rather than those which attacked the ecclesiastical hierarchy. These latter could be regarded as constituting mere copper-fastening. The desuetude into which they quickly fell speaks less of the intentions of the penal legislators than of the social beliefs which directed them.

Even if the destruction of a Catholic elite was the central element in the campaign against Catholicism, in this, too, success was less than complete. Revision of a historiography which tended to depict the eighteenth-century Irish Catholic body as an undifferentiated peasant mass began with the work of Maureen Wall in the 1950s. More recent work has allowed the assertion 'that the period 1690–1760, far from being a "penal era" in which Catholics were uniformly downtrodden and oppressed, in fact witnessed a considerable Catholic resurgence'.[21] Louis Cullen has suggested 'not only that a catholic and near-catholic [i.e. chiefly convert] interest existed but that it actually flourished during the period of the penal laws'.[22]

Such statements, it must be conceded, are open to some criticism. Their rather overemphatic correction of previous perceptions of the condition of eighteenth-century Catholics is apparent, for example in Cullen's inclusion with the Catholic interest of those who had actually abandoned their Catholic allegiance.[23] This overemphatic correction may, in some respects, mislead. It is true that there were groups which successfully thwarted the intentions of the framers of the penal laws. This Catholic interest may have flourished; but *the* Catholic interest (i.e. that defined as the threat offered to Irish Protestantism) certainly did not. For this had been broken by the land settlements and the deprivation of military and political power which had taken place in the course of the sixteenth and seventeenth centuries. In speaking of the restricted impact of the penal legislation, Cullen is careful to define it as that which was enacted from the reign of William and Mary onwards.[24] For modern historians the definition is acceptable. However, in the early eighteenth century the distinction between this and previous legislation, notably that which confiscated land, was as little noted as it is in modern popular reference to the penal era. It was a distinction largely brought into existence by the protagonists of Catholic relief in the latter part of the century, who were anxious to assure their Protestant audience that Catholics had no design to recover their forfeited property. To speak of a flourishing of a Catholic interest under the penal laws is a useful statement about Catholic property; but it may mislead about the state of the Catholic mind, conscious of a historical community which had suffered much affliction, and may obscure an understanding of the fervour and persistence with which the Catholic agitation was to be conducted.[25] While it is legitimate to speak of a Catholic resurgence, it should be pointed out that this was a resurgence from a very low position indeed.

The enactment of the post-Revolution legislation directed primarily against the Catholic laity began in 1695. Act was to be laid upon act, clause upon clause, some reflecting an immediate anxiety about security, some the desire to prevent any substantial acquisition of property among Catholics, some completing and reinforcing the structure of political exclusion. The process continued into the reign of George II. Later commentators have habitually singled out as the most significant measures the Act of 1704 and that of 1709, which sought to close loopholes and aid enforcement. The former both forbade Catholic acquisition of land, by purchase, by inheritance from Protestants and by the taking of long leases and attacked existing Catholic property by introducing the equal division of estates among heirs and by offering immediate advantage to heirs who became Protestant. Comprehensive as such measures may seem, they failed to complete the destruction of the Catholic landed interest, now, in the wake of the Williamite confiscations, the owners of only about one-seventh of Irish land. Good fortune, lack of enforcement, the holding of land in trust by friendly Protestants and the preservation of family solidarity in the face of the advantages offered by conformity all contributed to avert the essayed destruction.[26] True, the proportion of Irish land Catholics owned shrank from one-seventh to one-twentieth; but this is to speak only of land held in fee simple and leasehold land was also important. The law relating to this could be bent to allow what were in fact long leases. Even the mechanism introduced to ensure enforcement could be made use of to frustrate the legislators' intentions, by a process known as collusive discovery.[27] In any case, speculation in short leases could be profitable.[28] So it was that in the counties of Galway and Mayo, in Munster and south Leinster and in and around the old Dublin Pale a Catholic gentry, albeit a small one, did survive.

And behind them in rural society came a sub-gentry of middlemen (not infrequently the younger sons of gentry families) and strong farmers.[29] Not unrelated to the survival of a Catholic landed interest, was the growth of a Catholic trading interest. The penal laws weighed less heavily on those engaged in trade and, in some places, Catholics actually dominated the trading community. However, despite the impression given by some contemporaries, 'the Protestant commercial ascendancy' in Ireland was not in fact challenged.[30]

The impression left by recent revision of eighteenth-century Catholic history is of a community, certainly harassed and often humiliated, but whose chief sufferings were in the past and whose members, as individuals, were frequently capable of prospering and maintaining an appropriate social status. Similar conclusions might have been suggested simply by observation of the conduct of the Catholic question in the decades after mid-century. In the first place, it is worth remarking how restricted the debate was. Modern historians have been content to accept the view of early nineteenth-century writers, such as Thomas Wyse, and find the origins of the Catholic debate about 1750.[31] New voices, most notably that of the Franciscan priest Arthur O'Leary, soon to be joined by that of his more celebrated contemporary Edmund Burke,[32] began to be heard towards the end of the 1770s. Until then, the burden of representing the Catholic case in print lay on just two men. One was a Connaught squire and one of Ireland's best historians in the period, Charles O'Conor of Belanagare; the other was his intimate friend, a Dublin physician, John Curry. These two made a few efforts to recruit help; but even when they succeeded, it was they who supplied the ideas. We need only add the names of a few Protestants, such as parliamentarians and lawyers, who felt obliged by virtue of their duties in relation to the law to consider the Catholic case and whose considerations found their way into print. It is true that on the other side of the debate combatants were more numerous. Further, the conflict was not confined to print: it was continued in parliament. Still, the utterances of supporters of the penal code or of parliamentarians were but responses to Catholic initiatives. It was the Catholics who determined the dimensions of the debate and the Catholics, as a whole, were very quiet.

The limited Catholic participation in the early debate is curious. It is true that the Catholics were very hesitant to appear seriously divided among themselves. It is also true that O'Conor and Curry were very prolific authors, who presented the Catholic case with a good deal of skill and learning. Nevertheless, the failure of any alternative view of Catholic affairs to find its way into print is still noteworthy. Certainly, there was divergence from the views of O'Conor and Curry on the Catholic Committee which they had founded.[33] More generally, we hear of a good deal of murmuring about what was actually written, though some of it no doubt came from those who preferred silence to the necessary protestations of loyalty to the Hanoverians.[34] It was probably only very late in their careers as Catholic pamphleteers that O'Conor and Curry were able to feel that those in whose interest they wrote generally approved of their approach. At least it was possible for Curry to remark of their jointly prepared pamphlet of 1771, *Observations on the Popery Laws*, that that work anyway was 'Exceedingly liked Even by our Own People'.[35]

A conventional explanation of the silence of the Catholics about their condition lies in the reputed timidity of mid-eighteenth-century Irish Catholics. The theme is an old one. Wyse used it to set off the boldness he wanted to attribute to the founders of the Catholic Committee.[36] It has, however, been much overdone. It is true that Catholics were not habituated to expressing their views too loudly: still, they did express them. Religious debate, for example, even under the harsh conditions of the early part of the century, was always free. In the local political arena too, Catholic opinions were aired and Catholic influence was exercised.[37] In fact, Catholics had little reason to be nervous about making their views known. If they did not express those views too loudly, that was largely because such activity would have been counter-productive and not because they went in fear and trembling of the law. Blatant Jacobitism would, of course, have been checked. However, eighteenth-century Britain was reasonably tolerant of what it called 'guarded treason', so long as it was indeed guarded. Certainly in the third quarter of the eighteenth century, the mere advocacy of relaxation of the penal laws could not have brought down prosecution on anyone's head. Surprisingly, the contrary is still stated.[38]

There are, in fact, two substantial explanations for the limited extent of the Catholic debate in its printed form. In the first place, there was adherence to Jacobitism. Many Catholics were uninterested in seeking concessions from a Hanoverian government which, they continued to hope, would be overthrown.[39] However, there was undoubtedly another body of Catholic opinion, which entertained less faith in France and the Stuarts or more loyalty to the established order. Such Catholics may well have been restrained from agitation by an enduring adherence to the doctrine of passive obedience.[40] However, for the most part, their quiescence can only be taken as an indication of relative contentment. This is not, of course, to say that they were indifferent to the debate about relief. However, their conditions do not appear to have been so oppressive that any number of them were induced to devote the considerable amount of time and energy necessary to personal participation.

When one turns from the conduct to the content of the debate, what is to be observed here also supports the more recent assessments of the impact of the penal laws. In the first place, it is clear that Catholics were in agreement with Protestants that restrictions on Catholic practice could not be regarded as a grievance. Members of eighteenth-century ecclesiastical establishments had a tendency to use narrow definitions of the terms 'toleration' and 'persecution' when speaking of their own possible modes of conduct towards religious groups outside the establishment. 'Toleration' meant no more than granting permission for the bare existence of the cultus and whatever was strictly necessary to sustain it, such as priesthood. The term 'persecution' equally related only to the cultus and its necessary supports. By about mid-century, Irish Protestants had grown rather proud of their practice of toleration, in this sense. They were likely to be indignant at any suggestion that they persecuted.[41] In fact, though they may have wished to expand the definition so that they could, Catholics never accused Protestants of persecuting them. They willingly agreed that they enjoyed 'the free Exercise of their Religion'.[42] Statements to the contrary, that the penal laws violated 'the undoubted privileges of conscience', came only later, in the 1780s and 1790s.[43] So the bolder writers spoke; but they were speaking about a period then past.

Though they could not be considered to amount to persecution, restrictions were placed on Catholic practice. For example, specifically Catholic contributions to public life, such as Catholic charities, were not possible. Again, the Catholic cult was allowed no public display. However, the removal of such restrictions would have been, if they could ever have been contemplated, an infringement of the monopoly of the Church of Ireland. Assumptions about the privileges of ecclesiastical establishments were shared by all, Protestant and Catholic alike: consequently these restrictions on Catholic practice never became the subject of contention.

It is true that Catholics worried from time to time about the consequences of proposed legislation for their ecclesiastical structures. In the event, legislation which could have seriously disrupted those structures, such as the Priests' Registry Bill of the 1750s,[44] was never enacted. They also worried about the possible enforcement of existing legislation. Their fears, however, were strictly limited. Irish bishops did sometimes speak of the possibility of persecution when they corresponded with the Roman authorities; but the context generally makes it clear that they had in mind no more than a degree of harassment.[45] In Rome the term 'persecution' might comprehend almost any assault on the position of the Catholic Church. The bishops would not have used such a term when speaking to Irish Protestants. In truth, no one feared a return to the conditions of the early decades of the century. Catholics may have been wont, occasionally, to complain of the sword of Damocles that hung over them. It could conceivably have caused some injury if it had fallen; but, in fact, it was very blunt.

The Catholic debate of the late eighteenth century supports the now established view of the revisors in the field of ecclesiastical history largely by way of an *argumentum e silentio*. On the circumstances of Catholics, as opposed to the circumstances of their church, the debate speaks a great deal: the difficulty is knowing what to believe. Contemporaries were well aware of the doubtful character of the complaints which were being offered on behalf of the Catholics. Historians have frequently left them without serious investigation. No such unhesitating credence has been given to the defenders of the penal legislation, when they denied that their opponents had any serious grounds for complaint.[46] However, both views were presented for the purposes of political persuasion and, in fairness, there is no reason to accept one rather than the other without considerable enquiry. Meanwhile, it is probably best to assume that the truth lies somewhere between the two polemical positions.

Some of the contemporary literature does, in fact, give indication of this. There were fairly disinterested parties – those Protestants, for example, who looked favourably on the Catholic claims, but did not feel called upon to act as promoters of them. An interesting example is the litterateur, pamphleteer and newspaper proprietor, Henry Brooke. Brooke's career certainly illustrates his disinterestedness. In his earlier years he had enjoyed some celebrity in England as the author of *Gustavus Vasa*, the first play to merit prohibition under the Stage Licensing Act of 1737. The play was easily construed as Jacobite in tendency.[47] Consequently, on his return home to Ireland, and especially when he was seeking the post of barrack-master at Mullingar, worth £400 p.a., he thought it advantageous to publish a series of anti-Jacobite and anti-Catholic tracts, *(The Farmer's) Letter to the Protestants of Ireland*. The years passed, with Brooke changing political sides a few times as interest demanded,[48] and in 1760–61 he was producing pamphlets on behalf of the Catholics. A series of four very unprofitable pamphlets, bearing the title *The (Farmer's) Case of the Roman Catholics of Ireland*, were followed by a more successful work, *The Trial of the Cause of the Roman Catholics*.

Brooke was well paid by the Catholics to write on their behalf and wrote according to the instructions given him by O'Conor and Curry.[49] Substantially, the views he expressed were theirs and, in the earlier pamphlets especially, he depicted the situation of the Catholics as constituting an overwhelming danger to the nation. The penal laws, he explained, were part of a malignant English design to destroy Irish prosperity and they had done their job well: all of Ireland's economic ills could be attributed to them.[50] He must, however, have cast doubt on this rhetoric when he spoke more precisely about those laws which were still operative against the Catholics.[51] Alongside these economic arguments, Brooke developed another theme: he argued that the penal laws had alienated the Catholics to the extent that now, in the midst of the war against the French, they might constitute a serious military danger. Though he was careful to add that Catholic disloyalty was more potential than actual, this came rather close to confirming Protestants' worst fears. Catholic writers would have been very hesitant to use such an argument. Still, it did fit in very well with their desire to magnify the importance of their disabilities.[52]

All this, however, was Brooke as Catholic apologist. At about the same time as he was so employed, he produced another work, *An Essay on the Ancient and Modern State of Ireland*. This work too showed the influence of O'Conor, but as one of Ireland's more prominent historians, not as a Catholic pamphleteer.[53] Brooke declared, improbably, that he had 'nothing besides the Honour and Advantage of Ireland in View' when he wrote.[54] He eulogised her ancient glories and lamented her recent misfortunes. A new age, however, had dawned with the accession of George II. Brooke's aim in the latter part of the work was to show that in all areas of life Ireland had made immense strides and now compared favourably with other nations. Among recent changes for the better was the development of a more benevolent attitude towards the Catholics. However, in contrast to the 400 or so pages he was to devote to the subject of the Catholics when they paid him, here he dismissed the matter in a page and, by the context he placed it in and the way in which he treated it, suggested that it was unlikely to give much more difficulty.[55] The condition of those few Catholics who were affected by the penal laws was, indeed, a matter of concern. Apparently, however, it was of no more concern than the condition of the University or even (let it be remembered that Brooke was a playwright) the condition of the Irish stage, to which he devoted more space.[56] He certainly did not suggest that Catholic disabilities were likely to ruin the economy: there was no mention of them when he spoke of trade and agriculture.[57]

Brooke is by no means the only writer in whose works it is possible to discern not an inexplicable indifference to the existence of the penal laws, but a fairly realistic evaluation of their importance. Gorges Howard is one who might be expected to be capable of such an evaluation. In addition to being a pamphleteer, he was a lawyer who undertook a study of how the Popery laws operated in particular cases. The work was tendentious: Howard was opposed to the penal laws. The grounds which he offered for his opposition are interesting. He repeated, in very general terms and only as a matter of personal opinion, the usual pro-Catholic claims that the national economy was damaged by the laws and that they tended to alienate the ruled from their ruler. However, he indicated what he thought to be the extent to which this was the case by giving equal prominence to much more trivial disadvantages: the laws, he thought, had a potential for provoking family quarrels and they also tended 'to reprobate the mind by encouraging informers, those horrid pests to society'.[58] Howard's work illustrated the latter disadvantages, not the former.

Howard's work reveals what was, in fact, the dominant mode of thinking about the penal laws in the third quarter of the eighteenth century among those who were opposed to them: that they constituted a nuisance which ought to be dealt with by lawyers, rather than a great political problem which required the attention of statesmen. Thus one sympathetic Protestant was able to advance as his reason for raising the topic simply the fact that there were 'in the House of Commons of our new Parliament, more of that considerable and learned Body of the long Robe, than any Man now living can remember'.[59] The same thinking was present among parliamentarians when they did take up the matter. It is noticeable that the parliamentary advocates of relief were not content to advance merely the arguments to hand in the pro-Catholic pamphlets, which depicted the condition of the Catholics as a great social and political evil. They were careful to add arguments more calculated to appeal to those who perceived themselves to be called upon simply to remedy a faulty and inconvenient body of law.[60]

In outlining above the tendency of recent thought about the situation of eighteenth-century Irish Catholics, it has been possible both to express agreement and, on the basis of consideration of the pamphlet literature, offer some additional confirmation. However, acceptance of the position now held by historians provokes an awkward question. It is, in fact, this question which is the *point de départ* of the main argument of this study. Granted that the penal code remained to a large extent unenforced and that those parts of it that were enforced inflicted no extraordinary hardships on the Catholics, how did this body of law succeed in generating difficulties of the magnitude and intractability of those which attached to the Catholic question? Why – to put the matter another way – were writers like Brooke and Howard quite wrong in their belief that the problem of the Catholics was going to yield to easy, legislative solutions?

It might be answered that the penal laws, while lacking importance in the mid-eighteenth century, acquired it later – chiefly in the minds of those who agitated the Catholic question.

This owed its existence certainly to the penal laws, but just as much to the political developments of the late eighteenth and in the early nineteenth century. There were the continuing assertions of Irish rights against what were perceived as English encroachments; the demands for reform which emerged after the rights of the Irish parliament had been vindicated in 1782 and intensified with the growth of at least proto-democratic views in the wake of the French Revolution. It seems significant that the Catholic question's emergence coincided with what has been observed as the beginnings of the later eighteenth century's near-constant political disturbance – a contrast to the relative calm of the earlier decades of the century.[61] True, Catholics had been constantly possessed of a sense of personal affliction, smarting under the 'psychological effects' of the penal code, used as a means of 'humiliating' them.[62] Some, no doubt, also possessed a sense of communal grievance against the code as the crown of their people's historical misfortunes. But this protracted turmoil, with its politicisation of a wider section of the Irish population, was both the incentive Catholics required to develop this sense of communal grievance and their opportunity to express it with hope of redress. The code now assumed a new importance. It now occupied centre stage; for the land and dynastic settlements could not be challenged in acceptable political discourse. It was also unambiguously a political rather than personal grievance, occasioning ideologically supported zeal rather than mere psychological distress.

Redress did come, first amidst the agitation associated with the American war and the triumph of the Patriots in the early 1780s. The movements which now, in the last two decades of the century, appeared and sought political reform brought another change in the Catholic view of the penal laws. A particular section of the code, that which secured their political exclusion, became important. Much of this was removed by the relief acts of 1792 and 1793 and what remained derived its capacity to dominate political life, in a considerable measure simply because the Catholics themselves were more important. Their numbers had begun to matter. The increasing attention to and then participation by the lower strata of society quite changed and magnified the Catholic question's significance. Now the difficulty in making concessions lay as much in who sought them as in what was sought, though this too, beneath the level of parliamentary motions, had changed, as access to parliament for Catholics assumed the character of a panacea or even a millenarian deliverance.

An account of the relationship of the Catholic question to what have been identified as Ireland's progressive contemporary forces, as given above, needs to balanced by a declaration of the autonomy of the question and also a recognition of the influence of circumstances outside of Ireland on its history. The emergence of the Catholic question owed more to the eclipse of Jacobitism than to the rise of the Patriots.[63] It was the military demands which the American war placed on the Hanoverian Empire which brought the beginnings of relief legislation, as it was the demands of the French war which brought the eighteenth-century consummation of the concessions.[64] A new emphasis on political rights was inevitable in the 1780s, merely by virtue of the substantial nature of what had already been yielded. And democratic notions would have penetrated Irish minds without the aid of the United Irishmen. Still, whatever the influences at work, it remains true that the penal code, as it lost its effectiveness as law and was reduced in bulk by relief legislation, gained in ideological importance among those who opposed it.

But what of those who supported it? If we are to state why the Catholic question was of importance, its importance to the participants on both sides of the debate must be estimated. Indeed, it can be said that an understanding of the anti-Catholic view is the fundamental one to be attained. But here we enter a neglected field. Writing more than forty years ago about the 'political and religious prejudices' of eighteenth-century Irish Protestants, Patrick Rogers observed that it was 'much more difficult to understand than to condemn'.[65] Though since then Rogers' own practice of avoiding condemnation has become general, few have followed the hard course of trying to understand. As in considering the Catholics, a preliminary to reaching judgements about the significance of the Catholic question for the Protestants is an assessment of the real impact on them of the laws themselves. Until this problem, rather than the general impact of the laws on the Irish economy, is addressed, the assumption that the penal code itself was unimportant or incapable of generating conflict is indeed merely an assumption. At present, it can at least be suggested that, again as in the case of the Catholic community, the ideological dimensions of the code were of considerable importance. In attempting to communicate a general understanding of penal legislation Sean Connolly offers a modern parallel in 'the policies which successive governments since 1922 have adopted towards the Irish language'.[66] It may indeed be that the overwhelmingly dominant motivation in the attempt to maintain the penal laws was, like the motivation in the attempt to maintain the Irish language, ideological. The parallel is made more suggestive if it is borne in mind how important the cultivation of a Gaelic and Catholic ideology has been for the justification of the existence of the modern Irish state. But whether an ideological motivation for the attempt to preserve the penal code is to be judged primary among those which can be considered or not, the study of ideology will be useful in its own right and in offering access to other areas. For ideologies are not to be studied apart from their relationship to the intellectual, political and economic realities of their societies.

To a considerable extent, an acceptable, if incomplete account of support for the penal laws can be obtained even with the focus on the Catholics which existing historiography adopts. Indeed, this belief underlies large parts of the present work. Explanations of change in the anti-Catholic stance are to be found in the advances made by the Catholic cause and in the circumstances that helped to bring those advances about. The ideology of eighteenth-century anti-Catholicism can be, in a measure, explained from the writings of the apologists for the Catholics, both in what these attack and in their revelation of the world Catholics and Protestants alike inhabited. However, this approach represents an inversion of historical reality. The emergence of a Catholic agitation was certainly the occasion of manifestations of anti-Catholicism. Almost as soon as the Catholic question emerged, there was an increase in the quantity of visible anti-Catholicism.[67] But this certainly does not mean that the content of later eighteenth-century anti-Catholicism was a mere response to the Catholic case. On the contrary, it was this latter which held the negating position in the debate seen as a whole. After all, it was Protestants and a Protestant ideology that governed Ireland.

The negative phrase 'anti-Catholic ideology' and, worse, the condemnatory 'political and religious prejudices', used and quoted above, cannot be allowed to stand as the shorthand for the topic discussed here. It is better said that it is an ideology of the confessional-state that is being spoken of.

Such an ideology has indeed been described and its existence put forward as the substantial reason for the continued existence of the Catholic question until 1829. The reference, however is to England. The description and assertion are offered by Jonathan Clark in one of the most sweeping and erudite revisions of a long period of that country's history to appear in recent years.[68] Clark, in fact, goes well beyond speaking of the existence of a confessional-state ideology. He describes the ideology of an *ancien régime*, of which the confessional-state ideology is only a part. Since England and Ireland, to a considerable extent, shared a common political culture, Clark's study of that culture does a good deal towards explaining the nature and significance of the Catholic question in mid to late eighteenth-century Ireland, even if Ireland is not much adverted to. This omission is understandable. If England and Ireland shared much as sister kingdoms in the Hanoverian Empire, Ireland remained singular and requires separate treatment. It was not, though, as singular as Clark suggests, when he states that it was nationalist ideology that lay at the heart of the Catholic debate in Ireland.[69] This casual remark could not have been made by an Irish historian, nor is there any reason to refute it here.[70] However, it is hoped that as this study proceeds, both similarities and differences between the Catholic debates in the two islands will become clear.

Clark's work has proved exceedingly contentious.[71] It is neither possible nor appropriate to enter into this dispute among English historians here. However, a few points are worth mentioning in the present context. Firstly, Clark speaks *tout court* of eighteenth- and early-nineteenth-century England as an *ancien régime*. His initial reason for doing so is that 'the theoretic formulation of English society' in 'the public realm of ideology, law and political conflict' is such as to suggest this term.[72] Some critics are of the opinion that Clark's survey of the public realm has been inadequate and that much could have been found to conflict with the theoretic formulation he has revealed. However, even if Clark is right about the dominance of this theoretic formulation, further evidence must be offered to show that it corresponded with the realities of English life. In the absence of that evidence, though it may be legitimate to speak of an *ancien régime* ideology, it is hardly possible to speak of an *ancien régime*. There may well be a considerable gap between the perceptions of contemporaries and realities they are concerned with.[73]

Though the present study does speak of eighteenth-century Ireland as an *ancien régime*, this should not be construed as indicating that Clark's views are simply accepted as true and equally applicable to Ireland. All that is asserted here is that in the fields Clark has covered he has revealed the existence of an *ancien régime* ideology, or at least elements of one. Since the areas covered include the relationship between the state, the established church and religious dissenters, it seems not unreasonable to assume that an understanding of this ideology will explicate the nature of the Catholic debate in Ireland: that country's political culture, it has already been remarked, was very close to that of England. If the assumption is well-founded and the nature of the Irish Catholic debate is best understood as a manifestation of the existence of an *ancien régime* ideology, then this points in the direction of accepting the legitimacy of speaking of eighteenth-century Ireland as an *ancien régime*. There are, however, other pointers. It is impossible here to speak of these at length. Some, though, will be mentioned in the following chapter. Meanwhile, it is sufficient to say that Clark has provided an interesting hypothesis. However, a hypothesis can only be tested on the assumption that it is true and it is unexceptionable and convenient when discussing it to speak of it as if it were.

2 The Irish *Ancien Régime*

The prospect of placing the history of Ireland within a well-established interpretative context derived from the study of European history as a whole is singularly attractive. In the wake of the revisionism of recent decades, Irish history lacks the broad vistas that nationalist historians once gave it. Still, there is good reason to hesitate somewhat before making the effort to see the modern history of Ireland as the history of the rise and fall of an *ancien régime*. The most obvious reason for caution is that the term *ancien régime* is notoriously difficult to use. Some may even consider that it possesses such a degree of comprehensiveness of reference that it is not profitable to use it at all. If it is used, it is incumbent on the user to make some remarks about its definition. There are, in fact, a very large number of definitions available. This *embarras de richesse* derives in part from the number of states to which the term has been applied, but more from the variety of disciplinary approaches to the topic. The sub-disciplines of history, such as economic, social and political history, produce different emphases, as do attempts to synthesise the conclusions of the practitioners of these sub-disciplines.[1]

Marxist and other definitions of the *ancien régime* generated by economic history are hardly difficult to apply to eighteenth-century Ireland. If, following convention, demography prefixes economics, it may be pointed out that the demographic conditions of the period yield obvious parallels between Ireland and other countries, such as France, and that there is temporal coincidence of demographic change. The years immediately before the mid-eighteenth century were as significant demographically in Ireland as they were in France: these, in the former, mark the beginning of the well-known gap between the famines. There is thus in the case of Ireland the same possibility that exists in other cases, of relating an increased population to that acceleration of social and political change which allowed a consciousness that the recent past had indeed been left behind and become *ancien*. Equally obvious parallels can be drawn when speaking of economic structure and the class structure perceived as springing from it. Little controversy is likely to arise over descriptions of the eighteenth-century Irish economy as one dominated by its agricultural sector or of Irish society as dominated by rentiers whose wealth was derived from that sector.[2] Irish landlordism will give ample scope for reflection by Marxists on the final stage of feudal society.[3] Such an emphasis on landlordism gives clear temporal definition to the Irish *ancien régime*. Its origins can be ascribed to the sixteenth- and early seventeenth-century plantations, though the more important period of establishment is in the late seventeenth century. Its substantial destruction is to be placed at the end of the nineteenth and the beginning of the twentieth century. Some historians are inclined to think along these lines. Margaret MacCurtain sees a 'recognizable ancien régime model' of landholding emerging as a result of the Cromwellian–Williamite land settlement.[4] Joseph Lee deals with the other end of the span of landlordism. He adopts 'modernisation' as a key term which sums up the nature of the developments in the period he is concerned with. It is clear from the definition he gives of this that he is using it to speak of what could easily be described as the demise of the *ancien régime*.[5]

In the end attempts to define the *ancien régime* in economic terms, while undoubtedly revealing, are inadequate and frequently misleading. The difficulty lies in the fact that the primary reference of the term *ancien régime* is to the early modern period's political and juridical systems. Even for those most deeply committed to economic determinism, any such system simply contains too much that cannot be adequately related in terms of causation to the economic base on which they hold the system to have been raised. They can say much by way of explaining the origins of a system and may wish to claim that they are capable of substantial explanation of what is most important in it. Comprehensiveness, however, cannot be their forte.[6] Thus Kenneth Connell could relate a number of Irish peasant cultural traits in the eighteenth and nineteenth centuries to 'the elasticity of rent' with some degree of credibility.[7] Equally, MacCurtain can credibly comment on the impact of landlordism on the Irish landscape or even claim that landlordism gave rural society some of its dominating features. However, when she speaks of 'the permanent forms of administration and government' or 'the land legislation... generally referred to as "the penal laws"', then these must be described as consequences of the particular, the Cromwellian–Williamite land settlement, which brought the abstract, landlordism, into existence.[8] Since it is difficult to conceive of a discussion of the Irish *ancien régime* which does not speak much of 'forms of administration and government' and the penal laws, it is difficult to see how a definition of the *ancien régime* based on economic history and devoting particular attention to landlordism could be considered the most useful.

It is curious that in definitions of the *ancien régime* derived from the study of political history, the presence of a powerful monarchy should still occur as an element, as, for instance, in Clark's implicit definition discussed below.[9] He clearly assumes that by demonstrating the importance and power of the monarchy in eighteenth-century Britain, he is contributing to the justification of the use of the term *ancien régime*.[10] Yet, were the Venetian republic and the Polish-Lithuanian *rzeczpospolita* not *anciens régimes*? The notion of absolutism must indeed come into the definition of the *ancien régime*. However, in the case of some states it is the very absence of absolutist government which contributes to the description of them as *anciens régimes*. What must, in fact, be included as an element in the definition of the *ancien régime* is not simply the presence of absolutism, but the presence of a political polarity, in which absolutism constitutes one of the poles. The political and military conflicts in which absolutist governments had been embroiled in the seventeenth century had been resolved and absolutism had generally triumphed. Yet until the coming of the French Revolution and the new divisions this created, these conflicts continued to set the basic paradigm for political thought and activity. Not only in France, but throughout Europe, a *thèse royale* continued to oppose a *thèse nobiliaire* and in these were provided the motivations or justifications for political action.[11] Everywhere a tension existed between an absolutist tendency and a desire to uphold the particularisms of place, from kingdom to parish, and of social grouping, from noble estate to peasant commune, with what may be called a corporative–representative ideology.[12] Even where a high degree of constitutional stability prevented that tension from generating extensive political conflict, it continued to exist in political thinking and to some extent in political action. Even in those states in which absolutism had convincingly won the day, the corporative–representative tendency remained – necessarily, given the legal and geographical decentralisation of power in all states. Even where absolutism had been checked, it could not be ignored: it was, after all, the dominant political doctrine of the age.

Britons acknowledged their country's conformity to this continent-wide paradigm. The acknowledgement took a particularly coherent form in the notion of the Gothic constitution.[13] This allowed them to see the struggle against royal absolutism on a European scale and magnify their own role in it. Once, a free constitution, the work of Englishmen's Teutonic ancestors, had prevailed throughout the continent. Now, perhaps, Britons were 'the only remaining Heirs of Liberty upon Earth'.[14] More usually it was acknowledged that at least remnants of that free constitution were to be found elsewhere.[15] A blow against the Gothic constitution anywhere was a blow which Britons might feel. When Robert Molesworth wrote his Account of Denmark he was, it is true, aiming to give political lessons that could be applied in late Stuart Britain.[16] Still, he did not write an allegory. The book was also about Denmark; and with that country and the destruction of its free constitution he was genuinely concerned.[17]

Of course, the Gothic constitution was primarily a device. Among a few, like Molesworth, it was a device to attack the absolutism of the British monarchy; more commonly it served as a patriotic celebration of the existing constitutional arrangements. However, it was not merely a device. It was also believed in as a true statement, about the historical origins of the Hanoverian constitution, about a contemporary or near-contemporary continent-wide struggle against absolutism and about Britain's place in that struggle. We may, of course, dismiss it as a historical statement about the remote past: as such it was being called into question even in the eighteenth century.[18] However, there was, or at least recently had been, a struggle against absolutism. Britain's place in that conflict was not, perhaps, what the upholders of the Gothic constitution asserted: there are good reasons for describing the eighteenth-century Hanoverian Empire as an absolute monarchy.[19] Still, whatever their outcome, the seventeenth-century struggles to establish or overthrow absolutist rule did take place and determined the shape of British political thought and behaviour in the following century. Britain, in other words, conformed to the *ancien régime* paradigm.

Both historical circumstances and much English historiography have served to obscure this fact. The historical circumstances, to be specific, are the reign of James II, the Revolution of 1688 and the change of dynasty in 1714, together with the effects of these events on the political parties and their ideologies. The series of events which began with the accession of a Popish king and ended in tory proscription changed a toryism which seemed set fair at the end of the seventeenth century to act as a champion of absolutist tendencies into a toryism which opposed them. The same sequence of events produced precisely the opposite developments in whiggery, which had the mantle of the court party thrown over its shoulders by its own success. Both parties in the eighteenth century were the heirs of ideological traditions unsuited to the roles they were called upon to play.[20] What in fact occurred was a certain degree of ideological coalescence between, on the one hand, those whigs who maintained more continuity with primitive whiggery, thus adopting an oppositionist stance, and, on the other, tories induced by circumstances to adopt such a stance.[21] Thus did the Patriots emerge.[22] Confronted with the confusion created by the events of the last decades of the seventeenth century and the early decades of the eighteenth century, historians, understandably, have been divided. Are eighteenth-century party labels to be taken seriously? Should one not look beyond them to descry the true line of division, as one between court and country? Was there serious ideological division at all in eighteenth-century Britain?[23] Despite this confusion, however, the *ancien régime* political paradigm is still clearly visible.

Equally obscuring the fundamental conformity of England and Ireland to the pattern of European political thought and activity is the absence in these islands of a modern historiographical tradition prepared to observe absolutist tendencies with less than disapproval. There have been few modern British or Irish exponents of a *thèse royale*, few tory historians. Tendencies capable of being labelled 'progressive' have been assumed to lie on one side of seventeenth- and eighteenth-century political debates and there has been a consequent unwillingness to take seriously the archaic nature of the views propounded on the 'progressive' side. To revert to a previous example: Molesworth as a whig critic of the regime established in 1688, and thus one of that British band who were 'the spiritual heirs and ancestors of revolutionaries everywhere', has been found worthy of attention.[24] It has been overlooked that Molesworth's *Account of Denmark* was a plea for nothing more than a return to the constitution that country enjoyed in the early seventeenth century and a protest against the destruction of noble privilege.[25] Behind these political views lay attitudes that say much about neglected aspects of English whiggery; the aristocratic hauteur displayed in speaking of the Danish bourgeoisie, for example, or the enthusiasm for noble egalitarianism, reminiscent of the attitude of the Polish and Hungarian nobilities.[26]

The political mark of the *ancien régime*, the possibility of relating political positions to the two poles of absolutism and corporatist–representativism, cannot be missed on even the most superficial acquaintance with the political thought and activity of eighteenth-century Britain. It is clear throughout. It appears in the most fundamental political ideas of the period – in the notion of political balance between crown and estates, for example. Reed Browning is undoubtedly right in calling the eighteenth century in Britain 'the great era for the worship of constitutional equilibrium'.[27] The idea was of singular importance and is to be found in far more contexts than that of grand speculation about constitutional theory. It was, for example, the commonplace of debates about municipal politics, or again, of the historiography of the period. Browning explains its importance by pointing to its place in the network of contemporary ideas which supported it and flowed from it. Indeed, abstract justifications for a belief in political balance could be given. However, it was not political philosophy as much as historical experience that gave the idea its importance. And the historical experience in question was the conflict with absolutism. It was the same experience as that which gave rise to the belief in political balance articulated by Fénelon or Montesquieu.[28]

The omnipresence of the *ancien régime* political paradigm might again be illustrated from what have been taken to be the dominant themes in eighteenth-century Irish political history: the emergence of the Protestant nation, the rise of the Patriots and their leading of that nation to its political and constitutional triumphs of the 1780s. What has obscured the essentially *ancien régime* character of this struggle is the nationalist historiography of the nineteenth and twentieth centuries. The desire to perceive a continuity between the Patriot politics of eighteenth-century Ireland and the nationalist politics of nineteenth-century Ireland is as old as the latter itself. After all, the emergent Catholic nation of the early nineteenth century possessed no other native political language than that of the Patriots in which they could articulate their grievances and desires. The language adopted was not without some ability to determine the content of what was said; but it was far from being the major determinant. The illusion of continuity thus created has never been sufficiently dispelled by historians. Dismayed as he was as he watched the consequences in his own day of the entry of the Catholic population into Irish politics, Lecky could not have brought himself to reject the dominant tradition of his own century entirely. O'Connell, if not his repellent successors, was given the legitimacy that only continuity with the enlightened Protestants of the eighteenth century could give.[29] Among those more wholeheartedly at one with the Catholic nationalism of their own age than Lecky was, there was no desire to be rid of a Protestant inheritance. In the manner of contemporary nationalists everywhere, they claimed spiritual ancestors where they could. The honouring of eighteenth-century figures had the particular merit of assisting in the refutation of accusations that their politics were sectarian in character. It must be acknowledged that the very claim of nineteenth-century nationalists to continuity with the Patriots of the previous century served to create such continuity – in a degree. However, any assertion that continuity was more than superficial cannot but produce a gravely distorted understanding of the nature of eighteenth-century politics. The differences between that oppositionism which existed within the political spectrum characteristic of the *ancien régime* and the politics of those who in the following century sought to destroy the *ancien régime* as it endured must be emphasised.

In fact, what may, by way of concession, be called the proto-nationalist politics of late eighteenth-century Ireland had the same ingredients that such politics had elsewhere in the period. Protagonists of Enlightenment-inspired reform, now coming under the influence of the Romanticism which was growing out of Enlightenment, entered into a tactical, but often also ideological alliance with the protagonists of 'retrograde patriotism', to use the term of Margaret Ives, speaking of the Hungarian resistance to Joseph II.[30] It is the presence of the latter group which can be regarded as chiefly marking off the proto-nationalist politics of the late eighteenth and early nineteenth century from the nationalist politics of a later era. The 'retrograde patriots' were primarily concerned with the maintenance of corporative privilege and with opposition to what threatened it, such as religious toleration. Less abstractly, centralising, enlightened governments also threatened it, and the defence of *ancien régime* principles not infrequently found focus in the defence of the rights of the local estates or assembly as a barrier against the central power.

Defence of local political autonomy was always an element in the contest against monarchical power. Its presence as a part of the British oppositionist position, among the Patriots, is therefore not extraordinary. The rights of local parliaments in the British Isles, of colonial assemblies, and of those who possessed heritable jurisdictions, were all traditional objects of concern to those who held to an older version of whiggery than that espoused by the court whigs.[31] Of course, the English Patriots were not, most of the time, confronted with such issues. The Irish, who were, showed in the early eighteenth century rather less than wholehearted enthusiasm for the defence of local autonomy. Among those whom Caroline Robbins discusses as Irish counterparts of the English whig Patriots, some, notably William Molyneux[32] and Charles Lucas,[33] were certainly zealous for the rights of the Irish parliament. However, others whom she mentions, Henry Maxwell, Arthur Dobbs and Samuel Madden, favoured a union with England.[34] Enthusiasm for a union was in fact quite widespread among the Irish. Its economic advantages were not lost on them, any more than they were on the Scots. At any rate, the defence of Irish constitutional liberties tended to be associated with the Papists. It was the Catholic lawyer, Patrick Darcy, who had been the leading advocate of this cause in the seventeenth century and his views had been endorsed by James II's parliament of 1689.[35]

The situation which prevailed in the early eighteenth century, when the Irish might well have welcomed a union but could not hope for English agreement, was reversed as the century wore on. Then the Irish Patriots overwhelmingly adhered to the traditional position of the English Patriots and found general support for their stance. British governments, on the other hand, increasingly attempted to exercise effective control over Irish affairs. In fact, the latter circumstance must be offered as a foremost explanation of the former. In those disputes which 'provided a focus and accelerator for gathering patriotic sentiments', from the Money Bill dispute of the early 1750s through to the period of the American War, conflict was chiefly generated by the central government's increased involvement in Irish politics.[36]

Seen in this light, the Irish struggles which culminated in the constitutional settlement of 1782 seem quite conformable to the pattern of opposition to central authority manifested by the activities of the French *parlements* or by the activities of Joseph II's subjects in Hungary or the Austrian Netherlands in the same period. Indeed the parallels between the Patriot movement in Ireland and the anti-absolutist movements in other countries are often very striking. For example, no one acquainted with the history of the Volunteer movement in Ireland can fail to be struck by a strong feeling of *déja vu* on reading accounts of the *banderium* movement in Hungary.[37] All that obscures these parallels is the insistence that the Irish Patriot movement is to be regarded as 'progressive', while the importance of 'retrograde patriotism' is very clearly seen in the parallel movements on the European mainland. The distinction cannot be convincingly maintained.

What has been said here about the fundamental structure of English and Irish political thinking and activity assists an understanding of the nature and significance of the Catholic question in late eighteenth-century Ireland. The Catholics were associated with a pro-absolutist position. There was, of course, their historical identification as Jacobites: and before the last decades of the century it was, to say the least, very difficult for the opponents of the penal laws to state that this had no foundation.[38] Still, the threat to Britain's 'free constitution' from Stuart absolutism, real as it may have been until well after mid-century, was a declining one. The Patriots, as the years passed, became more concerned about the threat they perceived to come from the Hanoverians and their ministries. Once again, however, the Catholics, as the Patriots perceived the matter, were on the wrong side. Of course, lines of division were far from clearly drawn. Many Catholics were sympathetic to the Patriot cause and, like others, became more so as the Patriots' struggle drew on towards its climax in 1782. Equally, many Patriots found no difficulty in including the Catholic case among those it was proper for them to defend. Still, Catholics concerned with obtaining relief generally looked not to College Green, but to the Castle and to London.

As early as 1755, as the Money Bill dispute subsided, O'Conor made it clear where the Catholics sought support, by declaring in print that they, 'in Case of any future Intemperance in the Conduct of any Persons warmed with the Spirit of Liberty, might be useful in counterpoizing the Scales'.[39] The Catholics had no wish to alienate any potential supporters among the Patriots and so spoke in this vein only occasionally and generally temperately. Still, declarations of their hostility to the 'Independents' were repeated and they managed to make it clear what side they were on.[40]

Events of the 1770s served to confirm Irish Catholics in this stance. Lord North's government showed every sign of believing that the Catholics could be useful allies. There was the Quebec Act of 1774, by which the Catholic Church secured an establishment status in the newly acquired province. Patriot passions were inflamed by the threat this offered to the English-speaking colonies, but rather more by the thought that this treatment of Papists might serve as a precedent elsewhere in King George's dominions. Then, during the American War, it was proposed to raise Catholic regiments in both Ireland and Scotland, proposals which led to the passage of relief measures in England and Ireland.[41] To many the matter was plain: a despotic government was, as a century before, plotting to use Papist troops to crush the rights of free-born Britons, first in America and then, no doubt, at home. Once again the Patriot cause in Ireland received an impetus. Meanwhile the Catholics were happy to have the opportunity to declare their perfectly sincere hostility to the American rebels and Charles O'Conor wondered if it might not be appropriate to petition the king for the confiscation of the lands of the Protestants of Maryland and the restoration of the colony to the possession of Catholics.[42]

If Catholics, like everyone else, were swept along by the enthusiasm that attended the winning of the constitution of 1782,[43] the more so since the Patriots of the period found cause to favour them, yet generally they still did not look to the Irish parliament for a sympathetic hearing in the following years. The history of the relief measures of the early 1790s – demanded in London and unhappily and grudgingly accepted in Dublin – vindicated their judgement. At the end of the century, probably most politically-conscious Catholics were looking forward to the establishment of the new Union constitution with considerable enthusiasm.[44]

When the primary concern in defining the *ancien régime* is not with economics or politics but with social structures, attention inevitably focuses on the concept of privilege. This, in a degree, is unfortunate, in that the term 'privilege' is rarely a neutral one in such circumstances. To assert that the *ancien régime* was a society in which privilege was widespread is to assert more than that some people enjoyed more advantages than others. That hardly distinguishes *ancien régime* society from any other. The privilege spoken of is that which was distributed in such a way that an elite was created, capable of exercising not only political and economic but also cultural hegemony.[45] It is also privilege distributed on grounds which, since the eclipse of the *ancien régime*, have been widely held to be arbitrary and undesirable, such as noble birth or religious confession, for example. Of course, the *anciens régimes* themselves, in their vigour, possessed no aversion to elites and did not consider the grounds on which they distributed privilege to be at all arbitrary. It would be well if the historian could speak about the matter without adjudicating between the two views.

The moral shift which brought about the modern view, was, of course, already in progress during the eighteenth century and before. Indeed, it might be maintained that it was precisely this which brought about the destruction of the *ancien régime*. This change in moral perception was variously signalled. Among the French nobility, for example, there was the gradual abandonment of claims to privilege on the grounds of race and history in favour of claims resting on merit.[46] Again, in England, there was the Harringtonian dictum that power must follow property, which rose to the level of one of the most fundamental political principles of the age. The possession of property was becoming the preeminently rational and acceptable basis for the distribution of privilege. Such changes in thought had their correspondences in society. The description of French society as a *société d'ordres* had ceased to correspond at all accurately with social reality long before the Revolution dismantled the legal structures which still, in a measure, lent the description truth. Roland Mousnier found the essential characteristic of the *société d'ordres*, what distinguished it from the society which succeeded it, in the general lack of connection between the hierarchical arrangement of society and the roles played in the production of material goods by the groups so arranged. As the *ancien régime* moved towards its end the connection was becoming ever stronger.[47] The elite of the *société d'ordres*, the nobility, continued indeed to provide the most important element in the pre-revolutionary elite; but this latter was an elite 'qui s'élargit à la richesse, à la propriété et au talent'.[48] The French elite of notables, as it is now generally called, was not therefore substantially different from the elite of contemporary England. Here too the titled nobility and landed gentry stood at the centre of the elite; but around them were many more with good claim to be called gentlemen.[49]

Yet, for all the forces working towards the breakdown of older hierarchies, the principles on which those hierarchies had been established remained important. This was so not merely because they were reflected in laws that continued to be enforced. At all levels of European society innumerable groups were willing to defend those principles both because they held them true and as the foundation of their claims both to social status and to quite concrete advantages. The point needs little emphasis. After all, 'a counterrevolution that was not so much aristocratic as massive, extensive, durable and popular' was the consequence, for France among other countries, of the violent imposition of a new order based on the alternative, 'rational' principles of the revolutionaries.[50]

The claims to proprietary rights over reason made by the revolutionaries may be dismissed. The ways in which the *ancien régime* distributed privilege that were condemned by the revolutionaries were still, in varying degrees, intellectually defensible. Mousnier, by speaking of a *société d'ordres*, categorises the various grounds upon which privilege was claimed under the *ancien régime*. Preeminently it was claimed on the basis of social function. Thus, for example, its military function justified the privilege of the second order. This contention was becoming very difficult, though not impossible, to defend in the latter part of the eighteenth century, particularly in states, like France, which had a strong tradition of standing armies.[51] Even in states where noble opposition to standing armies had been attended with a measure of success, it was clear that militia forces, like the Polish *pospolite ruszenie* or the Hungarian *insurrectio*, were no match for professional troops.[52] On the other hand, the privilege possessed by the first order on account of its function was uniformly fairly easy to defend. The first order's function was now rather less to regulate the relationship between the heavenly and the earthly worlds and rather more to assist in the preservation of order in the latter by preaching morality. Still, this was no slight task and a privileged status assisted in it, as well as being an appropriate reward for it.

The distribution of privilege on the basis of the performance of such social functions created the *société d'ordres*. However, the *ancien régime* was never a pure *société d'ordres*. Other grounds existed on which privilege was distributed that were increasingly open to criticism. To name the most important, there were religious confession and ancestry. These principles for the creation of hierarchy were even more defensible than those just mentioned: for long and lively traditions of theological and historical learning came to the aid of the defenders.

Enlightenment influenced were not such as to alter the basic character of eighteenth-century divinity. Even when theology was not actually being used for controversy, its methods and emphases reflected the fact that controversy was its primary concern. Its tendency to generate declarations about the pernicious and dangerous nature of dissent from orthodoxy was inevitable. It never became necessary in the eighteenth century to explore the polemic of a previous era to be confirmed in the belief in the malignancy of Protestant heresy or Popery. Within this controversial divinity a great deal of attention was devoted to social relations, the nature of the state and the state's relationship to the church. This was necessarily so: for it was chiefly to divines that the eighteenth century turned for answers to abstract questions about society and its governance.[53] To state the matter plainly, eighteenth-century divinity was exceedingly conducive to a belief in the appropriateness of religious discrimination. Its discussion of the confessional nature of the state addressed the matter directly and at far greater length than was the case later. Moreover, the tendency of its arguments in this matter were thoroughly reinforced by its statements on almost all areas of religious concern.

There is no need to emphasise the importance which was ascribed in the *ancien régime* to the ancestry of the individual; to the genealogy which could be proven, either for the sake of material advantage or merely to satisfy pride. Contemporary historiography reflected and supported the attitudes involved. There was, for example, the tendency to concentrate on the martial and political exploits of illustrious individuals; or again, to reduce local history to an account of the distinguished families of the area.[54]

However, historiography came to the aid of privilege claimed on the grounds of ancestry in another way. Equal in importance to or perhaps more important than the ancestry ascribed to individuals, was the ancestry ascribed to the noble elite as a whole. *Ancien régime* historiography in many countries provided such an ancestry in the form of an origins myth.[55] These myths were generally based on historical events, medieval conquests, which, in a number of ways, provided matter for early modern political comment. Commonly, claims of conquest buttressed royal authority, while the counter-claim that there had been voluntary submission or acceptance of the rights of the conquered by the conqueror aided particularist elites. On occasion, the morality of conquest was even questioned.[56] However, claims of conquest might also serve the elite. It was possible to construct conquest narratives which showed, as the event took on the character of myth, how the ancestors of the noble elite triumphed over the ancestors of the relatively unprivileged. In this way the elite was rendered racially distinct from the rest of the population. It was also rendered racially superior: for the myths inevitably pointed to the martial prowess of the conquerors and the inferiority of the conquered. No doubt the most celebrated of these myths was that which French historians derived from the history of the *Völkerwanderungen* to sustain 'the distinction between noble Germans and common Gauls'.[57] However, the Magyar conquest of the Carpathian basin[58] and the German conquests in the Baltic region in the course of the northern crusades,[59] for example, were productive of very similar myths. By the end of the eighteenth century, however, new interpretations of old accounts and even counter-myths were coming into existence. Now the claim that the nobility possessed a distinct racial origin might be used not to exalt the nobility, but to denigrate it: what was demonstrated was not the nobility's superiority, but its alien character. So it was in France.[60] In Poland the long-established belief that the *szlachta* was constituted by the descendants of the warlike Sarmatians was now challenged by the equally dubious assertion that it had much less desirable origins – in Germany.[61]

What has been said above about the distribution of privilege in the *ancien régime* may be summarised. The characteristic feature of the *ancien régime* of the eighteenth century in this respect, is not merely the existence of modes of distributing privilege that later became unacceptable. Rather it is the undermining of these and a consequent conflict between those to whom they were important and those by whom they were attacked.

On first approach, the society of the Irish *ancien régime* appears to have possessed a character not dissimilar to that of its contemporaries. However, on closer investigation, it can be seen to have been somewhat deviant. This deviance is best explained by saying that in Ireland there existed two extensively overlapping, but distinct and in fact conflicting sets of beliefs about how the privileged elite ought to be constituted. Two theories of elite hegemony were in competition.

Most of the fundamental suppositions and beliefs about society and politics that prevailed in Ireland, at least since the overthrow of the Gaelic order, were shared with England. Thus an English understanding of the grounds upon which privilege might properly be distributed was substantially accepted in Ireland. This shared understanding was realised in an elite constituted in essentially the same way as the elite which dominated English society or, for that matter, the elites of France and other countries. It was an elite defined not chiefly by law, but by its possession of property and by social conventions, in particular those conventions which marked off the gentleman from others. True, this elite had an interest in securing traditional privileges held on grounds other than the possession of property. It valued, for example, the privileges of the nobility: after all, many of its members were noblemen and these, to a great extent, gave the entire elite its sense of identity and its theory of hegemony. It valued clerical privilege.

The assaults on this, in the form of assaults on the existing tithe system, were fiercely and successfully resisted until the second quarter of the nineteenth century. Significantly though, it was possible and found necessary to identify clerical rights to tithe with simple property rights.[62] Again, there was a willingness to preserve the privileges of Protestants *qua* Protestants. However, in the end, compromises on these matters were possible. The elite could take its stand simply on the rights of property, and ultimately privileges which rested on any other basis than the possession of property could, if necessary, be dispensed with.

This, of course, was not the view of those further down the social scale. For them the privileges derived from sources other than the possession of property were frequently of crucial importance. One such source was of far greater importance than any other. This was membership of the established church. It is, in fact, the importance which the Irish *ancien régime* ascribed to religious confession as a basis for the distribution of privilege, which, above all, distinguished it from the *anciens régimes* of other countries. Of course, other *anciens régimes* possessed laws relating to dissenting religionists which were very similar to those of Ireland. Most obviously there were the anti-Catholic laws of England and Scotland and the laws against the Huguenots. However, the Irish laws had a far greater impact on society than similar laws elsewhere. The laws of other states against heterodoxy operated in a predominantly negative way: they denied privilege to dissenters. The Irish laws too did this. The extent to which they did so in practice has been the major concern of recent historians of the penal laws. However, as suggested above, it is also worthwhile to ask about their positive effect, their effect, in other words, on the Protestant community.

A number of circumstances made the Irish laws against religious dissent different from the apparently similar laws elsewhere. Firstly, though they did not in practice grievously afflict most, their nominal and potential scope included the bulk of the population. Also, they operated against people who could be distinguished not only by religion, but also often by ancestry, language, social mores and the like. Further, they operated within a society in which valued privileges, such as the bearing of arms or political participation, extended rather further downwards than was commonly the case elsewhere. Because of these circumstances, out of that section of the population which they did not discriminate against, the Irish laws created a minority conscious of its distinct identity and its privileged position. In other words, they created an elite.

Thus Ireland came to possess two distinct sets of beliefs about how its elite ought to be constituted. One it held in common with England and other *anciens régimes*. The other was peculiar to itself. The former justified the existence of an elite which was certainly aristocratic, but which received into itself others who were qualified to enter by virtue of their property or ability and were willing to adopt its traditional ethos. Protestantism was, of course, a characteristic of this elite; but it was not its Protestantism which essentially constituted it as an elite. There were Catholics, the nobility and gentry, the wealthier merchants and the like, who had a claim to membership. Their exclusion by the penal laws was perceived, in some quarters anyway, as incongruous. In this lay the origin of the Catholic agitation.

The real difficulty for the Catholics lay in contending with the alternative set of beliefs about elite composition. As remarked, this, to a considerable extent, overlapped with its rival. It did not directly challenge any of the existing criteria for the distribution of privilege. It did, however, give singular emphasis to one of these, namely adherence to Protestantism. In opposition to the notion of an elite which was certainly Protestant, but only accidentally so, eighteenth-century Ireland evolved the notion that Protestantism was both a necessary and a sufficient qualification to gain access to the elite, that hegemonic rights belonged to the entire body of Protestants by virtue merely of their Protestantism. Such thinking, though, had not reached its full fruition even by the end of the century. Then the spread of near-democratic ideas and propitious political circumstances brought it to articulacy and the concept of 'Protestant democracy' emerged.[63] Before this had come another rallying cry: 'Protestant ascendancy'. The phrase entered Ireland's political vocabulary in the 1780s, to be adopted, developed and propagated as their own a few years later by Protestants hardly close to the landed aristocracy and gentry with whom it was later to be associated.[64] But for most of the eighteenth century the assertiveness of the lower ranks of the Protestant community had difficulty in finding expression. After all, Ireland shared the common political culture of the Hanoverian Empire and such a curiously-constituted elite existed nowhere else in King George's dominions. However, the claim that was being made was clearly understood by those who rejected it, such as Burke. If Catholics continued to suffer exclusion simply on the grounds that they were not Protestants, Burke asserted, Ireland would be in 'the condition of all countries in which an hereditary nobility possess the exclusive rule'. Burke, of course, had no objection to aristocracies. But he emphatically rejected the notion that the Irish Protestants as a whole could be regarded as constituting one. They were 'too numerous to answer the ends and purposes of an aristocracy' and, in any case, were 'to all outward appearance plebeians'.[65]

In the context of his own British political culture, Burke may well have been right. The idea that Irish Protestants should be regarded as a noble elite was quite unacceptable, at least when the matter was stated so plainly. However, polities unlike England's also existed.

An outstanding feature of most nobilities was a membership which reflected the whole social spectrum: as well as nobles with impressive titles, great estates and important political functions, there were noble shopkeepers, peasants, artisans, shepherds, labourers, professional men and officials.[66]

To nobilities which included within them a *petite noblesse*, and in particular to the so-called popular nobilities of eastern Europe or Spain, the Irish Protestant body did bear a distinct similarity. It possessed privileges very similar to those possessed by the mainland nobilities; privileges relating to landownership, the bearing of arms, access to education and the professions, political participation and so on. Looking at the history of the Irish parliament especially, it can be seen that it possessed similar political means of defending its possession of those privileges.

Striking too is the similarity of the ideological defences that were used. Indeed, they were often precisely the same. Such a comparison may appear strained. The arguments used by Irish Protestants in defence of their elite status were, after all, generally drawn from the political culture of Britain and not from that of the European mainland. However, the important point in the present context is not the sources of the argumentation used by the Irish Protestants, but the purpose to which that argumentation was put. Positions which were enunciated, for example, to defend the confessional nature of the English state, or by the English Patriots when they spoke about a standing army and a militia, were adhered to and repeated in Ireland in part because Irishmen were involved with the issues which agitated political life throughout the Empire. However, in an Irish context these positions inevitably took on a rather different significance from that which they possessed elsewhere. They became assertions of the Protestant right to hegemony; and the fact is revealed when comparison is made with the defences of the traditional modes of distributing privilege in use at the same time elsewhere in Europe. Among these, conservative thinking accorded pre-eminence to those which referred to the nobles' military role and their ancestry, albeit that the persuasiveness of such defences was diminishing. The Irish Protestants too spoke much of their military role and their ancestry. Their case, however, was more convincing.

The venerable oppositionist tradition of hostility to a standing army and enthusiasm for a citizen militia, the intellectual origins of which have been traced to the civic humanism of the Italian renaissance, was common to England and Ireland.[67] In Ireland, just as much as in England, it found frequent opportunity to express itself, at all moments of national military crisis and whenever augmentation of the army was proposed.[68] However, while it is quite proper to point out that the content of these Irish debates owed much to traditions of political thought in England and elsewhere, what was singular to Ireland should not be overlooked. The distinctive element in the Irish debates derived chiefly from the close connection, indeed often inseparability, of the pro-militia case and an anti-Catholic position. In other words, the claim to a significant role in the defence of the state was, like the similar claim of the nobilities of the European mainland, closely related to a claim to a superior position in the social hierarchy. It may be added that the connection between the pro-militia case and anti-Catholicism was the former's major strength.

In Ireland, as in Britain, popular calls for the abolition of a peacetime standing army became increasingly unconvincing as the eighteenth century progressed. However, the case for a permanently established militia remained strong. This, though, was much more the case in Ireland than in Britain. For Ireland had, or was perceived to have, military needs that, clearly, were best answered by a militia. Most obviously, there was the agrarian violence which was endemic in late-eighteenth-century Ireland. However, in the view of most Protestants, this was but a manifestation of a greater threat – the threat which justified the existence of the penal laws – the active disloyalty of the Catholic population. In fact, Irish agitation of the militia issue was always, implicitly or explicitly, bound up with this.[69] Nor did such arguments in favour of a militia fall on deaf ears: for the reality of the Catholic threat to the state was believed in almost as firmly by those charged with the government of Ireland as it was by the Protestant population at large.[70]

If the claim of the Irish Protestants to possess a significant military role was more convincing than that of nobilities of the European mainland, so too was their claim to possess an ancestry distinct from that of the substantially unprivileged part of the population. This latter claim, like parallel claims on the mainland, was closely associated with a conquest myth, as it has been called here. More accurately, in the case of Ireland, one might speak of conquest myths. The Norman invasion in the twelfth century, like that of England in the previous century, was disputed matter on account of the rights it was held to give or not to give to the crown.[71] However, accounts of it also served well to assert the superiority of that part of the population which was of English descent and the barbarous nature of that part which was not. As one pamphleteer put it:

How great then was the Undertaking! How glorious was the Work of Henry the Second, and those first *British* Adventurers, who, like Gods, engaged in the arduous Task of reforming this *Chaos* [of pre-Norman Ireland], of restoring the beautiful Face of Nature, of suppressing Tyrany, and making a Nation happy? – I care not to boast of what is not my own: Yet I must acknowledge, that I feel a secret Joy in the Thought, that my Ancestor was one among these Heroes...[72]

Not all Protestants could claim Norman ancestry, though, while many Catholics could. This first conquest then, was associated with later ones; with the Elizabethan conquest, when 'the Protestant Religion and Liberty was [sic] established among us' in the teeth of the resurgent 'old *Irish* Tyrants'; with the Cromwellian conquest, which took place after the unprecedented display of barbarity by the Irish Papists in 1641; and with King William's conquest, when the Irish, those 'bloody Cut-throats', again displayed their incorrigibility.[73]

The accounts of these conquests served the same purpose as the accounts of the origins of the mainland nobilities. They denigrated the descendants of the conquered and exalted the heirs of those who, by valour and divine favour,[74] were able to pass on to their descendants a claim by sword-right to the land. However, the close temporal proximity of the events referred to gave the Irish myths a force that could not be matched elsewhere: for these myths operated on the minds of Protestants who had reason to believe that the property they held was still fiercely coveted by the heirs of the dispossessed.[75] If this was not sufficient to reinforce them, then there was also the daily experience of the cultural divide which existed in a country that was still predominantly Irish-speaking: an Irish Catholic was clearly alien to Irish Protestants in a way that a French bourgeois, or even peasant, was not to his superiors.

Arguments of a sort becoming dated in Europe generally, arguments that sought to show that military function and ancestry gave a right to privilege, retained more force in Ireland. Nevertheless, Irish Protestants still felt the need to adopt, if they could adapt them, those defences of elite privilege which were becoming more fashionable. Ultimately the acceptance of the principle that privilege should be distributed on the grounds of the possession of property or merit was destructive of the *ancien régime*. Burke perceived that the dictum that power must follow property was a serviceable one in the cause of the Irish Catholics[76] and his view was shared by many Catholic and pro-Catholic writers of the late eighteenth and early nineteenth centuries. The Catholics possessed property and were thereby entitled to participate in the constitution.[77] However, as long as the balance of property lay with the traditional elite, the Harringtonian dictum was still capable of being used in defence of conservative positions; and indeed it was used in defence of Irish Protestant privilege. The Protestants as a whole, it was maintained, possessed by far the greater part of the property of the kingdom and their ascendancy was thus just.[78]

Of course, the most substantial and fundamental ideological supports of Protestant privilege were taken from the tradition of controversial divinity which defended Protestantism and the Protestant state. The conviction that Popery was no true religion, but a tissue of falsehood constructed to advance the material and political interests of the Roman priesthood,[79] was held to constitute in itself sufficient grounds for preserving the social relationships which the penal laws helped to maintain. If argumentation in defence of Protestant privilege went beyond this controversial divinity, it did not forget it. Theologically grounded anti-Catholic beliefs remained as presuppositions. It is true, of course, that religious argumentation constituted an important element in the intellectual defence of the *ancien régime* everywhere. However, Irish Protestants were singularly advantaged among the privileged elites of eighteenth-century Europe in being able to make such extensive use of the most important area of contemporary divinity, controversy, immediately in the defence of their privileged position.

Some exception has been taken to the acceptance by historians of the popular practice of using the late-eighteenth-century term 'Protestant ascendancy' to refer to Ireland's dominant elite around mid-century and earlier. The objection is not without some justification. It is no doubt always desirable for the historian to be aided in the adoption of the mind of the period being discussed by the use of contemporary vocabulary. However, 'Protestant ascendancy' is a near-contemporary term and its use appears acceptable, if its primitive significance is held in mind. It must be recalled that the phrase originally denoted a polity – or rather a variety of desired polities – as much as it denoted a body of persons and that that body comprehended a wider social and perhaps religious spectrum than nineteenth- and twentieth-century literary usage suggests. Use of the phrase, with its primitive significance, renders it ambiguous in a number of respects and reflection on those ambiguities is revealing, irrespective of what part of the century is being considered. The change in the usage of 'ascendancy', from use as primarily an abstract noun to use as a collective noun, is at least suggestive of the role of confessionalist beliefs and laws in determining Irish social structure. To note the diversity of opinion about precisely what legal and social status those who accepted – or at an earlier period would have accepted – the term 'Protestant ascendancy' wanted to accord to Catholics is to begin to investigate the extent of the century's commitment to its Protestant constitution. The most important question raised by historical probings of the term's use, however, relates to its religious and social extension. Did the collective noun signify Protestant dissenters as much as it did Anglicans; signify merchants, members of the professions and even operatives as much as it did the landed interest? To ask this is to become aware of Ireland's longstanding ideological difficulty in the matter of the composition of its *ancien régime* elite.[80]

In the foregoing survey of approaches to the question of definition of the *ancien régime*, it is hoped enough has been said to establish a preliminary case for speaking of the existence and dominance of, if not an *ancien régime*, an *ancien régime* ideology in eighteenth-century Ireland. It is also hoped that enough has been said, if again only in a preliminary way, to indicate the importance which the question of the role to be played by Catholics in society and state had for those who espoused that ideology. The rest of this study will attempt to establish more firmly what has already been advanced.

The ideology which will be discussed expressed itself in a variety of ways. It expressed itself, for example, in the ecclesiastical and civil liturgy of the period. Any acquaintance with eighteenth-century Dublin in particular, reveals a year studded with fasts and feasts with a strong political character kept by the City's churchmen, dignitaries, common citizens and inhabitants. Some were transient, devised to seek divine aid in a moment of national crisis or for the celebration of a triumph; others, like the celebrations of royal birthdays or the annual commemorations of significant events in the history of the Protestant and monarchical state, were more enduring.[81] In some cases, like those just mentioned, the political character of these solemnities is obvious; in others it may not be so clear. There were, for example, the festivities organised exclusively by the corporation and the guilds. In fact, these too carried a political message. One Dublin historian, speaking of the most important event in the City's calendar, the riding of the franchises, remarked:

> It was at once a commemoration of defiance against the Irish enemy outside the city's confines and an assertion for the benefit of the unfree and inferior in the city, that the guilds were determined to hold and perpetuate the privileges they enjoyed.[82]

All this activity would bear examination by those interested in the political ideology of eighteenth-century Ireland.[83] It is probable that it commu-

nicated that ideology more clearly and effectively than anything else could
to eighteenth-century Irishmen. However, modern historians are doubtless
better served by the literature with which this study is primarily concerned.

Before offering an explanation of how the findings of the study of this
literature is presented in the remaining parts of this work, it will be
convenient to refer to two other approaches to the problem of definition of
the *ancien régime*. Amidst their disputes about definition, historians of the
French *ancien régime* have mostly been able to agree that the object of
their investigation is what the Revolution destroyed, or, at least, what it
attempted to destroy.[84] It thus seems possible to offer a definition of the
term *ancien régime* which is based on an enquiry into its original significance: for the term emerged in the political discourse of the revolutionary
period. In short, the *ancien régime* was what its enemies considered it to
be.[85] Stated in this way, the approach sounds less than acceptable. There is,
however, much to be said for it. After all, it is not possible to define the
ancien régime without comparing it with what came after. Nevertheless,
if one is prepared to accept the view of the late-eighteenth- and early-
nineteenth-century revolutionaries as guidance in determining what the
most important elements in the constitution of the *ancien régime* were, it
would appear not unreasonable also to consider the view, as it were, from
within the *ancien régime*. Such an approach would, of course, necessitate a
discussion of the three, or more, traditional orders. This is not so simply
because of the conventionality which attached to the notion of a tripartite
division of society, by virtue of its venerable antiquity,[86] and the consequent
frequency of explicit reference to the notion in contemporary sources.[87]
Rather, it is so because the major institutions of *ancien régime* society, as
that society is described by contemporaries, whether they make explicit
reference to the three orders or not, turn out to resemble closely the
traditional estates. Quite simply, when those who lived under the *ancien
régime* described their society, they inevitably devoted considerable attention to such institutions as the monarchy, the church and the nobility.[88] This
approach to definition appears to have been the one adopted by Clark in his
study of the English *ancien régime*. To a discussion of the roles of the
monarchy and the church in eighteenth-century English society, he adds a
reconstruction of the period's theory of elite hegemony. Discussion of a
theory of elite hegemony might indeed be regarded as providing convenient
access to consideration of the two remaining orders.[89]

It is assumed in this study that the various approaches to the question of
definition of the *ancien régime* mentioned in the course of this chapter are
in fact complementary. They do, after all, emerge from the examination of

different aspects or areas of social life or, in the case of the last two mentioned, from the understandings possessed in different periods. Thus, in attempting to show that the significance of Ireland's Catholic question lay in its relationship to an *ancien régime* ideology, this study varies its understandings of how such an ideology should be defined. Accepting the view that important aspects of an *ancien régime* are revealed by the attacks that were made on it, the third and fourth parts of the work examine pro-Catholic literature, from mid-century through the earlier decades of the Catholic question's history.[90] In the second part of the work what was referred to above as the view from within the *ancien régime* has been accepted as the basis of definition. Thus, Chapter 3 is concerned with the church and the monarchical state, while Chapter 4 is concerned with the question of the hierarchical ordering of Irish society. However, it will be seen that these two chapters also take up the themes which were touched on above in speaking of the contribution of political and social history to the definition of the *ancien régime*.

Part II

Part II

3 The Catholic Question and the Irish Confessional State

Prominent among the problems faced by the historian who wishes to speak of the *ancien régime* is that of periodisation. The solution any historian may offer will, it has already been suggested, depend largely on how he chooses to deal with the prior problem of definition.[1] However, if the term is applied to Ireland, a *terminus a quo* for the discussion appears easy to establish. So profound were the political, social and economic consequences of the Elizabethan, Cromwellian and Williamite conquests, that one would be unlikely to attempt to assign the origins of the Irish *ancien régime* to any other period than, broadly speaking, the seventeenth century.[2]

From one point of view this raises doubts about whether the term *ancien régime* should be applied to Ireland at all: for some hold substantial continuity with the medieval past to be an essential element in the definition of the *ancien régime*.[3] Such doubts can be resolved, however, if it is said that what occurred in the late sixteenth and the seventeenth century was the extension to Ireland, and consequent mutation, of the English *ancien régime*. What is under discussion when an Irish *ancien régime* is spoken of, is a British *ancien régime* as it existed in Ireland.

The discussion in the following pages of Irish thinking in the eighteenth century about the confessional nature of the state will serve to illustrate this point. To a great extent the views expressed by Irishmen on this subject sounded perfectly familiar in English ears: indeed, they were often intended for an English audience.[4] However, this Irish conformity to a common British politico-religious discourse can mislead. For when Irishmen addressed Irishmen and the reference of this discourse was to the phenomena of Irish religious, social and political life, the significance of what was said was inevitably changed, in general, by addition. It is not that the confessional nature of the state was unimportant to Englishmen; on the contrary, it was of fundamental importance. However, to Irishmen its importance was not only fundamental. It was also immediate and pervasive.

The basis of the pro-Catholic argumentation which emerged in Ireland in the latter part of the eighteenth century can be summed up in a statement which was, in various forms, constantly reiterated: 'That Disaffection to the *Religion* of the State, is one Thing; and Disaffection to the *Constitution* of our Country, quite another.'[5] If this point could not be established, then further discussion was in vain: religious dissenters were, by virtue of their religious dissent, bad subjects and the restraints laid on them thus justified. The responses made to the proposition advanced by the Catholics and their allies bear some examination. There were some, throughout the century, who were prepared simply to reject it.[6] This view, it is true, did not often find expression in print, though the constant discussion of the matter in the Catholic pamphlets suggests that even if it was not in Protestant writings, it was certainly in Protestant minds. By far the greater part of those who opposed proposals for Catholic relief in print were prepared to accept this fundamental point advanced by their opponents. They asserted, however, that it was simply not *ad rem* in discussing the case of the Catholics. In the abstract, it was conceded, religious dissenters could be tolerably good subjects. In fact, Catholics were not.[7]

This Irish debate, as outlined here, hardly displayed originality: it well reflected thinking which had become common throughout Britain. It is scarcely surprising that Irish Catholics came to adopt arguments for toleration founded on the conception of church and state as, at least theoretically, distinct. It is only surprising that it was not until the latter part of the eighteenth century that they commonly did so. It is true that the view of the relationship between church and state upon which Locke in particular founded his plea for the toleration of dissenters never won wholehearted acceptance in eighteenth-century Britain. Those who adhered to it in the earlier part of the century, such as Bishop Hoadly, were hardly representative of Anglican opinion. Such views, like the heterodoxy in the matter of Trinitarian belief with which they were associated, became even less acceptable as the century progressed.[8] However, whatever views were held about the general question of the nature of the church–state relationship, thinking about the particular and practical matter of toleration was but little affected. By mid-century Anglicans had reached a satisfactory *modus vivendi* with Protestant dissenters[9] and it would have been imprudent indeed to challenge the grounds on which they most commonly argued their case. In fact, when the Catholics began to make use of it, the body of argumentation which justified the toleration that these more favoured nonconformists enjoyed – at least when it was used for that purpose – had acquired something of the status of an orthodoxy.

What is revealed by the failure of Irish Protestants to challenge the fundamental principle on which the advocates of Catholic relief asserted their case, is the decay of the confessionalism of the British state as a whole. This decay was considerable in practice and practice required justification, though not fundamental rethinking of the church–state relationship. It is observation of 'society's ostensible account of its nature', rather than observation of how this was translated into practice, which must provide a considerable part of what justification there is for using the term 'confessional state' in speaking of eighteenth-century Britain.[10] Still, theory and practice were by no means wholly divorced. In some respects their union was preserved and no Lockean special logic was required.[11]

The description of eighteenth-century Britain as a confessional state is not only doubtful but also ambiguous. The practice of extending a toleration to those who, while indeed dissenting from the established church, could be comprehended under the name of Protestants, renders very doubtful indeed reference to an Anglican confessional state. However, the situation of those who could not be so comprehended, either on account of their Catholicism or on account of their lack of Trinitarian belief, provides a considerable initial justification for reference to a Protestant confessional state. No doubt this distinction between Anglican and Protestant confessionalism would have been lost on many contemporaries: for most practical purposes the rule of Fielding's Thwackum could be followed[12] and the Church of England and Protestantism assumed to be co-extensive. Of course, to dissenters, Protestant and non-Protestant alike, the distinction was quite clear. As the eighteenth-century advanced, their demands for relief obliged others to reflect on it too. The comparative ease with which Trinitarian Protestant dissenters at length achieved their aims and the resistance which others continued to meet constituted a predictable enough statement that it was Protestant, rather than Anglican confessionalism that was held to be the more important.[13]

Great as the importance of Protestant confessionalism was in Britain as a whole, its importance was greater in Ireland. Irishmen possessed many of the same motivations as Englishmen for preserving Protestant confessionalism. Preeminently, it justified the dynasty's occupation of the throne. It is probably but to put this in other words, to say that it provided an ideological *raison d'être* for the state and justified the social order established within it. However, their circumstances ensured that such considerations presented themselves to the mass of Irish Protestants in such a way that they conceived their own immediate interests to be intimately related to the maintenance of that confessionalism. Those same circumstances – chiefly the simple fact that the greater part of the population of Ireland was Catholic – also ensured that this conception was continuously present to their minds. In short, we have reason to hestitate over the description of eighteenth-century Britain as a confessional state. We need not be so hesitant in speaking about Ireland. Here, that aspect of British confessionalism which gives most substance to the description assumed an importance that removes any such hesitation.

What, therefore, the copious argumentation supporting the refusal to extend the benefits of the Lockean doctrine on toleration to Catholics constitutes, is a defence of the Irish confessional state. It is not, as is very often assumed, a mere expression of religious bigotry. Contemporary Catholics and their allies strove to depict it thus, as an unacceptable survival in the *siècle des lumières* of the 'Party-rage' of the Reformation era.[14] On the other hand, the defenders of the Protestant cause constantly asserted that the hostility they showed towards the Catholics was 'not on Account of their religious, but *their political faith*'.[15] Since the suppositions of their argument were Lockean, it was hardly possible for them to do other than assert that their motivations were political ones. Nevertheless, such protestations can be accepted, provided that it is understood that the political beliefs their writings and statements referred to were such as were appropriate for the defence of a confessional state; that is to say, that they rested upon, and were not truly separable from, religious convictions.[16]

From the viewpoint of those who became hostile to the European confessional state, its most conspicuous characteristic was to be found in its attitude to, and treatment of, religious dissenters. A more positive view places this in context, as a consequence of an identification of the national – or generally more accurately, since we are speaking of *anciens régimes*, dynastic – interest with a religious one. Underlying and informing both this identification and its consequences was a further identification, that of a particular ecclesiastical body as the exclusive possessor of religious truth. When such convictions weakened, some alternative *raison d'être* for the state had to be found – it was generally supplied by nationalism – and the distribution of privilege on the grounds of religious affiliation became arbitrary.

Both the Anglican and the Protestant confessionalism of the Hanoverian state rested upon such religious convictions. The traditions of controversy which supported such convictions remained, in both cases, lively throughout the eighteenth century. It would be quite wrong to suggest that a willingness to deny the status of a legitimate form of Christianity to Protestant dissent was a peculiarity of high churchmen with old-fashioned intellectual tastes. Anglicanism's accommodation of contemporary intellectual trends allowed the suggestion that it possessed proprietary rights over reason and toleration.[17] Protestant dissent could be demonstrated to be false, just as Catholicism could, by its reputed rejection of the received doctrines of the age and its maintenance of enthusiastic – or, in the case of

Catholicism, obscurantist – and persecuting principles.[18] Nevertheless, in controversy, as in other areas, the decay of Anglican confessionalism and the continuing vitality of Protestant confessionalism provide a clear contrast. The moderation imposed on high churchmen by the advent of whig hegemony moved the parameters of debate in favour of those receptive to Anglicanism's comprehensionist and latitudinarian tradition.[19] Even in itself this stiffened the attitude of Protestant controversialists towards Catholicism: for the classical expounders of that tradition 'had based their hopes for Protestant unity not only on a broader spirit of toleration within Protestantism but also on a united front against Rome'.[20]

Fundamental to Protestantism's claim to the exclusive possession of religious truth was the conviction that its sole rival was such a thing as could not 'but for want of a better word to express it, be called a religion'. In so speaking, Andrew Marvell[21] was not indulging in mere polemical hyperbole. He was summarising the conclusion of the controversial Protestant divinity of the sixteenth and seventeenth centuries, as it flowed directly from the central tenets of Reformation theology. Luther's solfidianism produced an ecclesiology in which the church was simply an invisible *congregatio fidelium*. As such, it clearly could not exercise jurisdictional powers and certainly not in temporal affairs.[22] The Roman church's essential fault was to claim such powers. It had done so to the extent that what now existed was, in fact, a political system, rather than a religious one, though it made use of false religious doctrines and vain or harmful religious practices to advance its interests.[23] This view determined the shape of Protestant controversy. If the papacy's claims to a *potestas jurisdictionis* were successfully refuted, then, it seemed, little by way of further argumentation would be required.

Of course, history as well as theology served controversy. In view of Enlightenment distaste for dogmatic argumentation, it is not remarkable that it was the former that was somewhat preferred in the eighteenth century's anti-Catholic writings. Indeed, the anti-Catholic historiographical tradition itself was not uninfluenced by the fashions of the age. A distinctively eighteenth-century statement of the core of this tradition is set out in the writings of Francis Hutchinson, an Englishman of historical bent, who in 1720 obtained the bishopric of Down and Connor. Called to present the most salient points of anti-Catholic argumentation, in a sermon before the House of Lords, he took leave to lay before his hearers 'the strange course of the *Church of Rome*'.[24] He found the beginnings of the emergence of Popery from Christianity in the reaction of the patrician families of the old Rome to Constantine's establishment of a new capital on the Bosphorus. Chagrined by their loss of influence, they resolved to recreate their city's empire in ecclesiastical guise. From the 'Commonwealth of LXXII Cardinals', which they established, emerged the papal monarchy. Partly by perverting Christian doctrine to serve its own purposes, this institution accumulated political power until, at length, the pope 'undertook by Office to set up and pull down and dispose of Kingdoms, and give them away to whom he pleased'. The bishop went on to trace the reverses suffered by the court of Rome, not only at the Reformation but also at the hands of contemporary Catholic princes of Gallican inclination: it was the challenging of the worldly power of the papacy, rather than the defence of the doctrines of the reformers that was central. Hutchinson retained this stance when, a few years later, he published a work on Irish historiography. He dismissed the notion that national sentiment or religion was the cause of conflict between Irishmen and Englishmen: the only cause of division was papal power.[25]

Hutchinson's obligation to the anti-Catholic historiography of the sixteenth and seventeenth centuries, and in particular to the English tradition and its most eminent representative, John Foxe, is obvious. It was from these sources that the bishop took his dating of the rise of Popery. He also accepted their explanation of that event – but only in part. The concern of the earlier polemicists was not with ecclesiastical history in any modern sense of the term, but rather with *Heilsgeschichte*. Obliged to come to terms with the enormity of the changes which they had brought about or supported, the early Protestants were constrained to interpret their Reformation – and by extension the circumstances that led up to it – in terms taken from an apocalyptic tradition which had meant little to the Christian church since the days of Constantine and Augustine. The events they spoke of became part of the cosmic struggle between good and evil. The most important actors in them were God, Satan and the Anti-Christ.[26] All of this was quite absent from Hutchinson's exposition. Popery, in his account, was merely the product of human desire for power and wealth, rather than the instrument of an unmixed supernatural evil. He could thus hope for an end to it, not in eschatological conflict, but in peaceful change. Papists might, at length, become merely Catholics – in other words, adopt a clear Gallican stance – and the way be thus prepared for the papacy itself to abandon its unreasonable claims and accept reform.[27]

Mild as Hutchinson's anti-Catholicism may appear when seen in comparison with that of earlier writers, it was nevertheless quite able to sustain the belief of Protestants that they were the exclusive possessors of religious truth. Popery was not denounced as the artifice of the Anti-Christ; but it was clearly asserted to be something other than religion. In any case, Hutchinson said nothing which directly contradicted the traditional Protestant view that, since the High Middle Ages, the Anti-Christ had reigned in Rome. Such a contradiction would have been highly contentious, as the reaction, around mid-century, to the views of John Hutchinson, the natural philosopher, and his Oxford followers demonstrated.[28]

Enlightenment influence moderated somewhat the anti-Catholicism of earlier eighteenth-century figures such as Bishop Hutchinson. Is it not possible to assert that the same benign influence reduced both the intensity and extent of Irish anti-Catholicism as the century progressed? It may be; but the qualifications which must be added are so substantial that the assertion may be judged more deceptive than helpful. In the first place, it is not contested that popular anti-Catholicism retained its intensity and adherents. This popular anti-Catholicism took up and developed those themes of Protestant controversy which could be related to common experience; but it retained the central convictions expressed by the divines. The pope's insatiable desire for political power was of less interest than the avarice and petty despotism of the priest, the perversion of Christian doctrine of less interest than the perversion of Christian morality.[29] The essential point made, however, remained the same: the religion practised by Catholics was not, in truth, religion at all.

However, it is not a diminution of this anti-Catholicism in the later eighteenth century that has been asserted or assumed, but that of the elite, as they came under Enlightenment influence. The very existence of the Catholic relief acts of the last quarter of the century has not infrequently been regarded as the most conspicuous evidence of such a diminution and such an influence. In fact, the relationship between Enlightenment thought, anti-Catholicism and Catholic relief is not nearly so straightforward. Firstly, it is not to be assumed that Enlightenment influence necessarily worked against anti-Catholicism. It did much to revivify it: Voltaire was more readable than sixteenth- and seventeenth-century divines.[30] To the extent that anti-Catholicism was assailed, it was assailed in a weak, largely negative way. Irreligion, indifferentism, or distaste for serious discussion of Christian dogma tended to reduce both the quantity and the acerbity of anti-Catholic rhetoric. A zealous controversialist, one clergyman complained, now ran 'the Risque of giving Offence to the most genteel Part of his Congregation'.[31] Catholicism was less attacked; it was not more commended. Casting around for Anglican divines who did display an inclination to adopt a positive view of at least some aspects of his religion, one Catholic apologist could mention no one more respectable than the Nonjuror, Thomas Deacon, and James II's bishop of Oxford, Samuel Parker.[32]

If Enlightenment influence in some cases sharpened and increased anti-Catholicism, this was certainly not the only factor at work in insuring that a loss of zeal among some was compensated for by an increase of it among others. The existence of an eventually successful Catholic agitation and the rise of agrarian violence seen against alarming European backgrounds were much more important in forming an anti-Catholic resurgence, which, as already pointed out, appeared very quickly after mid-century.[33] But the relationship of this renewed anti-Catholicism to relief is, like the relationship of Enlightenment thought and anti-Catholicism, more complex than might initially be thought. Just as Enlightenment thought did not necessarily reduce anti-Catholicism, so anti-Catholicism did not necessarily induce opposition to relief.

The relief acts do not provide evidence for the kind of change in the communal mind of the elite which has often been suggested. In the first place, it must be pointed out that the relief acts can fairly be described as simply the products of the military needs of the British government transmuted into political pressure on unwilling Irish legislators.[34] But this allowed, can it not be said that some change of common mind must have occurred to make recourse to relief in military or political necessity thinkable? Perhaps a positive answer to this can be allowed in discussing the English governing elite; but it will hardly do in speaking of Ireland. What change of mind occurred in a section of the elite by the end of the century must fundamentally be seen as the product of a pragmatic acceptance of a new situation chiefly created by the relief acts. In speaking of the positive relationship between a diminution of anti-Catholicism and relief, the former should generally be regarded as effect rather than cause.

The argumentation in favour of Catholic relief in the period, though adorned with rhetorical references to the enlightenment of the age, was intended to appeal to a pragmatic attitude, rather than to men willing to alter their beliefs fundamentally. It commended the encouragement of a section of the population which was depressed; it did not commend those people's beliefs or even, in general, a more tolerant attitude to them. It was thus possible for the promoters of relief to adopt anti-Catholic stances. Henry Grattan, for example, in arguing against the clergy who opposed the reform of the tithe system, could casually recite the core of the argument against Popery:

> The care of religion is placed no where better than in the legislature. Popery will tell you, that when it was entirely left to the care of the priesthood, it was perverted and destroyed.[35]

Nor should it be assumed that the anti-Catholicism of those who supported relief measures was merely casual or generated by habit. To accept the desirability of relief did not at all imply an abandonment, from either principle or discouragement, of a belief in conducting a struggle against Popery. It was precisely to advance it, their supporters claimed, that relief measures were brought forward. 'Hopes of uniformity' were not to be abandoned; previous legislators had simply mistaken 'the means of con-version'.[36] What was required was a less harsh approach, congruent with the attitudes which, it was now clear, rendered inevitable the demise of superstitions as gross as those which constituted Popery. Some, while sup-porting a new approach, may have been less disposed to deny the usefulness of the old one – at least in its time. Catholic apologists were in the habit of declaring, in public, that the penal laws had failed and would thus continue to fail in their avowed purpose of conversion.[37] In private, they were probably more pessimistic, at least with regard to the more consequential part of their community. One correspondent of O'Conor in the 1750s gave his opinion that 'in another Century, if the present penal Laws subsist, it is likely that all the Farmers of the Irish or Strongbonian Races will be Protestant'.[38] There was indeed an increased conversion rate in the 1750s and the upward trend was to continue.[39] In short, among some, the inclination to repeal penal legislation may well have been stimu-lated by a renewed, Enlightenment-inspired anti-Catholicism, nurtured amidst convictions that much had already been achieved in the struggle.

Nothing in this discussion is intended to demonstrate that there was no diminution of anti-Catholicism in later eighteenth-century Ireland. There certainly was. However, there was also an intensification of anti-Catholicism and this may well have been a more important phenomenon. The matter remains to be judged. Meanwhile, the mere existence of the Enlightenment and the relief acts should certainly not be taken as a counter-indication.

Religious conviction provides the essential basis of confessionalism. It does so when it provides the state with an ideological *raison d'être*. The way in which Protestant – in particular anti-Catholic – religious conviction provided such a *raison d'être* in late Tudor and early Stuart England has been described by writers such as William Haller,[40] William Lamont[41] and Carol Wiener.[42] The religio-political ideology of which they speak inevitably suffered change over the course of the following century-and-a-half. The latter part of the seventeenth century saw, for example, the abandonment of its chiliastic elements.[43] Again, with the Revolution and the coming of the Hanoverians it resumed its role of providing justification for the dynasty, a role inevitably lost in the Restoration period: Charles II and his Popish brother hardly fitted the image of the godly prince. Despite such changes, however, the core of the ideology endured and remained immensely influential in many quarters in the mid-eighteenth century.

Britain had remained, on account of its role in the defence of the Protestant cause and 'upon this account alone..., since the blessed Aera of the Reformation, *the Chosen People of the Lord, whom he has formed for himself – and to shew forth his Praise*'.[44] As when the conspiracy against it was centred in Habsburg Spain,[45] so now when it centred in Bourbon France, the latter-day Israel was still confronted by a monolithic Catholic enemy, plotting untiringly. The Protestant state in 'The little *British* Isles, hardly the size of a *French* Province' was still, by human reckoning, bound to be defeated. Yet those who were its enemies were, in truth, engaged in theomachy: their fate was certain.[46] The truth of this belief was vouched for by the numerous examples of divine intervention on behalf of Protestant Britain that were commemorated in the anniversary sermons.

The extent and degree of adherence to this understanding of the British state and its place in the world is difficult to state precisely. Jeremy Black has spoken of the eighteenth century's continuing 'habit of discussing relations [between states] in religious terms.'[47] The habit was not often permitted to become an important factor in determining Britain's foreign policy. However, it was not banished. The elder Pitt found it advantageous to make much of Britain's duty to Protestantism to gain support for Frederick II, who rapidly rose to the status of a latter-day Gustavus Adolphus. British interests, for the moment, coincided with the 'Protestant interest', so dear to the hearts of the popular pamphleteers. However, by 1761, with a rising demand for peace, they had ceased to do so. 'Just as suddenly as the popular enthusiasm for Frederick in Britain flared up, just as rapidly did it disappear'.[48] Even among the populace, anti-Catholicism had lost some of its power as a determinant of how Britons saw the world. However, it would certainly be wrong to dismiss this Protestant worldview by placing it under such a heading as 'popular attitudes'. Central elements in it, at least, were the commonly-received views at all levels of society. When, around mid-century, O'Conor and Curry began to attack, in particular, the historical myths which sustained Protestant belief in perpetual Catholic conspiracy, they understood their task as an assault on an unchallenged scholarly consensus rather than on a mere vulgar prejudice.[49] They were certainly right: they faced a prolonged struggle against the views of some of the most acclaimed writers of the period, such as Hume and, later and nearer home, Thomas Leland.[50] Nor was the prevalence of such views without political consequences. The fears evoked by a belief in the desire and capacity of Catholics to overthrow the state influenced the actions of both the legislators and governors of Ireland. They were to do so for many years to come.

The description given here of the Protestant confessionalism of the Hanoverian state does it less than justice. For its anti-Catholicism, important as that was, was but one of its elements. When viewed from an English perspective, its concern with the preservation of the social and political order and with the non-Trinitarian dissent which was perceived as threatening it,[51] might well appear just as important as its concern with Catholicism. This is not to suggest that such concerns were alien to the Protestants of Ireland. Nevertheless, the circumstances of eighteenth-century Irish Protestants made a preoccupation with Catholicism inevitable. It was this preoccupation which rendered Protestant confessionalism a far more important phenomenon in Ireland than in England. In this, in the significance of the role it assumed, rather than in any very distinctive content, lay the major difference between the confessionalism of Ireland and that of England. An understanding of the distinctiveness of Irish confessionalism thus requires an understanding of the circumstances in which Irish Protestants stood.

Preeminently, there was the fact that Irish Protestants constituted only a minority of the population. This, though at one level of thought constantly and no doubt sincerely regretted, had been and remained a necessary condition for the enjoyment of privileged status by the community as a whole.[52] The maintenance of that privileged status rested, ideologically, on the doctrines of Protestant confessionalism. This topic must be taken up later.[53] The present concern is with the negative consequences for Irish Protestants of their condition as a minority – in particular, the fear which that condition engendered.

The extent and importance of the fear which afflicted eighteenth-century Irish Protestants have been little adverted to by historians. This is hardly because of any lack of evidence in primary sources, most notably – but certainly not exclusively – pamphlet literature, which constantly appealed to fear of disloyalty and conspiracy among Catholics in arguing against legal concessions to them. However, expressions of this concern have not been regarded as true indications of Protestant motivation in preserving the penal code.[54] In explanation of this disregard of the declared views of contemporaries, it is possible only to suggest that historians, being themselves unable to take the Catholic threat to the Hanoverian state in Ireland seriously, find it difficult to believe that contemporaries might have done so. It is not to be wondered at if Irish Protestants shared the anxieties of most contemporary Europeans about conspiracy among religious dissenters.[55] Indeed, they were among those whose anxieties had substantially reasonable foundation.

It has been presumed that, if by revolt anything more than agrarian disturbance is meant, eighteenth-century Irish Catholics possessed neither the capacity nor the motivation for such a thing. It is certainly true that they did not possess the former. If indeed they possessed the latter, what was the cause that supplied it? Jacobitism, it is suggested, was not, even in the early decades of the century, regarded as a serious threat.[56] Certainly, the failure of the '45 ensured its demise.[57] The sources which most obviously refer to it are not to be credited. The Protestant attributions of Jacobitism to the Catholics were intended to conceal the self-interest which motivated the maintenance of the penal code. With regard to the works of the politically conscious Irish-language poets, the one source which might represent popular Catholic sentiment, it is pointed out that expressions of Jacobite sympathy were conventional and their presence dictated by literary form.[58] Further, expressions of disillusionment with Jacobitism among the poets can be cited.[59]

It is doubtful, however, if this evidence of Jacobite sentiment needs to be explained away. Assertions about the absence of Jacobitism in mid-eighteenth-century Ireland rest on little but the acceptance of the claim that Jacobitism was no longer taken seriously as a political doctrine in England in the period. This being so, Irish Jacobitism was hardly likely to have been able to sustain itself. This argument is doubly doubtful. In the first place, Irish Jacobites may have considered their cause sustainable, irrespective of events in England.[60] More importantly, it must now be held questionable whether English Jacobitism was as moribund at mid-century as it has been held to be. It is now confidently asserted 'that [in England] the Tory party survived until the 1750s, and its survival had much to do with Jacobitism both as a tactical option and as an ideology'.[61] Even after Jacobitism ceased to be a 'tactical option', its history 'as an ideology', espoused among both the gentry and many lower on the social scale, apparently continued for some decades.[62] If these views are accepted, then, that Irish Catholics did persevere in their traditional loyalty, is an inevitable supposition.

The supposition may receive support, but will hardly become clear, lacking quantifying statements. Were sources relating to the period more extensive than they are, they would still be unlikely to permit anything that approached authoritative comment on the extent of an underground and largely passive loyalty.[63] However, what may be said about the matter does tend to a confirmation of the view that Jacobite sympathies remained widespread – they were certainly not universal – among Irish Catholics in the third quarter of the eighteenth century.

It was probably among the Catholic clergy that Jacobite loyalty survived best. This was certainly the view of Protestant commentators, though it is sometimes difficult to separate the hostility towards the priesthood expressed on these grounds from a more generally grounded hostility to what was the perennial focus of anti-Catholic sentiment.[64] In view both of the continental formation and continuing continental connections of many of the clergy and the influence in the matter of Irish ecclesiastical appointments which was exercised by the Jacobite court until the death of James III, such loyalty would hardly be inexplicable.[65] Casual references to it are not difficult to discover.[66] The most notable manifestations of it are associated with attempts to allow or oblige Catholics to make some declaration of loyalty, particularly in the form of an oath, to the house of Hanover.[67] For the first time in some decades this matter presented itself with urgency in connection with the proposals of Viscount Limerick (later Earl of Clanbrassil) in 1756–57 for the registration of the clergy. The oaths proposed at that time proved quite unpalatable in ecclesiastical circles. In public, it was strenuously denied that it was Jacobitism that lay behind this clerical hostility.[68] In private, Charles O'Conor was willing to state that this was indeed what created the difficulty with such declarations of loyalty.[69] This was but a decade after the '45 and at a point, at the beginning of the Seven Years War, when Jacobite hopes might well have been high. It is rather more surprising that Jacobitism was still an obstacle to the introduction of a test of Catholic loyalty some twenty years later. It is true that those who opposed the taking of the oath which was introduced by an act of the Irish parliament in 1774 had good reasons unconnected with Jacobite sentiment for adopting the course of action they did: the oath had merited condemnation by Rome.[70] Yet in some cases, such as that of the bishop of Ferns, Nicholas Sweetman, we may be fairly certain that it was loyalty to Charles III that prevented subscription.[71] Defending the propriety of the oath, Arthur O'Leary was at great pains to put to rest anxieties entertained about it on account of its denial of the Stuart claims. Surveying seventeenth- and early eighteenth-century Irish history, he pointed out that Irish Catholics had little reason to be grateful to the Stuarts and then proceeded to a long refutation of the doctrine of indefeasible hereditary right.[72] By now, however, what Jacobitism there was cannot have been more than merely residual. In the 1780s, though Protestants continued, at times, to associate Catholicism with Jacobitism,[73] Catholics themselves felt easy enough about their former loyalty to speak of it freely, even boasting of its long persistence as an indication of the firmness of their adherence to monarchical principles.[74]

It may be that a distinction should be made between clergy and laity in speaking of the persistence of Jacobitism among Irish Catholics. If self-interest must have inclined at least the more ambitious of the clergy towards Jacobitism, so it must have inclined surviving Catholic land-owners in the opposite direction. They certainly had more to lose in the event of an unsuccessful Jacobite attempt. Their anxiety to declare their loyalty to the Hanoverians, which they displayed as early as the accession of George II,[75] is not particularly surprising. However, such a cautious attitude may have been untypical of the Catholic body as a whole. Pamphlets which urged that Catholics should be permitted to acquire landed property constantly pointed out that it was this only which would prove a certain bulwark against their disloyalty to the established order.[76] The argument was an old one and had been used by Locke; but observation of variation of opinion among Irish Catholics may well have lent it force. Charles O'Conor has been cited as one whose concern to preserve what was left of his property disposed him to adopt a pro-Hanoverian stance.[77] Certainly it is interesting that his stance remains less than clear until the mid-fifties, at which time his County Roscommon property was actually threatened by action under the penal laws.[78] He was to remain embroiled in law-suits until 1783.[79] It is not inappropriate to mention also his close friend and collaborator, John Curry. Perhaps it is significant that it is Curry, a medical practitioner unencumbered with the difficulties which attended a Catholic landowner, whom we can much more readily identify as a Jacobite. His first work on the rebellion of 1641 took the form of a Jacobite tract. This was written during the '45, with the intentions of reminding Catholics of the injustice of the land settlement[80] and persuading tories that the true threat to the state came not from Catholics, but from the heirs of 'the *regicide* party', the Protestant dissenters.[81] Curry's later writings on the rebellion of 1641 were less contentious and might be seen as simply appeals for a change in the attitude of a Hanoverian government. However, it is possible that it was still primarily a tory audience that he had in mind. In a series of anonymous or pseudonymous pamphlets published in the late 1750s and the 1760s he developed – with reference to both the past and the present – the central theme of his *Brief Account*, the loyalty and innocence of Catholics contrasted with the disloyalty and guilt of dissenters.[82]

By virtue of the nature of the phenomenon, argument about the importance of Jacobitism in the mid-eighteenth century will persist. However, even if it is not the case that Irish Protestants of the period lived under a regime rendered unstable by dynastic conflict and under particular threat by virtue of the stance taken in that conflict by their Catholic neighbours, the reality of their fears should not be doubted. How else, for example, is it possible to account for the fact that such fears were permitted to determine the shape of the Irish parliament's legislation?[83] Nor should such fears be dismissed as merely irrational and incomprehensible. Their belief that Irish Catholics were capable of engaging in a successful or at least dangerous conspiracy against the state may have been false. It is, however, understandable in view of their prior belief 'that the popish population are entirely under the influence of their priests'[84] – the priests in turn being wholly under the power of the ecclesiastical hierarchy. No zealous Protestant could doubt that that hierarchy desired the destruction of Protestant Britain. What was there, therefore, other than Protestant vigilance, to prevent the conspiracy in potency becoming a conspiracy in act? Moreover, did the course of events not constantly confirm that this was happening?

It is not alone their constant circumstances – most importantly their position as a minority of the population – which must be mentioned in accounting for the intensity, and also persistence, with which Irish Protestants adhered to the confessionalist principles of the British state. Particular historical circumstances must also be mentioned in accounting for Protestant anxiety. The Jacobitism of mid-century has already been spoken of and the causes of alarm which the 1790s produced need hardly be elaborated on. What, though, were the stimulants of Protestant fear in the decades between the decline of Jacobitism and the rise of Jacobinism? A brief answer can be given by looking at the content and circumstances of what was one of the clearest, and certainly the most celebrated and most effective, assertion of confessionalist principles in the period – that made by the bishop of Cloyne, Richard Woodward.

In 1787 Woodward published his *Present State of the Church of Ireland* with the primary intention of demonstrating the Anglican church to be 'so essentially incorporated with the State, that the Subversion of one must necessarily overthrow the other'. As a theoretical defence of this fundamental assertion of confessionalism, the bishop's effort is hardly memorable. The theoretical part of his work certainly succeeded in proving the actual incorporation of the church with the state in law – a point presumably not contested. Beyond this, there was an almost bare assertion of the commonplace that the ecclesiastical polity which prevailed in England and Ireland was particularly 'conformable to the genius of the Civil constitution' of those countries and an observation on the value of religion as moral preceptor, 'a collateral aid to the check of Law'.[85] This last point, the only substantial one, might have been regarded as adequate for a defence of the establishment of Anglicanism in England. It was hardly appropriate in Ireland where the Anglican church's instruction was refused by the mass of the population. To be fair, Woodward did state that a learned discourse on the principles underlying the existing church–state relationship was not intended. Nevertheless, by mentioning the theoretical considerations that came most readily to his mind, he opened himself to attack from the establishment's Presbyterian critics and duly received it.[86]

Had the task set before Woodward been the defence of Protestant rather than Anglican confessionalism, it would hardly have proved so difficult. The mutual advantage to both Protestantism and the state of their union was uncontentious. Certainly an assertion that 'the destruction of Great Britain...must involve the Ruin of the Protestant Religion'[87] could pass without challenge. This, of course, was to speak of the state's service of religion rather than mutual dependence. However, Woodward's tract did succeed in demonstrating the state's need for adherence to Protestantism, not theoretically, but in a characteristically Irish emphasising, in response to immediate anxieties, the anti-Catholic elements of Protestant confessionalism. In so far as the work succeeded in identifying the cause of the Church of Ireland with that of Protestantism, it may be deemed wholly successful. In brief, Woodward scored his points when he moved on from theory to speak of the circumstances which brought him to write. His success in argument, though also no doubt the level of Protestant anxiety at the time, is at least suggested by the celebrity his work achieved.[88] It ran through eight editions before the end of the year of its first publication and provoked a veritable pamphlet war waged in defence of Anglican, Catholic and Presbyterian interests.[89]

The immediate occasion of Woodward's writing was the attack which was about to be made in parliament on the tithe system. What lent the attack of parliamentarians additional force was the attack being made simultaneously by the Rightboys in Munster.[90] The Rightboy campaign sought little more than lower tithe rates and the restoration of older modes of levying them.[91] This, however, was not how the bishop perceived it. Substantially, he adopted the view which had been expressed by the canon lawyer (and later parliamentarian), Patrick Duigenan in his *Address to the Nobility and Gentry of the Church of Ireland*. The Rightboys sought not merely the abolition of tithes. They were engaged in a Popish plot to bring about, as Duigenan declared, 'the utter subvertion of the Constitution in Church and the State'.[92] The Rightboys, the bishop believed, had it in their power, by driving out the Protestant clergy, 'to suppress entirely the Protestant Religion in Munster, Connaught, and even Leinster, Dublin excepted'.[93] There was a threat to 'Protestant ascendancy'. Here Woodward was adopting something of a neologism.[94] It has been pointed out that he was already using it in a very extended sense, that he 'identified Protestant ascendancy with Protestant control of land, dominance in the constitution, the security of the Church of Ireland and the maintenance of the British connection'.[95] This is true; but another phrase could have been chosen to refer to these abstractions of confessionalist thought alone. The merit of the term 'Protestant ascendancy' was that it encompassed also the immediate interests of his readers and thus called them to action. 'Protestant ascendancy' meant not only the principles they professed, but also Protestant control of the population in their own localities and the security of their own property.[96] For the overthrow of Protestant power at a local level was the necessary first stage on the way to the insurgents' ultimate goal – the overthrow of the Protestant state. Indeed, they were already under arms for this purpose.[97] Woodward had demonstrated his point. The subversion of the Anglican establishment, now identified with the immediate interests of Protestants, would lead to the subversion of the state – at least in the present instance.

However, Woodward's argumentation was of more general application. He had reminded his audience that as long as there were Papists, they would desire control of the state. The struggle to diminish Popery and thus the maintenance of the Church of Ireland, as the only alternative to it,[98] had to continue. The Church of Ireland, the bishop allowed, was not at present a realistic alternative to the Church of Rome in the minds of the Irish population. This was, however, mostly due to its poverty and the lack of support it received from its laity.[99] In other words, Woodward had pointed out that the conflict was an essentially religious one – motivated by the beliefs of the Catholics. In such circumstances, the Anglican church was ultimately the only defence the Irish state had. The two were indeed mutually dependent.

The effectiveness of these adversions to the Irish situation as defence of Woodward's proposition about the inseparability of church and state is reflected in the responses of his Protestant opponents. Campbell accepted the most important parts of his case. He acknowledged that the bishop's 'concern for the general safety of the Protestant religion...[was] laudable in itself' and took exception only to the assertion that it was the Church of Ireland that was best able to ensure that safety. 'Our established clergy', he objected, 'are not and never have been, a defence of the Protestant religion'. A new establishment, one which comprehended the Presbyterians, was what was required.[100] Barber, an enemy to all ecclesiastical establishments, could only offer the manifestly false assertion that 'Protestant dissenters have no fears of the Roman Catholics' and add that these could, if they were to gain an ascendancy, prove no worse from a Presbyterian point of view than Anglicans.[101]

Duigenan and Woodward, in adopting their view of the Rightboy disturbances, were following in a well-established tradition of Protestant interpretation of agrarian unrest. Whiteboyism had been similarly interpreted.[102] This movement emerged in the early 1760s after a long period in which Ireland had been substantially free of agrarian unrest. At precisely the point at which Britain could begin to allow Jacobitism to pass into the background, it re-emerged to provide a new source of fear for Irish Protestants. Protestant fears remained, of course, unrealised and by the 1780s it was generally accepted that the Whiteboy movement had been no Popish plot. This, however, in no way prevented Rightboyism being so perceived. For one thing, Rightboyism did not look as though it was concerned only with the grievances of the Cork peasantry. It was, as contemporaries were acutely aware, much better-led and much more efficient in achieving its local objectives than the earlier movement had been.[103] More importantly, Rightboyism was not thought of in isolation from the political events of the period and these were a cause of deep unease about the future of Protestantism among many.

It was not to the priests alone that the increased competence of the rural insurgents was attributed. Woodward and others, notably Dominic Trant, believed, not without some reason, that the Rightboys enjoyed the leadership of some of the local gentry none-too-well-disposed to the church.[104] Here was a manifestation, at a local level, of the distemper in the Irish body politic that so alarmed the bishop – the adoption of positions in fact hostile to the established order by many of those who by virtue of their background and station ought to have been to the fore in defending it. And what could better have pointed to the alarming origin of these positions – in the political theology that came from extreme, non-Trinitarian dissenters – than the disorder in Munster?[105] It was, after all, the church which was the primary target of the Rightboys and their reputed sponsors. Further, it was the new tactics of the heterodox opponents of the Anglican church–state that were being demonstrated. Was it not now well-known to Anglicans that there was a 'confederacy of...[their] ancient enemies, the Puritans and the Roman Catholics'?[106] Woodward's ultimate fear was of the Roman Catholic Church: it was that which, by virtue of the numbers it commanded, would finally reap the benefits of the subversion of the state. However, there were also the Presbyterians, to all of whom the bishop was inclined to attribute the extreme doctrines that in truth were espoused only by some.[107] Worse still, the alliance between these one-time foes was being given encouragement from within the political establishment. The result was the two-pronged attack on tithes, in the Munster countryside and in parliament.

In the event, parliament held firm and the double assault was resisted. On going up to Dublin for the parliamentary session of 1787, Woodward was pleased to learn that the government, under the duke of Rutland, was 'taking a very proper decided part' and one that was certainly to his liking.[108] As a consequence, the session of 1787 produced no change in the tithe system. Neither, despite the efforts of Grattan, did the sessions of

1788 or 1789. There did emerge from the session of 1787, however, two severe measures that were most effective in restoring order to Munster.[109] The Irish confessional state, despite the assaults upon it, was still very much intact as it faced the intensified threats of the 1790s.

Woodward, we may say, defended his confessionalist position by asserting that the groupings hostile to the established order had the character that almost inevitably belonged to those who offered fundamental challenge in the *ancien régime*. In an *ancien régime*, confessional state, which defended itself effectively with religious argumentation and was, in its local manifestations at least, identical with the church, fundamental opposition was necessarily religious. The bishop's assertion provides a key to the understanding of the arguments of the zealous defenders of the established order throughout the closing decades of the eighteenth century. These, with their constant anxiety about conspiracies, have been treated with scant respect. Yet, in many ways, they came close to the truth; and the events of the 1790s, even more than those of the 1780s, did much to vindicate them.

Certainly the belief that Irish political conflict was about religion was amply vindicated.[110] The new politics of France and England were quickly adapted to the needs of the Irish religious parties. The enthusiasm which the progress of the French Revolution generated was far greater among the northern Presbyterians than in any other section of the Irish population. The body of extremists which sprang from this enthusiasm, the United Irishmen, implicitly indicated by their constant attempts to identify with the cause of the Catholics – now urging the Catholics to support them,[111] now urging their Protestant sympathisers to support the Catholics[112] – their own acceptance of the fact that it was their religious identity that came first with their fellow-countrymen.[113] Explicitly, this was a declaration to Anglicans of consolidation of the agreement between their enemies which they feared. The United Irishmen also did much to confirm Anglicans' understanding of the character, as well as the tactics, of their adversaries. Certainly, the blanket condemnation of the United Irishmen on the grounds of infidelity – the eighteenth-century term for atheism – was unjust. Indeed, some apparently believed revolutionary zeal not incompatible with even firm adherence to orthodoxy. While speaking of the published sermons of William Jackson, an Anglican clergyman executed as a French agent in 1795, one contemporary was constrained to comment on 'the perpetual recurrence [in them], whatever be the subject, of the peculiar doctrines of orthodoxy'.[114] Jackson devoted his time in prison to writing a refutation of Paine's *Age of Reason*. However, such hostility to Paine was hardly typical. Among many the *Rights of Man* approached the status of a sacred text, though its Deism was almost as clearly stated as the later work's.[115] And if Deist ideas contributed much to the politics of the United Irishmen, so did other forms of heterodoxy. Among Presbyterians there was the New Light movement, which can, without much misrepresentation, be described as Arian.[116] The nineteenth-century historian, William Killen, in his edition of Reid's *History of the Presbyterian Church*, was surely not wrong when he suggested a close association between New Light theology and extremist politics.[117] The overthrow of the Anti-Christ who had established his throne at Nicea was the true significance of the revolutionary activity of the 1790s for some at least.[118] True, there were subscribers to the Westminster Confession who failed to see in this a justification for withholding their support for such activity;[119] but the broad identifications of heterodoxy and political dissent, of orthodoxy and defence of the established order were hardly less widespread in the 1790s than they were when they did much to shape the Presbyterian conflict of the era of Henry Cooke and Henry Montgomery.[120]

There is much to be said for the understanding of their situation that zealous upholders of the Protestant order possessed; but it was flawed. Though religion was still of preeminent importance, secular concerns were present also to motivate political action. It was true that Catholic rural insurgents did desire 'to destroy the Protestant religion';[121] but that was not their only motive for revolt. It was true that politically-active Catholics generally gave their first loyalty to the Catholic body; but it was as much the Catholics as a legally or socially disadvantaged group as the Catholics as religionists that concerned them. In any case, they had little choice of political activity, in view of the exclusion they suffered. The first step, giving access to the political nation, had to be taken first. It was true that their unorthodox religious beliefs did lead some Protestants into disloyalty; but there were other influences at work. There were certainly orthodox Protestants who had reached the same point. The politics of such people was at least in the process of becoming distinct from their religion. However, the defenders of the established order could hardly engage with such politics in any meaningful way: the idea of an autonomous politics remained a strange one.[122]

What gave significance as a persuasive to Woodward's assertion about the religious motivation of the enemies that were to be faced was the assumption that this constituted proof of conspiracy to rebellion. In defence of this assumption Anglicans were most likely to point to the persecuting and monolithic character of Popery, the persecuting and fanatical character of dissent and the historical record of Popish and fanatic rebellions. Further evidence was unnecessary. Still, the events of the 1790s provided it for those disposed to see it and accordingly sharpened fears. In the early years of the decade, proof of Catholic ability to organise in support of their publicly declared aims – and thus, it could also be assumed, to plot rebellion – was present in abundance. Never had the Catholics been so well-organised as they were when their convention met in Dublin's Tailors' Hall towards the end of 1792. The advantages gained in the relief acts of 1792 and 1793 by such skill – and, it must be said, Burke's skill in persuading Pitt's government of the need, as war approached, to make concessions to the Catholics – were considerable. The constitution now allowed everything except access to the higher levels of political power to the Catholics. Equally alarming was the violent activity of the Catholics. The Defender movement of the 1790s attained a measure of conspiratorial competence unknown to the agrarian secret societies which had preceded it. Its activity was also more widespread than theirs.[123] Fearing strong repressive measures, Catholics and pro-Catholics tried, in public, to play down the extent of this disorder.[124] In private, they acknowledged it, though attributing the conflict to causes quite different from those put forward by their opponents.[125]

Those most fearful for the future of the Anglican church–state in the 1790s were not fundamentally in error. There was indeed a widespread conspiracy afoot which endangered it and, in some respects, they understood what had engendered this conspiracy rather better than later historians were to do. Their mistake, understandable in view of the way in which the Catholic activity of the period confirmed traditional perceptions, lay in their belief about where it was centred. The mistake was not corrected even by the events of the closing years of the century. When one of the great Protestant champions of the period, Sir Richard Musgrave, came to give his massively detailed interpretation of what had taken place in 1798 and in the years leading up to it, he consistently rejected the truth that the conspiracy was that of the United Irishmen, propagated, directly and through the Defenders, among the Catholics. The origin of rebellion lay less with 'the infidel leaders', than with

the Catholic Committee, that intriguing body, which sat long brooding in grim repose, and unnoticed in Dublin; but came forward when the French revolution took place, and endeavoured to avail itself of the shock and fermentation of opinion, which that event produced, to advance the interest of its own order.[126]

At another level, it could be said that the rebellion sprang

From the envenomed hatred with which the popish multitude are inspired from their earliest age by their clergy to a protestant state, their protestant fellow-subjects, and to a connection with England, and which has appeared in various shapes, such as levellers, white boys, right boys, united Irishmen, and defenders.[127]

It was this clerically-inspired hatred which Musgrave's entertaining narratives of the events of 1798 constantly sought to bring to the surface.[128]

The Irish confessional state had suffered permanently debilitating blows in the last decade of its distinct existence. In truth, of more importance than the rebellion were the concessions made to the Catholics earlier in the decade. This legislation was important in itself. True, it was merely permissive; but to some considerable extent the Irish Protestant body showed itself willing to act on it. If it was important in itself, it was also important for the divisions that ensued over the Catholic question in the Protestant county communities up and down the country.[129] Musgrave was not, as Woodward had been at the end of the 1780s, addressing himself to a consensus from which some dissented. It may be that it was this division of its elite which was the most serious blow delivered by the 1790s to the Irish confessional state. Still, for all its troubles, the old Irish polity could still offer to its successor state its ideological gift – now enhanced by new historical interpretations – of a distinctively fervent anti-Catholicism, emphasising the themes of conspiracy and violence. That, Musgrave made plain as he wrote in the wake of the Union, was his motive for writing.[130] The gift was far from being wholly rejected.

4 The Meaning of the Quarterage Dispute

In September 1792 Dublin Corporation made a memorable statement of its views on the Catholic question in a *Letter to the Protestants of Ireland*. These now found themselves confronted with a British government actively concerned, as it reflected on both domestic and international affairs, to conciliate Irish Catholics. The *Letter* is remembered chiefly for the definition it offered of 'Protestant ascendancy'. Bishop Woodward had used these words to refer to what were, in acceptable political discourse, uncontested principles and to elements in a social order, which were equally beyond challenge. Though it annoyed Burke and Grattan among others, the term remained as an expression of consensus. Inevitably, a number of claims of identity with the consensus were made and a corresponding number of definitions of the term were offered. In brief, it came to signify whatever it was that Protestants could not reasonably be expected to abandon. In Dublin Corporation's view, this was a good deal: Protestant monopoly was to extend a long way down the social scale. However, just as interesting as the opinion offered about the exclusion of Catholics, was the opinion offered about the inclusion of Protestants. 'Every Irish Protestant', the *Letter* declared, 'has an interest in the government of this kingdom'. This had been inherited from forebears, who had 'won [it] with their swords'.[1] In the concrete, the claim being made on behalf of 'every Irish Protestant' was a modest one: mere Protestantism bestowed no more than a 'capacity' to possess specific political rights. Yet the tenor of the *Letter* is significant of what was to come. If a claim to participation in political life could be made on behalf even of Catholics, it would be increasingly difficult to advocate the exclusion of any Protestant, most especially if he was zealous in the Protestant cause. The years between the 1790s and Catholic emancipation would see a willingness to accept, albeit tacitly and only in so far as it was necessary for an effective defence of Protestant ascendancy, something of the thinking provoked by the agitation in favour of parliamentary reform in the 1780s. In this way, the notion of an elite constituted simply by its Protestantism and nothing else would come to fruition, with the attribution to that elite of the political power with which it could defend itself. In other words, the last decade of the eighteenth century and the early decades of the nineteenth would see the foundations of what was to be called 'Protestant democracy' laid.[2]

It is true then that, before the last years of the eighteenth century, mere Protestantism was not advanced as justifying the possession of privilege in the political sphere. The hierarchical gradations within the elite remained, in this respect, substantially unchallenged. There were, however, strong assertions of the political rights already possessed by those in the lower ranks of Protestant society and even calls for an increase of such rights. Further, mere Protestantism was regarded as adequate grounds on which to seek other kinds of privilege. It was quite simply their Protestantism, their identity as heirs of the British conquerors, which provided the most fundamental argument in support of the various causes that rallied Ulster Presbyterians in the course of the century.[3] It was this which was fundamental to their campaign for the repeal of the sacramental test, for example. Again, the sympathy which the Hearts of Steel received in their campaign against the working of the landlord system in Ulster[4] was to a large extent induced by the reflection that

> The brave Forefathers of these...Men...were, perhaps, amongst those who suffered and bled for our Religion and Liberties, at the Boyne, Aughrim and Enniskillen, or nobly stood in the gap at Derry, encountering Famine and the Sword, to make their Posterity, and us, free and happy.[5]

Presbyterian anti-tithe agitation too derived benefit from this line of argument. Samuel Barber declared that the payment of tithe by Presbyterians suggested that they were 'a conquered people', rather than the equals of their fellow Protestants, having 'fought at their side and conquered with them'.[6]

Outside of Ulster, the Protestants of Ireland were a predominantly urban people and it is in the history of the towns – particularly of Dublin, where members of the established church actually constituted the majority of the population in the early part of the century[7] – that a further prolegomenon to the claims of Protestant democracy is to be found. Here the privilege enjoyed by inferior members of the Protestant body was considerably more extensive than elsewhere. For in addition to the privileges which they possessed in common with all their co-religionists, there were the privileges associated with membership of the urban corporations. In the first place, there were the privileges derived from the control exercised over much of the towns' trade by the lesser corporations, the trade guilds. There was also the privilege of political participation, largely exercised through these guilds as the constituent parts of the municipal corporations.

The freemen of the towns had interests to defend, their urban environment was conducive to politicisation and they were possessed of sufficient political rights to make the views that reflected their interests and political education of some importance. Thus emerged a distinctive politics, the most memorable exponent of which was Charles Lucas.[8] Local particularism and a concern to preserve what had been inherited from the past were the most prominent features in its character. In its content, it was a blend of anti-Catholicism, zeal for corporate privilege and enthusiasm for popular causes of the sort that in England at about the same time attracted the supporters of John Wilkes or a little later, in the Netherlands, the supporters of Joan Derk van der Capellen.[9] In what may be reckoned as the first campaign of the eighteenth - and nineteenth-century Catholic agitation, the quarterage campaign, the Catholics struck at what was both the primary object of concern and the chief channel of influence for the upholders of these views – the guild system. There can scarcely be a better illustration than this, that what eighteenth-century Catholic activists pitted themselves against was their country's *ancien régime*.

In 1756 O'Conor, Curry and a member of a Waterford gentry family, Thomas Wyse, established the Catholic Committee. It was to be the instrument by which the Catholic body would become what it had not been since the previous century – a Catholic party. The Committee, when established, had a general concern to present an image of the Catholic body which would render it an object of sympathetic concern to the country's legislators. Among its specific concerns, quarterage was the one which was clearly dominant.[10] The importance of the quarterage issue in the early stages of the Catholic agitation can be explained. The issue was not quite the only one affecting the Catholics receiving parliamentary attention in the 1760s and early 1770s; but it was the one on which the Catholics and their allies were able to gain enough support – though sometimes just enough – to carry the day.[11] Further, it was an issue which was of immediate concern to the overwhelmingly urban membership of the Committee.[12] Nevertheless, some puzzlement over the importance attributed to victory in the quarterage dispute remains. For, as the substance of the dispute has hitherto been described, it appears decidedly picayune.

Wall, in her account of the dispute, gives a brief but adequate statement of what quarterage was. It was a regular, involuntary payment made to the trade guilds by their freemen and by others known as quarter brethren or quarterers. These were persons who practised the trades with which the guilds were concerned, but were either unable or unwilling to become freemen. Most commonly, they were Catholics, unable on that account to take the requisite oaths. Dispute arose, according to Wall's account, for no other reason than that Catholics regarded the payment they were obliged to make 'as an unjust and illegal levy'.[13] In fact, it was not the quite small payments,[14] quarterage itself, which first generated the conflict. Rather it was what these payments betokened and effected, the partial integration of Catholics within the guild system as quarter brethren, that was important.[15] For if any substantial group of tradesmen was permitted to leave the guild system, what control of trade the guilds were able to exercise was lost. And their primary *raison d'être* gone, what then would be the standing of the guilds? In view of their functions outside the economic sphere, in particular their constitutional and political functions, that was a question of no small importance.

If this matter has not been understood, it is chiefly due to the assumption that virtually all control of trade had already been lost by the guilds well before the period of the quarterage dispute. This view has been adopted since John Webb published his study of the Dublin guilds some sixty years ago.[16] The guilds, Webb held, brought about their own demise by abandoning 'the fraternal spirit between masters and men' which had previously characterised them and abandoning too their interest in their trades, as they became engrossed in politics. The decay thus brought about was already far advanced 'more than a century' before the dissolution of the guilds in 1840.[17] If indeed the Dublin guilds were by the mid-eighteenth century in the doleful condition depicted by Webb, the circumstance would certainly be noteworthy. Guild life had not yet reached such a low ebb elsewhere in the British Isles.[18] In fact, there is little reason to accept Webb's view. It is true that the extent of the continuing influence of the Irish guilds in those areas with which guilds were still concerned in this period – small-scale manufacturing and the retail trade – is far from clear. The scarcity and the nature of surviving guild records precludes any precise statements on this topic.[19] However, if these records do not disclose the extent of the guilds' economic influence, they do disclose its existence.

In the case of some guilds the amount of evidence provided is considerable. The only record of the activities of a guild outside the capital to survive from the mid-eighteenth century, the minute book of the Limerick Guild of Masons, Bricklayers, etc., indicates that the guild exercised a very considerable degree of control over the building trade in the city. It regulated the activities of the trade's masters with regard to competition,[20] the kind of work they engaged in[21] and their employment of apprentices and journeymen.[22] Quality control was exercised by having guild officials 'view' buildings about which complaints were made.[23]

There is similar evidence from Dublin. In the late 1760s some of the Dublin guilds undertook a revision of their bye-laws. The action may, in part, have been motivated by a hostility to a prevailing oligarchical control.[24] More certainly, there was a need to adapt the guilds' codes to the situation which had been brought about by the defection of the Catholics during the quarterage dispute. The dispute, it is true, was still going on. But by now most guildsmen had probably come to accept that things could not be as they had been and were willing to settle for any triumph over the Catholics, even one which lacked substance. The consequence of the new attitude which had been imposed on the guildsmen can be seen in the sets of bye-laws now drawn up in the Guild of St Luke the Evangelist[25] and in the Guild of St Loy.[26] Virtually all attempt at trade regulation was abandoned. However, in another guild, the Guild of the BVM, there was no such intimation of surrender. Here too there was a revision. But the code drawn up contained almost six times the number of regulations which were accepted by the Guild of St Luke and almost half related to the detailed, indeed minute, regulation of trade. The aspiration to this degree of control was not abandoned until 1792, when a new set of bye-laws was adopted.[27] Why the Guild of Sadlers considered themselves able to retain their share of the control of Dublin's trade when other guilds were renouncing theirs, is unclear. The saddler's trade was reckoned a genteel one and very high apprenticeship fees were demanded.[28] It may have been that this guild had been more successful than others in excluding Catholics and consequently less troubled by their defection.

Before the quarterage dispute some of the Irish guilds were exercising extensive control over their trades. It would be imprudent to state firmly that all were doing so. It is not the absence of records alone that urges caution. In the first place, it must be presumed that there was variation from guild to guild and from town to town. Some trades were less easily controlled than others: and the larger the town, the more difficult the task of achieving control for all its guilds. Further, some of the surviving guild records are much less than explicit about control of trade. It is possible that such records witness to the unevenness of the guilds' economic influence. It is also possible, however, that the guildsmen simply did not consider it proper to clutter formal records with references to the commonplace, day-to-day activities of their corporations. Indeed, this latter interpretation should probably be preferred. For there are in these records occasional references which indicate at least a capacity to regulate trade. For example, in the late 1750s the Guild of St Mary Magdalene was obliged to deal with intense competition for the service of skilled journey-men among its master peruke-makers. Men were being lured away from their employers with offers of higher wages. Combination inevitably appeared and could not be dealt with, since masters were prepared to overlook the previous activities of those they took on. The guild, however, felt itself quite equal to keeping masters under control and established a strict code for the purpose.[29]

Even if reference is restricted to those guilds whose records afford but little evidence of effective control of trade, Webb's sweeping assertion that the mid-century Dublin guilds had degenerated into mere 'political clubs' cannot be justified.[30] Political activity there was. The role assigned to guilds by eighteenth-century municipal constitutions made their involvement in local politics at least not merely proper, but necessary.[31] And, of course, no clear line could be drawn between local and national politics. Still, it is quite untrue that politics were more important than trade in the years before the quarterage dispute or even in the decades imme-diately after it. The guilds were not flooded, as Webb suggests they were, with members who sought nothing else from them but the parliamentary franchise. The tendency to acquire such members existed; but it was a tendency which was deplored and opposed.[32] It seems to have affected the character of the guilds very little. Thus, to cite again the example of the Guild of St Mary Magdalene, in the late 1760s 'the Great Majority of the Body of the Corporation' was still made up of working barbers.[33] Since the guild dealt with trades other than the barber's, the number of those with no occupational justification for membership must have been small indeed.

If the degeneration Webb spoke of is not evident in the composition of guild membership, neither is it to be discerned in guild activity. No doubt politics of some kind entered into such matters as the election of guild officers and representatives. However, if the issues involved were those of the City's or the nation's politics, the point is well concealed by the sur-viving record. It is the records of the decade of the Lucas affair, the 1740s, which might be expected to yield the greatest number of references to local politics. There is indeed some reference to the conflict in the minute book of Lucas's own guild, that of St Mary Magdalene. In the transactions of other guilds, however, the public excitement registered hardly at all. The minutes of the meetings of the Guild of St Luke the Evangelist, for example, in the whole course of the decade make but one explicit refer-ence to the storm raised by the troublesome apothecary.[34] The issues of national politics apparently occasioned even less discussion in the decades around mid-century. The opinions of the guildsmen on these matters are occasionally made known by the grants of freedom made to politicians.[35]

The records do not otherwise disclose them. It was not until the late 1760s that the guilds began to acquire the habit of passing resolutions on the major issues of the day. Even then, these matters hardly dominated. 1782 found the Guild of Merchants, for example, much less concerned about the winning of the constitution than about the difficulties of exporting Irish woollen goods to Portugal.[36]

In brief, the Catholic campaign against quarterage was directed against a guild system which was still of some considerable importance in the economic life of Irish towns. This system was, however, under strain and it may be that some guilds were in the process of giving up the struggle to retain this influence. None, though, showed any inclination to acknowledge such a situation by abandoning their primary *raison d'être* in favour of a political one.

This view is amply borne out by the known content of the debates associated with the attempts of the guilds to impose affiliation on Catholic tradesmen with the aid of a proposed new law. The matter first came before parliament in the mid-1760s, in the form of a series of petitions from the freemen of almost all the important corporate towns.[37] A number of these petitions, following a pattern text into which appropriate local variations were introduced, made, explicitly and implicitly, extensive claims about guild control of trade.[38] The freemen's case as presented by the City of Cork, for example, makes it plain that, not long before, the guilds had possessed and, at least sometimes, exercised considerable power over tradesmen, by virtue of their right to fine delinquents and distrain their goods. The ends for which they exercised this power – or at least the ones they wanted to point out – are indicated by the doleful consequences which were represented as ensuing upon the successful challenge which the Catholics had been making. The guilds had been able to regulate the quality of goods, keep prices up and check combination.[39] The Catholic replies to these petitions, the counter-petitions of the non-freemen of the several corporate towns, are also instructive. Had it been possible to deny that the practices mentioned in the freemen's petitions had consuetudinal force, they would certainly have done so. They did not. Instead, they made reference to the deleterious effects those practices had on the towns' trade. The petitioners in Limerick, for example, reminded the House that trade could not be extended by monopoly and declared

that the bare suspending of the unwarrantable Power of imposing and exacting Fines and Quarterage, has already extended the Trade and Manufactures of the said City, and the Revenues of the Crown, to a pitch unknown before this Period... .[40]

The argumentation in the petitions and counter-petitions of 1766 probably represents a second phase of the quarterage debate. In the beginning,
the Catholics had probably sought full membership of the guilds. This, at
any rate, is what is suggested by the petition of the freemen of Youghal.
The enactment which this advocated was not one which would affirm the
right of the guilds to fine and levy quarterage, but one which would place
the local bye-laws by which the Catholics were excluded from municipal
freedom beyond dispute.[41] But if, at the emergence of the conflict,
Catholics did indeed entertain the hope of being admitted to all the
benefits of the guild system, they must soon have been brought to an
understanding that such a degree of indulgence was, in fact, well beyond
reasonable expectation. An easier, if less desirable way forward was to
attack the system. Contemporary thinking on economic matters was not
favourable to it. Again, at a popular level, the guilds were resented not
only because of their ability to regulate prices, but also on account of the
corruption and extravagant display which were associated with them.[42]

The Catholics were thus possessed of acceptable arguments. These were
listened to; but they were not the only ones which were relevant. The
legislators had the duty to consider not only how the trade and manufactures of the kingdom were to be advanced, but also how the Protestant
interest was to be safeguarded. Proponents of a quarterage bill could thus
depend on very considerable parliamentary support and, sometimes, a
parliamentary majority. But in order to achieve this, they were, it seems,
obliged to abandon substance and settle for appearances.[43] Only a few
years after the first of the quarterage bills was brought before parliament,
its supporters wholly ceased to make reference to the desirability of guild
control of trade. Instead, they spoke only, for the most part, of the need to
'restore harmony and concord', by putting 'non-freemen in some sort
upon a level in contributions, with the freemen, who purchase their freedom and bear the burden of public offices'.[44] This hardly convinced their
opponents, who continued to believe that the true objective of the guildsmen was effective control of trade.[45] They may well have been right.
Nevertheless, in the latter part of the 1760s the quarterage dispute did in
some degree assume the appearance of being about nothing more consequential than local taxation. In truth, though, the matter was a good deal
weightier.

When the freemen of the Irish towns began petitioning for a quarterage act,
the Catholic historian Sylvester O'Halloran was moved to declare that if

the 'monopoliers and oppressors' were successful, the end would surely be 'the Extinction [of] Religion and Industry'.[46] Clearly, acrimonious debate was producing exaggeration. Yet, if a Protestant triumph in the quarterage dispute would hardly have inflicted a fatal wound on the nation's economy, neither would it have left the economic development of Irish towns unaffected. Similarly, if the fate of Irish Catholicism did not hang in the balance, the fate of the guilds was still a matter which concerned Catholics, as Catholics, very much indeed. To some extent the reason for this is obvious. The guilds not infrequently used their power to exclude Catholics from trade and manufacture and to bring about conversions. Their regulation of apprenticeships, for example, gave rise to such activity. The freemen of Youghal boasted in their petition of 1766 that

> upwards of 200 Papists who served their Apprenticeships in this Town within this few Years, went to Church or Meeting during their Servitude, and continued so to do when they had served their Apprenticeships.

However, apparently they had been less successful in restricting the number of Catholic merchants and tradesmen. This had increased to the extent that Protestants believed that it was they who were in danger of exclusion from the town's trade.[47] In places where such Protestant anxiety existed – Youghal was certainly not singular in this respect[48] – the guilds' anti-Catholic activity, and consequently Catholic resentment, were no doubt considerable. In other places, it is true, feelings ran less deep and opportunities to harass the Catholics were commonly let slip.[49] It is probable that, if such a step could have reconciled their defecting quarter brethren, many guildsmen would have been prepared to forswear this harassment altogether.[50] Yet even when Catholics found it possible, either by virtue of their own ingenuity or by virtue of the degree of tolerance or laxity that existed among the guildsmen, to circumvent the guilds' anti-Catholic measures, the possibility of application continued to exist. This and the instances of actual application were quite capable of sustaining the considerable zeal manifest in the Catholic conduct of the quarterage campaign. There was, however, more than the practice of the guildsmen, in fear or in fact, to spur Catholics to action. The true motive for Catholic hostility to the guilds lay not in their activity, but rather in their character. They were now not merely accidentally, but essentially anti-Catholic – a cornerstone, at one level of society, of what would be called Protestant ascendancy. An understanding of this probably came but slowly to the Catholics: so at any rate the slight evidence of a desire at a late date to enjoy full membership of the guilds indicates. In the end, however, it was clear to them that they should seek nothing less than the guilds' destruction.

If the Catholics by no means underestimated what was at stake in the quarterage dispute, neither did their Protestant opponents. Lucas was persuaded that 'the good and credit of our Trade and Manufacturers, the Support of the Protestant religion and the Very Existence of this [City of Dublin] and the other Cities and Towns Corporate in this Kingdom' depended on a victory for the freemen.[51] He may, of course, have been wrong in his belief that a Catholic victory would have a detrimental effect on Ireland's trade and manufactures; but, this aside, he spoke little more than the truth. The City of Dublin – if by that is meant what Lucas meant – was indeed in danger, even if its fall was much longer delayed than Lucas might have feared. What Lucas had in mind when he spoke of 'the Support of the Protestant religion' is unclear. Ireland's Protestant state itself was hardly under threat. Some of the most important of the principles which upheld it, however, certainly were. In brief, when the Catholics attacked the guild system, they called into question, albeit in a degree unintentionally, the prevailing understanding, not only of civic life, but of the appropriate organisation of Irish society in general.

Nothing indicates more clearly than the character of the country's municipalities the appropriateness of the application of the concept of the *ancien régime* – considered in this case as a corporatist society – to the study of eighteenth-century Ireland's institutions and the thought which upheld them. The cities and towns of the period were still primarily neither geographical areas nor aggregates of population, but corporations of which the guilds were the 'constituent Parts or Members'.[52] They were constituted essentially by their possession of freedom. To borrow the words of Johan Huizinga, this was 'vrijheid opgevat als een samenspel van vrijheden gelijkbeteekenend met een aantal regelen, elk geldig binnen beperkt terrein, – regelen van: ik mag doen wat gij niet doen moogt'.[53] To state the matter shortly, civic life reflected the wider society. As the nation as a whole was but those possessed of substantial privilege,[54] so the city or town was but its freemen. In none of this, of course, were Irish modes of thought and institutions singular. They were those of the *ancien régime* everywhere. What was distinctively Irish was the way in which they reinforced and were reinforced by confessionalism. The congruence of the principle of exclusion which was integral to the concept of a municipality or a state with the principle of exclusion enunciated in the penal laws resulted in an intertwining which gave strength to both principles and to the institutions which they justified.

That it was adherence to this ordering of civic and national life which motivated Protestant activity in the quarterage dispute is made clear by the writings of the freemen's champion, Lucas. The designation of Lucas as an exemplar of Irish *ancien régime* thought may, at first, appear strange. The commentators on his career have uniformly seen him in another light, as an heir to the radical whig tradition and 'the forerunner of the constitutional nationalism of Grattan and O'Connell'.[55] Lucas stands, in other words, not as a witness to an order that was passing, but as a herald of what was to come. That he was 'bitterly intolerant to his Catholic fellow-countrymen', has stood as the solitary objection to ranking him among the virtuously progressive.[56] However, a recent writer on the subject, Seán Murphy, has brought even this reservation into question, declaring that Lucas's anti-Catholic zeal has been 'greatly exaggerated'.[57]

That Lucas was indebted to whig writers, can hardly be questioned. However, contemporaries were a good deal less sure than later writers have been that he himself could be identified as a whig.[58] When the mixing of ideological strands that was characteristic of mid-eighteenth-century oppositionism is borne in mind,[59] it may well seem best to let this ambiguity of contemporary reference to Lucas's position within the whig–tory spectrum stand. If some shorthand description of Lucas's politics is sought, then the term already used in this study to explicate the nature of political division throughout the Europe of the *ancien régime*, corporative-representative, seems especially appropriate.[60]

Much more objectionable than the attempt to identify Lucas unequivocally with one of the traditions of which he made use, is the attempt to place him within a supposed tradition which brings together eighteenth-century Patriots and nineteenth-century nationalists. In fact, Lucas's thought displays very well many aspects of Irish 'retrograde patriotism', which has been referred to above.[61] Because of this and because his thought 'was in no way original',[62] Lucas serves particularly well as an exemplar of eighteenth-century oppositionism in its historical specificity.

It is, perhaps, not inappropriate to begin an examination of Lucas's thought by commenting on his anti-Catholicism. For, *pace* Murphy, its strength has by no means been exaggerated. Further, contrary to what is suggested by Lecky, it was neither at variance with nor accidental to his thought as a whole. It is his *Barber's Letters* which are usually taken to be the clearest witness to Lucas's anti-Catholicism. These pamphlets are, indeed, noteworthy, largely because of the form which their anti-Catholicism assumes – a form particularly appropriate to Lucas's role as the freemen's champion. Theologico-political argumentation about toleration was, at first anyway, quite absent. Instead Lucas dwelt on that theme which so flatteringly elevated the inferior Protestant and confirmed his claims to a participation in the life of the political nation – the barbarity of the Catholics as the descendants of the Gaels and degenerate English and their status as a conquered people.[63]

The dispute which occasioned this polemic was indeed a trivial one. It had its beginnings in January 1747, when a drunken young man by the name of Edmund Kelly interrupted a performance at the theatre in Smock Alley and went on to make indecent advances towards one of the actresses. As a consequence he received a thrashing from the celebrated actor–manager, Thomas Sheridan. That a gentleman – for Kelly came of a good County Galway family – should be thus treated at the hands of a mere player, was a cause of outrage, at least among some. Others resolved to take Sheridan's side. Rioting ensued and spread to the streets of the city.[64] It may be that the disturbances owed something to the fact that Kelly was a Catholic, or at least of a Catholic family. But if this was rioting in support of Popery and the Pretender, the fact was not adverted to by any of the authors of the many pamphlets which discussed the affair[65] – except Lucas – or noticed by the citizen body at large.[66] It fell to Lucas to raise the alarm among those 'whose Ancestors came to subdue the Barbarity of the Natives of this Island'. Danger was upon them yet again from those whose 'very Names to *Protestant* Ears, sound *Rebellion, Treachery, Murder, Rapine, Riot, Debauchery*, and every Vice that can deform human Nature'.[67] What had occurred in Dublin was nothing less than a preparation for 'a *foreign Invasion*, a *western Insurrection*, or an UNIVERSAL MASSACRE'.[68]

The anti-Catholicism of the first two *Barber's Letters* was so extreme that it gave offence. It was not that such things could not be said about Papists. They were said very frequently. But in this case they were being said about 'several Gentlemen of Rank and Distinction'.[69] Further, they were being said by a trouble-making tradesman, who compounded his offence by mouthing egalitarian rhetoric.[70] Anti-Catholicism, at least at this point in the history of the Irish *ancien régime*, could not serve as a justification for undermining the social order. In this reaction to the first two *Letters* is found one explanation of the moderate tone adopted in the third. It was a moderation in which Lucas was to persevere. To say this, however, is not to agree with Murphy, who detects in Lucas 'a change of heart' by which he became 'somewhat more kindly disposed towards Catholics' and even rather hostile to the penal laws.[71] Both the reasons for the adoption of a more temperate tone and the precise content of what was communicated in it ought to be noted.

The first two *Barber's Letters* were, quite clearly, composed in the heat of the moment. In consequence Lucas displayed more of the *bourgeois*'s resentment against the gentry than was prudent. He also displayed, at least in his own estimation, an egregious inconsistency in his thought. The assertion that the Protestant stood to the Papist as conqueror to conquered was one which sprang very easily to mind. It was indeed a commonplace in every Protestant's thought, corresponding as it did not only with his desire to assert his superiority on reasonable grounds, but also with Ireland's historical experience in the latter part of the seventeenth century and the social reality which had emerged from that. However, as Lucas had stated it, the position seemed singularly at odds with the views of one of his chief mentors in constitutional matters, William Molyneux. Molyneux was more concerned in his writings to vindicate the rights of Irish Protestants against the estates of England than to defend their position in relation to the Catholics. He consequently and, in view of his politics, naturally applied the whig interpretation of the Norman invasion of England to Ireland and anathematised the belief that it was a conquered nation.[72] When his deviation from his chosen orthodoxy was pointed out, Lucas recanted, declaring that 'he who confesses a *Conquest* is, in my judgement, a *Slave* and a *Villain*'. What others might speak of as conquests were, as Molyneux said, but suppressions of rebellions.[73] Lucas had encountered a conflict between the two uses to which the Irish Protestant elite commonly put conquest theory.[74] Could it serve against both monarchical power and the unprivileged? If a conquest was accepted, it seemed that the former was being justified: if a conquest was denied, the latter had gained a point. Lucas preferred denial. Thereafter, he was careful not to speak, at least directly, either of a conquest or of the barbarity of the Irish natives that justified conquest. Indeed, the maintenance of this caution led him close to a Catholic interpretation of the rebellion of 1641.[75] Nevertheless, he was unable to discard the notion completely and it can be found, though hardly expressed with clarity, in pieces written long after the *Barber's Letters*. Others were less sensible of the difficulty involved in asserting that the rights of Irish Protestants were the rights of conquerors or, disagreeing fundamentally with Molyneux, held that there was no difficulty and the point continued to be very frequently made.

There was yet a further imprudence into which Lucas had been led in his alarm over the Smock Alley rioting. By virtue of the preeminence which questions of religious toleration possessed in whig–tory conflicts, it was difficult to address any such question without making some display of party colours. This was true even when the discussion concerned Papists and not Protesant dissenters. Indeed, it was not unknown for a discourse on the treatment of the former – a topic on which all were in practice agreed – to serve as little more than a cover for the airing of opinions on the more contentious topic of the treatment of the latter.[76] Lucas had no desire to adopt any party label.[77] Even had he been willing to be described as a tory, it would have been foolish of him to take a stand on the question of religious toleration. This was a battle the tories had already, in practice if not in principle, lost.[78] Thus in the *Third Barber's Letter* he made it plain that his views on the treatment of the Catholics were founded on the dominant – in fact Lockean – line of thought.

In brief, if Lucas altered his mode of expressing his opinions about Catholics and Catholicism in his third pamphlet on the Smock Alley affair and retained a moderate tone subsequently, this was not due to any new-found affection for those he had been attacking. Moreover, the change was indeed one of expression and expression only. What was expressed, a belief in the penal laws, remained unaltered. Murphy is of the opinion that Lucas, in his view of the penal code, in the period after the writing of the *Barber's Letters*, 'was very close to Charles O'Conor'.[79] Undoubtedly, to a considerable extent he was. However, he had this in common with most anti-Catholic writers. For Protestant and Catholic alike generally argued on Lockean grounds. It was widely agreed that if the Catholics could convincingly demonstrate their loyalty to Britain's civil constitution, then the penal laws would become unnecessary.[80] The question at issue was whether Catholics, as a body, could or would demonstrate such loyalty. To this question, Lucas never offered a positive reply.

Enough has now been said to vindicate McDowell's statement, controverted by Murphy, that 'Lucas condoned the penal code'.[81] However, it is not the *Barber's Letters* and the writings displaying his adherence to the doctrines of Molyneux and Locke alone which are to be referred to if the extent and nature of Lucas's commitment to anti-Catholicism is to be understood. There was an anti-Catholic dimension to the whole of his thought. This existed by virtue of the inseparability of institutionalised anti-Catholicism and other structures of privilege in the Irish *ancien régime*. In defending the latter – and such defence was the whole content of Lucasian politics – Lucas could not possibly have avoided, even had he desired to do so, upholding the former.

Lucas's career as a parliamentarian, in the years after his return to Ireland in 1761, was dominated by his championing of a few popular causes:[82] he gave expression to the old tradition of hostility to the standing army by campaigning against abuses in the Dublin garrison and he agitated for the limitation of the duration of parliaments[83] and the reimposition of quarterage. His concern with this last matter resulted in the writing of a substantial pamphlet, which, in truth, gives a rather better insight into the nature of Lucas's anti-Catholicism than the *Barber's Letters*. This is his *Liberties of Dublin* of 1767.[84] The primary content of this piece is a list of grants of privilege recorded in Dublin's charters and in parliamentary statutes.[85] If the compiling of such a catalogue appears, at first, neither an obvious nor a particularly effective way of defending the case for quarterage, yet its relevance – or at least part of its relevance – to the dispute can be quickly grasped. By pointing out what valuable privileges the freemen of Dublin possessed, Lucas justified the imposition of charges on those who sought to participate in them. Further, as he cited the charters and acts, he was able to draw attention to specific references to the exclusive nature of the privileges and even to the practice of levying quarterage. If this were all that this pamphlet conveyed, it would still be of interest. Lucas at least, it may be concluded, regarded what the documents he cited established, the guilds' control of Dublin's trade, as a contemporary, if now threatened, reality. The *Liberties of Dublin* was no merely antiquarian tract. That fact alone may serve as a strong indication that the decay of Dublin's guild system has been exaggerated. However, the pamphlet's rather imprecise statement about the dating of the decline of the guild system contributes only a small part of its interest.

While the *Liberties of Dublin* is chiefly a cataloguing of the City's privileges, it is more than that. It is also a defence of them. In part, this defence is contained in the catalogue itself, inasmuch as this constantly refers to the antiquity of the privileges. Not that Lucas had need to be precise about this: a privilege, almost by definition, was something ancient. 'Consciously or unconsciously, the appeal to the privileges', the Dutch historian, Woltjer, has remarked, was always an appeal to those characteristic assumptions of *ancien régime* political thought, that 'the past had been better than the present' and was the source of right order.[86] And the more remote the period adverted to, the more capable it was of imparting legitimacy to that which sprang from it. Hence Lucas's insistence that the charters and acts he cited were no more than confirmations of privileges which already existed by prescription.[87] This appeal to antiquity was supplemented by more explicit defences of the freemen's rights. But here too it was the most traditional patterns of political thought which underlay Lucas's argumentation. Liberty, he assumed, was but the aggregate of liberties. For he argued that any assault on such liberties as the charters of Dublin recorded could well be taken as an intimation of an assault on that liberty that characterised the British state.[88] If others were coming to regard liberty as primarily the possession of the individual,[89] the corporatist view was still the one which appealed to Lucas.

For the present discussion, what is important is not merely Lucas's implicit and explicit attachment to characteristically *ancien régime* patterns of thought and legal structures, but also the anti-Catholic purpose which his argumentation served. By this is meant rather more than the specific and immediate purpose of defending the freemen's case in the quarterage dispute. A more general anti-Catholic purpose can be discerned. This, however, was not expressed with reference to the most common anti-Catholic themes of the period. The disloyalty of the Catholics and their inferiority as a conquered people were hardly adverted to.[90] Such matters were not *ad rem*. For, in this instance, the Catholics were not seeking access to political influence, as they would have been perceived to be doing if they had sought full membership of the guilds.[91] The corporate and individual role which the guildsmen had in political life might be regarded as the chief barrier to the Catholics' pursuit of this latter course. In all probability, however, neither Catholics nor Protestants clearly distinguished between the categories of privilege enjoyed by freemen. Privileges which bestowed economic advantage or even a mere sense of superiority, would have been just as zealously defended by Protestants as unalterably their exclusive possession as privileges which bestowed political influence. Ideological convictions about the inferiority of the Catholics, perceived both as depraved religionists enslaved to a noxious superstition and as members of an inherently barbarous race, were reinforced by a strong sense of self-interest. Catholic artisans and traders were, after all, competitors. Further, their continuing exclusion was the means of raising those Protestants with little claim to status a few rungs higher on the social ladder. In short, political prudence, ideological conviction and self-interest combined to render it unthinkable that guild privilege could be anything other than exclusively Protestant. This was the fact which the Catholics tacitly acknowledged in failing to pursue the clearly desirable objective of full guild membership. When this Protestant conviction and the reasons for its coming into existence are borne in mind, the whole import of Lucas's cataloguing of Dublin's privileges is clear. Not only were these privileges an exclusively Protestant patrimony; but they were, to a considerable extent, important precisely because they were so. In such circumstances the solemn rehearsal of them could only be regarded as triumphalist – a plain declaration of Catholic inferiority. Lucas's pamphlet was a verbal riding of the franchises.[92]

It is important to understand the full significance of the kind of discourse used by Lucas in the *Liberties of Dublin*, for it recurs throughout his writings. Indeed, it is hardly an exaggeration to say that it dominated his political thinking and determined his political activity. How else, after all, did Lucas conceive his career, but as a protracted defence of the liberties of his City? A discovery of precisely what those liberties were was, he assumed, the necessary prelude to all debate. Thus when, at the beginning of his career, he resolved to enter the lists with the aldermen, he first 'inspected, examined and abstracted all the *Royal Charters*, and other *Grants* made to this *City*'.[93] The result of his study was a pamphlet which looks remarkably similar to the *Liberties of Dublin*. Indeed, although in 1743 he had as yet no substantial reason to be anxious about Catholic assertion, Lucas could not let pass the opportunity the pamphlet of that year gave him to attack the non-freemen, as well as his chief target, the aldermen.[94] The inclination came naturally from the form of discourse adopted. This, it should be noted, was common to all the participants in the debate which followed. The City's charters and the precedents which offered an interpretation of them formed the basis of the argumentation of Lucas's opponents just as much as they formed the basis of his own.[95]

If indeed eighteenth-century Ireland was developing the concept of an elite constituted simply by its Protestantism, that concept clearly rested on two major principles: the continuing acceptability of the venerable anti-Catholic political theology and the appropriateness of maintaining, though modifying, traditional *ancien régime* modes of distributing privilege. The required modification was the downward extension of privilege into the lower ranks of Protestant society.

That this last also constituted an important part of the belief of those who followed 'the Wilkes of Ireland', as Lucas has not infrequently been dubbed, hardly needs emphasising. The attention which those who have commented on Lucas's thought have given to its egalitarian tendency is, indeed, understandable. The contrary tendency, to exclusive principles, was, it is true, just as fundamental. However, this latter had, before the 1760s, rather less occasion to find expression: in the 1740s Protestants perceived no Catholic threat other than a military one. Lucas was but rarely diverted from his efforts to resist an assault on the rights of his fellow freemen, not from below, as would be necessary in the latter days of his career, but from above. While the threat came from Dublin's oligarchs, who conspired with an aristocratic interest to exclude both the Corporation's lower house and the citizen body at large from their rightful degree of participation in the City's government, the expression of egalitarian sentiment was conspicuous. However, that this rhetoric, albeit sincere, was composed in the service of a limited end, the defence of the interest of the freeman body of Dublin as a whole, should not be forgotten.

If Lucas concerned himself with causes other than those of Dublin's freemen, this was largely because they were perceived to touch upon or parallel those which were of primary concern to him. That this placed him firmly in the tradition of oppositionism was inevitable and convenient. It was inevitable in that it was oppositionism that set itself to defend the rights of Montesquieu's intermediary powers, such as the corporate towns, and by such means restore, as Lucas sought to do in Dublin, the pristine balance of the constitution.[96] It was convenient in that the espousal of oppositionist causes – by virtue of their popularity – was a fitting complement to the expression of egalitarian sentiment.

In brief, Lucas displayed a firm adherence to a perfectly consistent set of principles in all his political stances. There was no contradiction between his hostility to Dublin's oligarchy and his hostility to its Catholic tradesmen and merchants: both groups had made themselves the freemen's enemies. Nor was there any contradiction between this twofold defence of corporate privilege and zeal in defence of the rights of the Irish legislature or hostility to a standing army and unlimited parliaments. In the maintenance of these causes the familiar Lucasite themes – anti-Catholicism, particularism and hostility to oligarchy – could all find expression.

When Lucas fled Ireland in 1749, he was wholly defeated. When he returned in 1761, all had changed. Now the objectives of his campaigning of the 1740s had been realised to a considerable extent by a Municipal Reform Act passed in 1760. More generally, Patriot politics, in the wake of the Money Bill dispute, were gaining strength. He himself secured election to the most prestigious seat in the nation's parliament. Nor, despite his failure to obtain a quarterage act, was his subsequent career a disappointment to Dublin's electorate. At the time of his death the troublemaking tradesman of the 1740s had become, according to the resolution of the Guild of Merchants (never well disposed to the old Lucas), 'that steady patriot' entitled 'to every mark of respect and esteem from the electors of this Kingdom in general and from those of this City in particular'.[97] Lucasite views had now secured something close to the position of an orthodoxy in municipal politics.

In the decades which followed, the causes which generated political excitement in Dublin were uniformly such as would have earned warm endorsement form Lucas. Most notably in the 1770s, of course, there was the cause of the Americans. Then there was the cause of the Irish parliament. A few years later, it was the rights of the City of Dublin itself which were seen to be threatened by the encroachments of the crown and its ministers. Chief Secretary Thomas Orde's Dublin Police Bill of 1786 provoked not only stiff opposition in parliament, but also a remarkably extensive and fervent public agitation. The proposal to establish a police force under the control of Dublin Castle summoned up old anxieties about standing armies and brought forth dire warnings about the decay of

Dublin's constitution which a continuing accumulation of power by the government would bring about.[98] Nor was it ever forgotten that the constitution which was being defended in these conflicts was a Protestant one. Lucas's anti-Catholic campaigning was kept up, both in the continuing efforts to obtain a quarterage act and in declarations of hostility to relief proposals.[99] These latter inevitably became more fervent when, in the 1780s, the question of yielding political rights was raised.[100]

When, in the following decade, that question was answered affirmatively, the foundation was laid for a realisation, in a degree, of the aspirations which Lucasite egalitarian rhetoric had encouraged. The fears which the Protestants of the early 1790s entertained proved, in the immediate anyway, to be groundless: in the country at large a social order based on deference ensured that the extension of the franchise to Catholics brought about no political upheaval; while in Dublin itself the guilds and Corporation fought a successful battle to exclude Catholics from the rights that the last Relief Act had promised.[101] Yet the fears were hardly diminished and allies were anxiously sought. Thus, side by side with the campaign to exclude Catholics from the urban polity, there was a sustained effort, reaching its peak in the 1820s, to include a greater number of Protestants within it.[102] The allies thus acquired were certainly dependable. Since their own position rested on little but their religion, their defence of its privilege-yielding character was zealous. However, this movement towards a realisation of the idea of an elite constituted simply by its Protestantism came at precisely the time, and precisely because, the political environment which nurtured the idea stood in danger of destruction. In 1840 municipal reform brought Protestant domination of Ireland's corporate towns to an end. The beliefs Protestants held, even at the lowest levels of their society, about their proper place in Irish life were not so easily eliminated and continued to find expression in a lively political tradition.[103] It was one in which Charles Lucas would certainly have found himself comfortable.

Part III

Part III

5 Questioning the Catholics

The Irish *ancien régime* was singular. It possessed characteristics that marked it off even from the English *ancien régime*, of which it was an outgrowth. Its singularity derived chiefly from the significance that confessionalism had come to assume. This gave it nothing but strength. Religious belief, it is true, supported the established order everywhere. In Ireland, however, it was that aspect of religion which most easily excited the public mind (what a later age would dub sectarianism) and its scholarly foundation, the heart and summit of the Christian intellectual endeavour of the age, controversial divinity itself which were engaged. Further, they served in a most immediate way – in defence against a perceived military threat to the power and property of the elite.[1] This emphasis on confessionalism, along with other factors, brought about a further mutation of the English *ancien régime* that the Tudor and Stuart eras had seen planted in Ireland. A basis was laid for a widening of the elite to include all or, at least, a much greater part of the Protestant body. The consequent self-assertion of tenant farmers in Ulster and artisans in towns throughout the country was an important element in fomenting political discord for much of the eighteenth century. In the longer term, however, its capacity to expand its elite strengthened the Irish *ancien régime* greatly. In the struggle to adapt to the new circumstances of the revolutionary era and the early nineteenth century, the acquisition of allies became crucial.[2]

When, around the middle of the eighteenth century, some Catholics launched an agitation to modify the Irish state's confessionalism, they were in fact assailing the ideological centre and strongpoint of their country's *ancien régime*. That their opponents had some understanding of this, is clear from the strong reaction which the new campaign provoked. The agitating Catholics themselves probably understood the matter less well. Since they had practical political objectives in view, their argumentation was conciliatory. Generally, they simply turned to their own purposes certain limited criticisms of aspects of their society already in use among Protestants, adding only a few well-supported points of their own.[3] Nor did they perceive their objectives as radical. They sought no more than a place for Catholics and, as time went on, their religion within the existing order. In truth, however, an acceptance of the principles on which they argued – essentially Lockean – would lead to a very profound alteration in the nature of the Irish state. It was only because their implications were not understood, that those principles appeared relatively uncontroversial.[4] The attempt to apply them, by making religious affiliation less consequential in the affairs of the country's municipalities, makes clear what was contradictory in the aims of the Catholic campaigners. The existing order of which they sought to be a part, rested to a substantial degree on their exclusion. Consequently, instead of effecting an entry into the existing municipal structure, the Catholics in effect destroyed one of its major component parts – the guild system.[5]

In brief, even from its beginnings, the Catholic agitation offered a far-reaching threat to the Irish *ancien régime*. Such a view must not, however, lead us to attribute to it more modern features than it actually possessed. The Catholics' desire for acceptance within the existing order – an implicit affirmation of it – makes precisely that point. After all, Catholics as a whole and those who campaigned on their behalf, even if they did desire change, shared most of the assumptions and beliefs of their contemporaries. They were thus upholders as well as underminers of the *ancien régime*, albeit not in that form which had in fact emerged in Ireland. It is the chief purpose of the remaining chapters of this study, as they try to explicate the writings of the Catholic campaigners, to make clear in what ways the Catholic agitation constituted an assault on the country's *ancien régime*. However, the more positive and constructive disposition towards the existing order which existed among the Catholics must also be described.[6]

In speaking of the literature associated with the Catholic agitation, it is worthwhile to ask what its beginnings were. The agitation itself was conducted chiefly by the Catholic Committee. Its establishment, in 1756, was due largely to the zeal of Charles O'Conor and John Curry, which had been expressed in their pamphleteering efforts over the previous years. Before mid-century the Catholics, it is frequently said, were silent.[7] The sole exception pointed to is the Dublin priest, Cornelius Nary, who in 1724 produced his *Case of the Roman Catholics of Ireland* in response to a proposal to introduce new penal legislation.[8] True, before O'Conor and Curry began to write, some Protestants had indicated a sympathetic attitude to changes in the law relating to Catholics.[9] However, until Catholics themselves took the matter up, such airing of opinions was hardly likely to issue in serious political activity.

This account of the beginnings of the Catholic debate gives, in fact, a very inadequate indication of what the significance of O'Conor's and Curry's pamphleteering activity was. Their pamphlets were not mere harbingers of political activity which was bound to emerge in any case. They were important because of the thought they contained, displaying some degree of awareness that a new political situation – one that made a Catholic question possible – was coming or, at least, could come into existence. Indeed, they were themselves part of this development and, in offering both Catholics and Protestants a way of responding to it, paved the way for further change.

It does O'Conor and Curry less than justice to speak of the mere existence of their works without enlarging on the matter of content; but it gives them rather more than their due to state that they were the first Catholics to write in the Catholic cause. Nary's *Case* did not, in fact, stand alone. Its author produced numerous substantial defences of the Catholic case, from his *Chief Points of Controversie between Roman Catholics and Protestants* to his published disputes with Archbishop Edward Synge of Tuam.[10] Or, again, what of the writings of the County Cork priest, Thady O'Brien?[11] If more such material was not produced, it was no doubt because the arguments of Bossuet, John Gother and the like were found adequate. Indeed, both in print and in their 'conferences held...to pervert Protestants' the Irish Catholics of the early eighteenth century put forward their case with considerable boldness.[12] It will at once be objected that the works just referred to dealt with questions of divinity and not politics. However active they may have been as religionists, as men concerned with public affairs, Catholics were indeed silent. Such an objection, however, misses the degree of identity between religion and politics which existed in the eighteenth century. Proselytism was political activity. The point was constantly made by Protestant pastors who became anxious about the actual or possible conversion of members of their churches.[13] Indeed, so long as the prospect of a Stuart restoration remained, proselytism, the occasional expression of 'guarded treasons' and actual conspiracy were the only political activities with which Catholics were likely to be concerned. These alone advanced the cause to which they were committed. Other forms of political activity could only have constituted an inconsistent and, indeed, pointless dallying with a political order whose overthrow was desired and expected. In other words, early-eighteenth-century Catholics, like their Protestant contemporaries, had no inclination to compromise. They looked for victory. While this was so, it was the submission of Protestants, and not accommodation with them, that was sought and the uncompromising discourse of religious polemic remained the appropriate one in the political struggle.[14]

Already at mid-century, however, such attitudes were beginning to wane. The lack of success which attended the rising in Scotland certainly did not kill Jacobitism, but it did diminish hope. Without political change, religious polemic, which was in any case becoming less than fashionable, was unlikely to bring about any substantial change in affiliation. One anonymous Catholic pamphleteer noted the altered needs of the times.

> My present Design is not to combat or weigh the *Merit* of the Arguments, which subsist between the *R. C.* and the *Protestants*. All that can be said of either Side is already exhausted, in the polemic Tracts written by those of each Party; the principle View now is, to remove the Prejudices daily insinuated against those of the *R. C.* Communion.[15]

This concern with the attitude of Protestants, who were likely to remain Protestants, towards Catholicism was something new. Some Catholics were now thinking of coming to terms with the permanence of the Protestant order.

A similar and related, though much less marked, development was taking place among Protestants. Irish Protestants had always been less than consistent in their stance in relation to the surrounding Catholic population. Certainly, though in varying degrees, the conversion of the Papists was desired. In the earlier part of the eighteenth century, the penal laws, the example of the upper ranks of society and the charter schools were the instruments chiefly looked to to achieve the desired end.[16] Yet along with the desire for conversion, Protestants had, since the early part of the seventeenth century, displayed an acceptance of the permanence of their position as a minority of the population. This was more than a mere bowing to Catholic intractability and political prudence. It also involved the adoption of ideologies which gave a positive meaning to minority status by turning it into elite status.[17] Whichever of these two attitudes or whatever balance of attitudes had prevailed, the position of Catholics in Irish society had not been problematic. It might be that Popery would, under constant pressure, diminish into insignificance. Even if it did not, those Papists who had grounds to seek admission to the nation could continue to be excluded.

Around the mid-eighteenth century, circumstances were changing somewhat. Protestants were perhaps only but little less inclined to be optimistic about conversion. Numbers of converts were increasing: old methods were not to be despised. But now what was increasingly hoped for was the natural death that superstition suffered when subjected to the glare of reason. Still, no means of encouraging conversion promised quick results, neither the existing laws nor the *deus ex machina* solution that the *siècle des lumières* offered. In the meantime, Catholics, sometimes rich and influential and generally disaffected, had to be lived with. Consciousness of this, by itself, might have done little to create change. It became important only when, in the latter part of the century, it combined with another phenomenon – the decline of Jacobitism. This, in the first place, drove the Catholics to abandon their aloof stance and seek a place in the existing order. It also, though more slowly, deprived Protestants of their preferred justification for the exclusion of the Catholics from it. The relationship of Catholics to the Protestant state was now becoming problematic. In other words, the Catholic question had come into existence.

All the factors which contributed to the emergence of the Catholic question could have been discerned in the trends of mid-century. It is doubtful, however, if O'Conor and Curry did discern them and resolve consciously to set a new course for the Catholics by attempting a dialogue with the Protestant community. The substantially new argumentation which they produced may well, at least initially, have been looked on merely as a response to an immediate situation (as Nary's work of 1724 had been), which might aid in reducing the difficulties Catholics had to deal with. As pointed out, Curry at any rate appears to have undergone no major change in his political outlook in the years around mid-century.[18] In view of this, it may be that the work of O'Conor and Curry should not be regarded as the manifestation of an already existing Catholic question. Rather, it might be said that in commenting on Catholic affairs when they did – in a period of change – and in displaying the possibility of dialogue with the Protestant community, they were important contributors to the creation of a Catholic question.

It is possible to state the significance of the work of O'Conor and Curry in a way more relevant to the central contentions of the present study. If the dialogue which the two publicists commenced was to be attended with success, it was necessary for the Catholics to make concessions, which in turn required considerable changes in outlook. After all, the Catholic community was not, as Irish historiography has conventionally suggested, a mere passive victim. Its own hostile stance towards Protestantism, the Protestant community and the Protestant state, contributed much to maintaining its disadvantaged condition. When therefore the Catholic agitation's critical and innovatory role is considered, it should be considered firstly in relation to the community which it sought to aid. The criticisms of the stances of their own community by Catholic apologists were inevitably made indirectly. Indeed, to some extent, they may have been made only accidentally. It was in the nature of a Catholic apologist to conceal, rather than expose, with a view to assault, the Catholic stances that invited hostility. In any case, they may not have wished to assault them. Inevitably, however, in the course of depicting Catholics in the most favourable light possible, the apologists indicated clearly what views could or could not be held by those Catholics who sought a positive relationship with the existing society. In the context of the present study, what is of importance is the nature of the Catholic views which were thus challenged. They are easily grouped into those relating to confessionalism, to dynasticism and to the relationship between land and political power. In a word, they related to matters central to the discussion of the *ancien régime*. Seen in this light, the work of O'Conor and Curry constituted a contribution to the establishment in Ireland of distinctively modern modes of political thought, firstly among their fellow Catholics, but also – since they were attempting dialogue – among Protestants.

What is spoken of here might be illustrated, pursuing a point already discussed, in the matter of confessionalism. In this O'Conor's and Curry's most fundamental contribution lay in their promotion of a strictly political discourse – as opposed to one which intermingled and identified political and religious arguments – in attempts to advance the Catholic cause. This, however, is to construe their work very broadly. They themselves construed it more narrowly. They sought simply to obtain a favourable hearing from Protestants and to prevent the strength of traditional Protestant religious polemic being brought to bear against them. The task of changing the mode of Catholic address to Protestants was formidable. For in the mid-eighteenth century, while religious discourse was construed as political, political discourse was construed as religious. The problem was made manifest in the course of debate. In 1767 a pamphlet entitled *Observations on the Affairs of Ireland* was prepared by O'Conor but published under the name of Viscount Taaffe, a Catholic nobleman who had gained distinction in the Austrian service and could move in the most influential circles. The work contained neither an attack on Protestant doctrines nor a defence of Catholic ones. 'Taaffe' put forward the now well-established arguments of O'Conor. Even if Popery was 'a compound of idolatry and superstition', it included 'no *civil evil* to the public' and was therefore 'not the proper object of pains and penalties'.[19] The unhappy effects of confusing civil with religious evil was pointed out by referring to the economic condition of Ireland. That Catholicism did indeed teach nothing dangerous to the Protestant state was argued by referring to its toleration by various Protestant princes.[20] This Lockean distinction which the pamphlet sought to establish was largely lost, however, on the clergyman who came forth as the Protestant champion. His reply to 'Taaffe' included a protracted denunciation of the religious evils of Popery, its doctrines relating to the sacraments, its cult of the saints, etc.[21] O'Conor, now forgoing the use of the viscount's name, attempted to make his point explicitly, stating that the discussion of such matters was irrelevant and denouncing controversy as 'an Exercise of Malevolence, of Wrath and of Fraud'.[22] His opponent was merely confused by such statements. Was religious controversy not what all parties to the discussion were engaged in? He declared that 'certainly it was as innocent in me to defend our Religion and Laws as for Lord *Taaffe* to attack them, and for me to defend again as for you to attack'.[23]

O'Conor might have been tolerant of such failures to distinguish between political arguments and religious controversy: for he himself had not always been able to distinguish sharply. In debate with Bishop Clayton of Clogher in the mid-1750s, he had devoted about half of a substantial tract to a traditional defence of papal authority.[24] He had, however, been unhappy to do so and stated his opinion that controversy was 'a task generally as unprofitable as it is irksome'.[25] He already knew that even the mildest and briefest defence of distinctively Catholic teachings would provide fuel for his opponents. Confused by his separation of the secular from the sacred, they inevitably seized upon whatever pieces of familiar apologetic they could find and directed their arguments against those.[26] O'Conor thus became more rigorous in the exclusion of such material.

The anti-Catholic writers, however, never found reason to abandon it. Their mixing of theology and politics was perhaps the product of an enduring general conviction that dogmatic truths had a unique, over-whelming importance and that consequently religious belief was the sig-nificant determinant of human behaviour. Certainly, this conviction was to emerge from time to time in Protestant writings. The view 'that the moral and political principles of men are an emanation from, and are modified by their religion'[27] often stood, stated or unstated, as the preliminary to a denial of the claim for political rights for Catholics. But even if the general conviction about the potency of belief was abandoned – or if that potency with which belief was still credited came to be looked on with distrust – it might still be denied 'that Roman Catholics, like other men, are governed by their passions, and their interests...by rules of common sense and expediency'.[28] Perhaps it was true that religion and politics ought be sepa-rated; but Popery confused them, using its perversions of Christian teaching to advance its political ends[29] and various political doctrines to secure the acceptance of such perversions.[30] If religion and politics were confused in Popery itself, how could they be separated in the discussion of it? Fear of Popery preserved a union of religion and politics in Protestants' minds, as it did in their state.[31]

While theological matters may have dominated the exchange between Catholics and Protestants in the period before mid-century, there were writers who could be drawn on for the creation of a new secular discourse. A comparison between those late-seventeenth- and early-eighteenth-century writers and O'Conor and Curry will elucidate further the character of the transition in the thinking of Irish Catholics which the work of the latter represented and advanced. Those few Catholics who wrote works dealing only with politics and history offer themselves as the most obvious forerunners of the two mid-eighteenth-century pamphleteers. Their works, however, were preoccupied with those matters – the dynasty and the land – that would have to be left aside if an effective Catholic politics was to emerge.

In the first part of the eighteenth century, Nary stands alone. There were, however, earlier writers, such as the Jesuit, Richard Archdekin, and the Jacobite lawyer, Hugh Reilly. Old as their tracts were, they were not considered as having passed beyond political relevance when O'Conor and Curry began to write. Archdekin's *Letter from an English Gentleman,* written in the 1660s, was still in use, in an updated form, at that time.[32] Reilly's work, written in the 1690s and originally entitled *Ireland's Case Briefly Stated,* but known later as *The Impartial History of Ireland,* was decidedly popular.[33] Both would certainly have been regarded by any Protestant as grossly seditious. They presented essentially the same case. It was argued on behalf of an Irish Catholic nation, which had suffered the injustice of the Cromwellian confiscations and the Restoration land settlement – 'the Settlement of Rebels and Traitors but the ruin of loyal subjects', as Reilly put it.[34] This was the work of evil ministers, who were part of a succession of latter-day Hamans. The most notable of these were the lords justices of the reign of Charles I, Sir William Parsons and Sir John Borlase, who, in provoking the rebellion of 1641, were motivated by greed for Irish land, hatred of the Catholic religion and disloyalty to their sovereign.[35] But if the tradition of false counsellors continued into the reign of Charles II, this did not exculpate that monarch. Reilly thought 'it no great matter for one whether he marches towards Hell of his own meer [sic] Motion, or is led thither by others, if he arrives there in the long run'.[36] King Charles's weakness, in allowing his enemies to gain at his friends' expense, was indeed the primary object of the tracts' complaint. Reilly drove home the point for the benefit of Charles's exiled brother. Like the sins of Saul, the sins of Charles were visited on his heirs.[37]

The pamphleteers' criticism was, of course, as unlikely to shake the loyalty of James III's Irish subjects, as it had been Charles II's or James II's. That their enemies were still the Stuart king's enemies, remained the Irish Catholics' only hope. Indeed, justification for loyalty to the Stuarts, or at least Catholic disaffection, had much increased, certainly since the

Restoration era. Archdekin's *Letter*, as it appeared in the eighteenth century, pointed to new injustices done by extending the line of anti-Catholic conspiracies and adverting to the violation of the Treaty of Limerick.[38] But the *Impartial History*, as its popularity in the period suggests, spoke more effectively to the eighteenth century. It was written, after all, when the War of the Two Kings had been fought and lost. If the fortunes of the Irish were to be mended now, it could only be by means of another war. The exiled author's bitterness and lack of inclination to adopt conciliatory views is apparent. The language of the tract was violent and Protestant sensibilities were wholly disregarded. Even the Protestant religion itself was derided.[39] Perhaps the influence of the war and its consequences can be seen also in the attitude Reilly expressed towards the Stuarts. That there was again, as in the Cromwellian period, a much worse alternative to them, sharpened Irish loyalty. Insofar as the central concern of the *Impartial History* with Charles II's failures allowed, the work took care to depict the Stuarts in a kind light.[40]

Nary's *Case of the Roman Catholics of Ireland* was a quite different sort of Catholic political argument from that of Archdekin and Reilly and much closer to that advanced from mid-century on.[41] Nary was concerned to prevent the passage of a bill which renewed the threat that the Catholic clergy had successfully faced fifteen years previously: there was to be another attempt to impose the oath of abjuration on them.[42] Since they could not take the oath, as their conduct in 1709 made clear, this amounted to an attempt to banish them. Since its object was to influence Protestant opinion, the *Case* did not mention the land settlement. Its protest was against the violation of the Treaty of Limerick by the penal laws. Such breaching of public faith threatened to reduce the world to 'a Chaos, an Haceldama, or a Field of Blood' and draw down the wrath of God.[43] This appeal to divine justice, reinforced by an explication of the effects of the penal code on Catholic gentlemen, lawyers and farmers, constituted Nary's chief argument. When, however, he came to speak of the proposed legislation which was his immediate concern, he added a few arguments from expediency. Further persecution of the Irish Catholics, he pointed out, would make representations to foreign princes on behalf of their Protestant subjects more difficult. It would also bring about a substantial emigration, which was likely to harm the country severely.[44] Very different as this address to Protestant opinion was from such writings as those of Archdekin and Reilly, it showed little more inclination to abandon Stuart sympathies. Its object, after all, was to defend Catholics from an anti-Jacobite oath. It also remained, to give the mildest interpretation, highly equivocal about Catholic loyalty. True, it was stated that Irish Catholics were 'loyal

Subjects to King *George*' and willing to take an oath of allegiance to him.[45] Elsewhere, however, it was suggested that they were disaffected and only likely to change if they were well used.[46] As for Nary himself, he made it plain that he considered the Jacobite case to be at least a good one.[47]

Although Catholic writers did provide themes which were used in the new Catholic case that emerged around mid-century, the views of Protestant writers were more influential. However, for the most part, those views, when first expressed, did not relate to the condition of the Catholics at all. It was the ingenuity of O'Conor that made them do so. Still, as already pointed out, a few Protestants did have observations – other than hostile ones – to make about the Catholics. They were, though, made casually in the course of works concerned primarily with other, generally social and economic matters. There were, for example, Samuel Madden's remarks on Catholic leases, made in his call for improvements in Irish agriculture.[48] Equally incidental – and not uniformly sympathetic – were the statements of the philosopher-bishop, George Berkeley, in his wider-ranging work, the *Querist*.[49] In short, while the origins of parts of the later Catholic argumentation may be sought among Protestant writers, it should not be suggested that there was, in the early eighteenth century, any substantial dissent from the anti-Catholic consensus that was characteristic of the Irish *ancien régime* in its strength.

There does appear to be at least one true Protestant anticipation of the Catholic argumentation of the late eighteenth century – in the writings of Bishop Edward Synge. For when, in 1725 as a prebendary of St Patrick's, Dublin, and chaplain to the lord lieutenant, the promising young ecclesiastic was charged with preaching the anniversary sermon on the Popish rebellion of 1641 before the members of the House of Commons, he chose to consider *The Case of Toleration...with Respect both to Religion and Civil Government*. This work was published as a substantial pamphlet the following year in London and Synge entered a pamphlet dispute about his views with the vicar of Naas, Stephen Radcliffe. It is true that Synge set out the fundamental contention of the later Catholic argumentation with clarity, declaring 'That all Persons in a Society, whose Principles in Religion have no Tendency to hurt the Public, have a Right to a Toleration'.[50] Indeed, he set out this point more fully and consistently than later Catholic writers, obliged to have regard for the teachings of their church, could or did do. From this he drew out conclusions about the appropriate treatment of Catholics and his opponent suggested that it was for them that the work was 'chiefly intended'.[51] This, though, was an accusation and need not be accepted without question. Certainly one object of Synge's preaching and further writing was to declare opposition to parliamentary attempts against the Catholic clergy – such as had alarmed Nary. The proposed legislation could not, he thought, be in any degree effective.[52] But Synge had, it seems, no other clear views about any piece of legislation, proposed or enacted, relating to the Catholics. Apologists for the Catholics later in the century would certainly limit their proposals; but there were proposals. Synge argued only in the most general terms, for a toleration, and often negatively, pointing out how limited this might be.[53] In any case, it was to be enjoyed only by those who could demonstrate, by an oath, their abandonment of principles dangerous to the state.[54] The offering of an oath acceptable to Catholics was a matter which was central to debate about Catholics and thus frequently discussed – a reminder of the religious underpinnings of eighteenth-century society.[55] It is just possible that, reflecting on a tradition of learned Jansenism among the Irish in the seventeenth century and on the recent Utrecht schism, Synge did entertain some hopes that Irish Catholics might at least divide over an oath which would be odious to Rome as well as to Jacobites. However, the reality was that in the eighteenth century Jansenism scarcely existed among the Irish, either at home or abroad.[56] In view of this and his stated conviction about the actual disloyalty of the Catholics,[57] it is most unlikely that Synge thought of a new oath as doing more than providing renewed justification for the measures in force against them. An oath such as Synge spoke of was not a realistic proposal. The fact is witnessed to, if by nothing else, by the complete failure of discussions of the matter to bear any fruit over almost the next half-century.

In brief, if Synge was arguing a Catholic case, it contained remarkably little by way of practical suggestions.[58] Indeed, both the sermon and the writings that followed, Synge's and Radcliffe's, contained only limited reference to Catholics, whether as persons worthy of relief or not. The chief concern of the authors was with the theoretical justification, or lack of it, for the toleration advocated. It is in the discussion of this that the context for the interpretation of the pamphlets is indicated. That context is not the problem of the Irish Catholics, but the Bangorian controversy. Synge took the opportunity offered by a sermon on the Catholics to rehearse the bishop of Bangor's – essentially Locke's – denial of the state's interest in acting and of the church's authority to act against religious – in fact Protestant – dissenters.[59] Lest his hearers were unaware of his sources, even the text of the sermon which had initiated the controversy, 'My kingdom is not of this world', was cited when the chief conclusion he wished to be drawn was reached.[60] Radcliffe, a clergyman as anxious lest 'FANATICISM prevail over our present Establishment' as about Popery, was not willing to let this aggressive display of extreme whiggery pass.[61] He no doubt sensed that

Synge's main weakness lay in the context in which he had expounded his Hoadleian views, that of a sermon about Catholics, and accordingly focused much of his attention on them. Yet there was still a considerable amount of argumentation directed against 'the Atheistical and Profane, and Enemies of all Religion'.[62] In short, Synge has no claim to be considered as a serious advocate for the Catholics.[63] As in the case of Madden or Berkeley, his very restricted plea was made quite incidentally. He differed from those two writers only in that, while their primary concerns were economic and social, his were religious and political.

The reasons for this lack of Protestant interest in the Catholics, other than as a threat to the nation's security, have already been discussed.[64] The penal code affected comparatively few, except in the matter of religion. Synge stated the point succinctly when he observed that the common people 'must continue *Hewers* of *Wood* and *Drawers* of *Water*, whoever prevails'.[65] As for that matter of religion, it was one in which the Protestants came quickly to acknowledge impotence. Synge's belief that 'they will always have *Priests*, whether they are allow'd or no' was shared by the legislature, which never did adopt the measures against the clergy proposed in the mid-1720s.[66] As for that part of the Catholic body which was affected by the penal code as it related to privilege and property, rather than religion, its burdens hardly seemed onerous, least of all to those who did not have to bear them. In any case, the Catholics themselves put forward no argument for relief. Instead, it seemed, they sought a foreign army and a king of their own religion, who would overthrow the whole social order which the land settlement had brought into being.

As already remarked, O'Conor's approach to the Protestant community[67] did not emerge ready-formed. There was the venture into traditional controversial divinity in his exchange of pamphlets with Bishop Clayton.[68] In earlier pamphlets, his *Counter-appeal to the People of Ireland* and his *Seasonable Thoughts*, O'Conor assumed the persona of a Protestant with radical religious and political views. The first of these had as its central objective the refutation of the accusation of barbarism made against the ancient Irish in the course of an attack on Charles Lucas.[69] O'Conor felt 'some disgust' towards the author of the *Barber's Letters*.[70] Nevertheless, an oppositionist stance, even if in Lucas's case it was inherently anti-Catholic, invited friendly tory gestures. Thus he added to his remarks on the civility of the Gael a commendation of the apothecary's cause and, indeed, of Lucas himself.[71]

A pamphlet O'Conor had published a few years later was rather more curious. This was his *Seasonable Thoughts Relating to our Civil and Ecclesiastical Constitution*. It presented most of the elements of the Catholic case that were to be amplified in later pamphlets,[72] founded on an

assertion 'That the present *Christianity* wanteth Reformation'. By
'reformation' was meant an abandonment of controversial divinity and its
replacement by rational historical investigation of Christian origins, which
would sweep away the accretions of the centuries. All might prepare the
way for the new Christianity that Englightenment genius would uncover,
by forbearing with those who differed from them and regarding them as
friends. Thus was the case of the Catholics introduced.[73] To all of this a
sprinkling of radical whig politics was added.[74] It seems difficult to accept
that O'Conor truly assented to the rationalism and political heterodoxy of
this pamphlet, any more than he believed in its declarations against 'the
Superstitions of *Rome*'.[75] Those who knew him well regarded him as a
good Catholic and a tory.[76] No doubt the views put forward in the earlier
pages of the tract were intended to convince the reader that the author was
indeed a Protestant. Certainly, such a task was difficult. When the work
was published, O'Conor's relative and agent in Dublin, Michael Reilly,
thought that probably most Protestant readers believed the author to be a
Catholic.[77] Still, the mere creation of a disguise hardly warranted such an
elaborate effort – extending over half of the pamphlet. Further, it was
hardly necessary for O'Conor to express the particular views which the
tract contained in order to assume that disguise. It is probably best to
regard the *Seasonable Thoughts* and the *Counter-appeal to the People of
Ireland* as standing in a tradition of Jacobite writing, which Paul Monod
refers to as 'pseudo-Whiggery'.[78] Such writings were sometimes satirical;
but they also displayed the ideological coming-together of the politically
excluded[79] and Jacobite hopes for a bipartisan restoration. This is not to
suggest that O'Conor's first political writings should be described *tout
court* as Jacobite; the cause with which they were primarily concerned was
that of the Irish Catholics, not that of King James. However, they may
well be regarded as reflecting a period in which the two causes were not
easily distinguished. In the event, the writing of the *Seasonable Thoughts*
proved unfortunate. Just a year after the publication of a second edition,
Bolingbroke, whom the work had lavishly praised and quoted, fell post-
humously into gross disrepute when it was disclosed that he was in fact a
Deist.[80]

This experience may have induced O'Conor to change tack somewhat.
So too might an understanding that the Catholic and Jacobite causes were
separable. In any case, a change there was and with the argumentation he
now adopted he appears to have remained satisfied. At least his later pamphlets were so uniform in their content that they are scarcely worth
describing individually. Variation between them was the consequence
only of a desire to advert to the issues of the moment or of the search for
new ways in which to express the same points.

After the writing of the *Seasonable Thoughts*, O'Conor adopted a decidedly moderate tone. If previously there had been identification with Jacobitism, it was now gone. And the Catholics, O'Conor appears to have decided, were unlikely to benefit from association with dissidents, such as the now-exiled Lucas or the heterodox, such as Bolingbroke. It was not until the 1780s that Catholics were willing to be seen in alliance with those who engaged in oppositionist agitation or in manifestly fundamental criticism of the existing order.[81] Their Protestant opponents at least had some understanding of the fundamental nature of the challenge offered by the Catholics themselves. It was hardly to the Catholics' advantage to allow others grounds for attributing to them a subversive character. To the extent that the radicalism of the early pamphlets was a mere disguise, it now seemed vain and, indeed, undesirable to take trouble over this. It was kept up, but very carelessly. When O'Conor produced his next major pamphlet, the *Case of the Roman Catholics*, he generally spoke in the person of a Protestant, but occasionally also in the person of a Catholic.[82] This practice he maintained in later pamphlets. It was, indeed, appropriate. It was important for the Catholic case to be presented from a Protestant viewpoint. Yet ambiguity about the religion of the author of a pro-Catholic tract was useful. If ambiguity remained, some might take it as the disinterested and thus more persuasive work of a fellow Protestant. More would assume correctly that it was the work of a Catholic. In that case, they would, it was hoped, accept the enlightened and loyal sentiments they found expressed as representative of the Catholic body as a whole or, at least, of some considerable part of it. If they considered themselves to have reason not so to accept it, then the possibility of attribution to a Protestant author served to defend against charges of Popish deceitfulness.

The adoption of a Protestant viewpoint meant, in the first place, dealing with Protestant fears. These, in part, were the fears Protestants everywhere in the British Isles and beyond entertained about Popery. They sprang from the complex of thought, dealing centrally with the question of who properly possessed *potestas iurisdictionis* in a Christian society, upon which Protestant dynastic confessionalism was raised. Essentially they concerned the means that Popery would use to attain and maintain the power which its head had usurped from Christian princes. They were commonly expressed by attributing to Papists, universally, a belief in the right of the Pope to depose heretical princes, in the moral acceptability of breaking faith with heretics and in a positive duty to persecute them, when opportunity permitted.

Eighteenth-century popes may have had little desire to see Britain's Hanoverian sovereign murdered or an inquisition established in Dublin;

but Rome was not inclined to denounce opinions, held by some Catholics, which constituted no danger to the Catholic faith and which indeed it itself had sanctioned. Nor was it well-disposed to others doing so on its behalf – especially if, as in this case, matters touching on the Holy See's authority were concerned.[83] Hence, when proposed texts for test oaths condemning the doctrines Protestants found alarming were produced in the late 1760s and early 1770s, the Roman congregation responsible for the affairs of the Irish church condemned them. There were Irish bishops prepared to disregard this stance: some took the oath of 1774. Others, however, were supporters of the Roman view. Bishop Burke of Ossory did much to confirm Protestant fears and dishearten proponents of relief when he went so far as to publish one of the condemnations.[84] While such a cautious, not to say equivocal attitude to the matters which troubled Protestants existed among ecclesiastical authorities, the task of the Catholic apologist was made a good deal more difficult than it might have been. Curry did his best in a series of short pamphlets produced between 1757 and 1760. His arguments, however, lacked the force that was required. He was able to state only that the beliefs which were attributed to Catholics were not universally held by them, but were only the opinions of 'particular Papists'.[85] In support of his statement he adduced as many appropriate examples of Catholic behaviour as he could. In the matter of the pope's right to depose princes, he displayed his tory sentiments by adverting at length to Catholic enthusiasm for passive obedience[86] and counter-charging Protestants, who had, after all, actually deposed two British monarchs in the previous century.[87]

O'Conor occasionally mentioned these matters,[88] but generally avoided dealing with them directly. His venture into traditional controversy[89] dealt with the more fundamental question, that of papal authority, by which and for which Protestants conceived the objectionable doctrines to exist. When, in later pamphlets, the attempt to justify papal power was given up, efforts were still made to emphasise its limited character in the eighteenth century.[90] O'Conor made use of other indirect approaches. The adoption of an Enlightenment doctrine of progress, for example, was useful. In contrast to the age which would 'make this long *Night* of *Prejudice* give Way to the *Lights* held forth by *Nature*',[91] there stood the era dominated, not by Gothic barbarism, but by 'rage of party'. In this period, stretching 'from the Commencement of the sixteenth Century to this Day',[92] political conflicts had taken on a religious guise.

In such Conflicts, *all Parties* act upon *one common Principle*; let them divide ever so much *on any other*. They *punish* and *reward*, as they *love* and *hate*; and they carry the Lust of domineering in *Church* and *State* to such excess, that they sacrifice not only the Good of *both*, but very often their own particular Interests, to the Gratification of this Passion; a Passion, in Truth, not more unworthy of our Natures, than detestable in its Operations.[93]

To this theme O'Conor constantly returned.[94] It was meant chiefly to explain the enactment of the penal laws and to display their otiose character in an age in which reason in the service of secular ends, rather than religious passion, was to govern. However, it was also meant to explain how his own co-religionists espoused and acted upon principles 'which the *Catholic* religion never warranted'.[95] If Catholics had once used unsavoury means to advance their religion, this had been but a temporary aberration. The enlightened eighteenth-century Catholic could now condemn all persecution on religious grounds.[96] In this case, the formal ambiguity about the author's own religion, rather than permitting an identification with Protestants, served to allow a freedom of expression that could hardly have been enjoyed in a Catholic persona.

In addition to the fears which afflicted Protestants everywhere, there were those of Irish Protestants in particular to be dealt with – the fears that sprang from concern about the dynasty and the land. What was to be said of the Catholic desire for a Jacobite restoration that would overturn the land settlement? The most eloquent intimation that such a desire had been abandoned lay in the very existence of a call for Catholic relief; or, rather, in the fact that that call was now made to the Irish parliament and not to the pretender. Yet that call was being made by very few. What of the silent bulk of the Catholic community? As in the matter of the attribution of immoral and dangerous doctrines to the Catholics, plain, universal denials that obnoxious principles were maintained were scarcely possible. It was quite possible to assert that Catholics were willing to yield obedience to their *de facto* sovereign and in that sense loyal. Such assertions could be given an unqualified form.[97] However, it was admitted that there were Catholics who possessed another loyalty, which they hoped would be rewarded.[98] In such circumstances, O'Conor seems to have found it best to avoid direct reference to Jacobitism altogether. Only in the 1770s was it possible to say: 'in effect, we have no Pretender to the throne at present'.[99] Yet it was still quite possible to create a strong impression that Catholics had come to accept the existing disposition of property and political power. The discussion could, for example, be moved to the level of principle. Thus O'Conor argued that the historical and existing association of Catholicism with 'arbitrary government' was accidental: the immutable religion of

Rome was something quite different from the politics of the court of
Rome;[100] that that immutable religion imposed no belief dangerous to the
British constitution;[101] and that there were examples, historical and
contemporary, of association between Protestantism and 'despotism', while
Catholicism had flourished under and had supported 'free constitutions'.[102]
This was all very well: Catholics, *qua* Catholics, had no reason to be
disloyal to the existing order. It hardly proved, however, that Irish
Catholics did not, in fact, continue to be well-disposed to such 'arbitrary
government' as might be imposed by James III. O'Conor introduced other
approaches, making use of the assumption that the pamphlets were indeed
by a Catholic or Catholics. No opportunity was lost to suggest that
Catholics now shared the more fundamental political convictions of the
Protestant community. There was explicit commendation of the Revolution
and whiggery,[103] together with the use of decidedly whiggish principles in
argument.[104] Again, there was much praise of revered Protestant figures
from the past, such as Queen Elizabeth, who, O'Conor reminded his
readers, had anticipated whig principles of toleration by distinguishing
between 'Papists in Conscience, and Papists in Faction'.[105] Even more
praise was given to King William. However, this was intended to do more
than merely indicate an acceptance of Revolution principles. The reign of
the Protestant hero was made to stand as an age in which, on the whole,
political wisdom and moderation had prevailed, in contrast to the reign of
the last of the Stuarts, under whom the bulk of the penal code had been
enacted.[106] The message was clear: Catholics no longer complained against
the confiscations and consequent loss of political power, but only against
the burdens that were later imposed on them. The limited extent of the
actual requests for relief was no tactic to be employed in the undermining
of the existing order, but represented a genuine acceptance of it.

O'Conor was not content to attempt to remove Protestant fears. The
Protestant belief that the condition of the Catholics constituted no very
serious problem also had to be combated. Regrettably, Catholics suffered
little that was likely to provoke a sense of moral outrage in any section of
the Protestant community. It was possible to speak occasionally of the
practice, which many found repugnant, of allowing those who disclosed
violations of parts of the penal code to profit from their activity;[107] but
more than this could hardly be found. An effective argument would have
to be founded on something other than Catholic grievance. O'Conor's
point de départ was the acceptance that Ireland was now a Protestant
nation, to be governed with a view to advancing the 'Protestant interest'.
He acknowledged that this meant advancing the Protestant religion, both
at home and by means of the perennial struggle between Protestant and

Catholic states. His own discussion, though, sought to secularise the term, 'Protestant interest', until it meant little more than 'common good':[108] and the good he spoke of was, almost exclusively, economic good. The Catholics had but one strength of which O'Conor could make use in argument – their numbers. Those numbers, it was emphasised, were not likely to decline. All attempts at conversion had hitherto failed. If numbers afforded influence nowhere else, they did so in the economic sphere. It was the Catholics, with 'their inconnection [sic], their disability, their laziness, their despondency, their beggary',[109] who were the chief cause of Ireland's unimproved condition and consequent poverty. Of course, the Catholics might at once be transformed into productive members of society by the repeal of the discouraging statutes. With this at its centre, the new Catholic argumentation was to be not a continuation of the religious and political polemic that Catholics had previously produced, but an addition to those very extensive writings of Protestants, such as Madden and Berkeley, calling for social and economic reform.[110]

O'Conor, as a political writer, was merely a pamphleteer, properly concerned only with the issues of the day. He sought simply to allay Protestant fears and offer such other arguments as might discourage anti-Catholic measures among the Irish legislators and promote more acceptable ones. He did so, however, as one well-read in the literature of the Enlightenment.[111] With such a task and such a tool, it was not possible to avoid at least implicit questioning of established beliefs of the Protestant community about religion, politics and society in general. The most salient features of his criticism related to the characteristically *ancien régime* concerns, confessionalism and dynasticism. Confessionalism was assailed in criticising the anti-Catholic tradition and, in particular, attempting to consign it to a bygone age; in extending the use of the distinction between civil and ecclesiastical allegiance; and, putting the principle implied at once into practice, in rigorously distinguishing between religious and political discourse. Implied, though not developed, in this assault on confessionalism was a criticism of the manner in which the Irish *ancien régime* distributed privilege. There was little advantage to be gained from threatening particular interests. In the matter of dynasticism O'Conor's argumentation was equally subversive, but less direct than in the matter of confessionalism. Dynasticism was not attacked; but its importance was undermined. If, as O'Conor said, the Catholics were no longer seriously concerned with the Stuart claims or the issues – chiefly the land settlement – which fuelled support for them, then Protestant dynasticism might fade, like any other set of beliefs that commanded consensus, into the political background.

The difficulty, of course, was whether what O'Conor said was in fact true. If Protestants were unable to believe that the views which he expressed were now those of the Catholics as a whole, then they were most unlikely to respond positively to his arguments. Indeed, this was so with regard to his attack on confessionalism also. Protestants were unlikely to abandon what they firmly believed to be merely defensive positions, unless they were convinced that Catholics had moderated the proselytising zeal of the previous era and learnt the principles of toleration. In brief, O'Conor's writing was vain if the views he expressed were not accepted by his own co-religionists. For this reason, it is probably best regarded as primarily an appeal to them, rather than to the Protestants who were the ostensible primary readership, to alter their traditional modes of thought.

The need for such an appeal could hardly be plainly admitted; nor, however, could it be wholly denied. O'Conor's assertion of Catholic loyalty and religious moderation could not be wholly convincing. He could, in the end, only claim to speak proleptically and assure his Protestant readers that the 'decrepid Prejudices' of some of his fellow Catholics were 'fairly on the Eve of losing...all their Edge' as tools to create dissension.[112] This statement, as events turned out, was not far from the truth. Yet, as O'Conor wrote it, he could only have regarded it as part evasion, part exaggeration. He would hardly have cared to state precisely what 'decrepid Prejudices' still held to by the Catholics he was referring to. For it was convenient if his Protestant readers included in this category rather more than he himself would have included. All of O'Conor's political tracts avoided clear statement of the Catholic community's, or indeed the author's own views. If Protestant readers concluded that these were now widely regarded as 'decrepid Prejudices', they were hardly to be blamed. Not only were Catholic views suppressed; every opportunity was taken to exhibit what were, in fact, peculiarly Protestant ones. On one occasion, lest his friend, Curry, be scandalised by his apparent betrayal of Catholic principles, he explained not only his praise of King William, but his approach to his work as a pamphleteer.

> You will dislike, perhaps, to see so much said of King William, but truth warrants most of it and our little *astutia politica* warrants the rest. We must take our adversaries in their own way and ply them, as you must some of your weak patients, with such remedies as will lessen the evil when the constitution will not bear such as are more effectual or when obstinacy will not yield to them.[113]

If O'Conor declined to express his true religious and political opinions in his tracts in defence of the Catholics, they are scarcely to be accurately

ascertained from any other source. His scholarly writings may occasionally be of use in this respect. However, since these were mostly concerned
with early medieval Ireland, they offered but little scope for reflection on
Catholic affairs.[114] His private correspondence too offers some insights.
But even in this he did not speak quite freely.[115]

It may at least be said of O'Conor that he believed, or at least came to
believe, that a rapprochement between Irish Catholics and the Protestant
state was possible and desirable. He could hardly, though, have regarded it
as other than an exaggeration to suggest that his co-religionists as a whole,
even if he excluded 'the common Herd', were 'fairly on the Eve' of
renouncing the attitudes and opinions that sustained a more intransigent
position. Even Curry, his closest collaborator in the work for the Catholics,
was, for some considerable time, ambivalent about the need to come to
terms with the existing order. If only because they were considerably less
original than O'Conor's, Curry's views should almost certainly be taken as
much more representative of those of Irish Catholics than his friend's.
There are, certainly, good grounds for attributing – as has generally been
done in the present study – the new Catholic argumentation of mid-century
to O'Conor and Curry jointly. The two men themselves saw their work in
that light. Each regarded the other's writings as complementary to his own,
rejoiced to see them published and gave what practical assistance he
could.[116] If O'Conor had any doubts about what Curry wrote, this does not
appear to have led him, on any occasion, to withhold the approval which
his friend sought.[117] Still, it is probably significant that no joint composition
appeared before 1771. The *Observations on the Popery Laws* of that year,
was entirely typical of O'Conor's works, but hardly of Curry's. Curry, in
his previous writings, showed a considerable movement away from older
Catholic positions; but he was certainly closer to the tradition of Archdekin
and Reilly than O'Conor was. His most substantial work of the 1750s and
1760s was the *Historical Memoirs of the Irish Rebellion*, which, in fact,
reworked much of the material of his Jacobite pamphlet of 1747. It was not,
unlike the tracts of Archdekin and Reilly, chiefly concerned with the mere
rehearsal of Catholic grievances. Instead, it sought to explain the Catholic
conduct which was used to justify the penal code. It was, like O'Conor's
work, intended to influence Protestant views in a way that earlier Catholic
works could not. Nevertheless, it has at least the appearance of standing in
the tradition of Archdekin and Reilly. It dealt with many of the same
historical events and expressed much the same opinions about them. It even
condemned the land settlement.[118] In short, if it differed from the works of
earlier writers, it could have given little offence to those who agreed with
them. Other pamphlets by Curry published in the 1750s and 1760s, though

again certainly intended for a Protestant readership, went as far and frequently expressed what must at least be taken as strong tory sentiments.[119]
O'Conor's Catholic pamphlets were a clear statement to his co-religionists
that the Protestants had to be approached and that thus a change in Catholic
political attitudes and stances was required. Curry was certainly willing to
make such an approach and understood what it involved. But he clearly
continued, perhaps until around 1770, to entertain the belief that Catholics
might, at the same time, put their hopes in something other than the good-
will of the regnant powers. Even if O'Conor no longer shared that belief, he
understood it and was, it seems, prepared to indulge the expression of it.

The history of Irish Catholic political writing in the eighteenth century is
certainly consonant with, indeed tends to confirm the assertion that
Jacobitism retained much influence until well into the second half of the
century. No alternative to Jacobite politics appeared before O'Conor began
to delineate one in the 1750s. The implicit call for change in his own
community made in his appeals on their behalf demanded a very great deal.
Further it demanded it of the whole Catholic community and not only of
that part of it which was zealous for the interests of the exiled house. Irish
Jacobitism was more than a simple belief about who ought to occupy the
throne. Behind this there were beliefs about the nature of monarchy. Both
adherence to the house of Stuart and to the latter beliefs were supported by
a loyalty to Catholicism. Then there was a particular understanding of Irish
history, in which a sense of injustice, centred on the matter of the land
settlements, held an important place. And if this complex of emotions, attitudes and beliefs supported loyalty to the Stuarts, the latter also supported
the former. It was hope of a Stuart restoration that gave hope of the
restoration of the Catholic church and of winning justice for the Catholic
nation. An Irish Catholic ideology without the Stuarts, without an instrument to turn that ideology into politics, made little sense. It would be
foolish to believe, however, that contemporaries who had, in fact, ceased to
hope for or care about a Stuart restoration perceived this with clarity or, if
they did, were capable of changing habits of feeling and thought accordingly. Those habits were, after all, communally held and supported not by
political expectations alone, but also by deepseated assumptions – those of
the *ancien régime* everywhere – about the necessity of confessionalism and
the importance of land ownership. In any case, traditional stances would
not be abandoned until positive alternatives were offered. It may well be
that what was most contentious in O'Conor's writings was simply their

intimation that loyalty to the Stuarts would have to be abandoned. But even if it is thought that such an intimation would have been otiose in the 1750s and 1760s, the pamphlets were still highly disruptive of existing patterns of Catholic thought. For some – perhaps still for most – they called for a change of dynastic loyalty and, consequently, the abandonment of hope for the re-establishment of the Catholic church. In any case, for all they were a declaration that politics constituted a secular sphere, in which it was inappropriate to regard Protestants as either potential converts or implacable enemies. An aggressive political Catholicism could not yield fruit. For some the new argumentation called for renunciation of the belief that a Catholic elite could simply replace an expropriated Protestant one; but for all it stated that Ireland was a Protestant nation, in which Catholics could only hope to possess the influence that their existing property – increasingly now obtained from trade – allowed. In short, it was put to Catholics that it was no longer advantageous for them to nurture an *ancien régime* understanding of the state as dynastic and confessional as the basis of their politics or to uphold the *ancien régime*'s more traditional convictions about the distribution of privilege.

Whatever success O'Conor achieved in persuading his co-religionists to abandon their loyalty to the Stuarts hardly mattered. The course of events accomplished his task far more effectively than he could have. The Hanoverians remained on the throne and the Irish Protestant state endured. At last, terms had to be made and were, as the response to the introduction of the new oath in 1774 testifies. Perhaps much the same can be said about the abandonment of other elements in Irish Jacobite ideology, but only with considerable qualification. True, a secular political dialogue aimed at the amelioration of the condition of the Catholics within a Protestant state was maintained. But O'Conor himself had conducted such a dialogue without, in all probability, genuinely abandoning a political Catholicism which took the form of a loyalty to the wronged Catholic nation. In O'Conor's case, that loyalty may have been weak for lack of hope. It should not be too readily assumed that, even had he not been constrained by political considerations, O'Conor would have expressed the kind of Irish Catholic zeal that the Abbé James MacGeoghegan disclosed to a French audience.[120] O'Conor's successors as Catholic champions had new reasons for optimism. The British state, confronted with external difficulties, had, when the prospects for change looked bleakest, in the 1770s, resolved to conciliate its Catholics. The pattern of external threat followed by generosity to the Catholics was repeated in the early 1790s. The consequent increase in Catholic influence was magnified by internal threats to the British *ancien régime*. Its Protestant confessionalism was now assailed, not by Catholics, but by those other dissenters whom it had excluded. Against these, Catholics could offer themselves as allies. This gave rise to a new kind of Catholic confessionalism. The possibility of the Catholic church being constituted as a 'subordinate establishment' was envisaged.[121] If, as has been argued,[122] it is in this assault on the British state's confessionalism that the origins of political radicalism are to be found, then the Irish Catholics were even further obliged to it. For it was certainly such radicalism that placed the concession of direct political power among the relief measures. In these circumstances, the Catholic assertiveness which O'Conor had shunned could re-emerge. Indeed, it had never gone far underground. Just a few years after O'Conor and Curry had, in the *Observations on the Popery Laws*, declared their acceptance of the fact that Ireland was a Protestant nation, to be governed in the Protestant interest, their fellow-historian, Sylvester O'Halloran, presented a rather different view. For O'Halloran, the Irish nation was constituted by both Protestants and Catholics, who were 'assuredly but one people'.[123] it was this view that was to be constantly repeated in the Catholic literature of the following decades. Yet side by side with it, there existed another. For Charles O'Conor's grandson, writing an account of his progenitor's life and accomplishments, Ireland was again a Catholic nation, more so now than ever, having been tried and tested by oppression.[124]

O'Conor and Curry would, no doubt, have rejoiced to see this new Catholic self-confidence. Certainly, they had done a great deal to begin the changes which brought it about. It would be quite wrong of course to regard Catholic argument as the chief cause of the relief measures. Still, even when they do exist independently of political discourse, social and political problems are not dealt with until they are articulated as such and convincingly spoken of as soluble. No doubt, even without O'Conor and Curry, Catholic grievances would have been articulated in some form – eventually. It is doubtful, however, whether without these spokesmen the Catholics of Ireland would have possessed a political outlook congruent with the forces of change in the late eighteenth century. It was this which enabled them to take advantage of the opportunities which that era offered them.

6 Land and History

The agitation of a Catholic question was an attack on what was ideologically central to Ireland's *ancien régime*. The success of such an agitation could not but bring about the most profound change. This would have been so, even had the emergence of proto-democratic and democratic ideas at the end of the eighteenth century not magnified the importance of the Catholics. Even in its beginnings, the Catholic agitation produced remarkable effects. In the Catholic community itself, it assisted considerably in bringing about the abandonment of confessionalist and dynasticist beliefs and attitudes which could no longer be of profit.[1] In the cities and towns of Ireland, much of the substance of corporate privilege was destroyed in the course of the quarterage dispute.[2] Yet these effects were, in a sense, accidental. The Catholics were urged to abandon their loyalty to the Stuarts and their aggressive Catholicism merely because this was an unavoidable preliminary to the construction of an effective case on their behalf. They would, in all probability, have assisted in the maintenance of corporate privilege, had Protestant intransigence not refused them a share in it. Results were achieved; but they were not the ones chiefly sought and argued for.

In the decades before the relief acts, Catholic objectives were limited indeed – by the realities of parliamentary politics. There were appeals that Catholics might be enabled to lend on mortgage and take long leases on land suitable for reclamation. The latter was acceded to in the first Relief Act in 1772. The Catholic pamphlets, when they made specific proposals, did not go beyond these matters.[3] Their argumentation in general, however, did. In effect, it called for the removal of restrictions on Catholic acquisition of property. Thus far it went; but no further. Its object, after all, was to persuade Protestants, not to alarm them. They were not, therefore, asked to concede participation in public office or affairs. This was 'an Indulgence never to be expected, and, no doubt, never to be granted'. Nor, O'Conor also made clear, were they being asked to give any status to the Catholic church.[4] Further, moderation was evident not only in the proposals, explicitly stated or to be deduced by the reader, but also in the manner in which they were advanced. There was, most obviously, the depiction of the Catholic community's loyalty and lack of religious fanaticism.[5] However, there was more in the Catholic argumentation than this reassurance: and in everything that was said, particularly by O'Conor, a desire to accommodate

112

to prevailing modes of thought was evident. What was advanced for the Catholics consistently rested on, or was assimilated to, argumentation which, if it was not beyond debate, was certainly established as part of the acceptable political and scholarly discourse of the time. Nevertheless, in itself and in its application to a Catholic question, the argumentation of O'Conor and Curry cannot but be seen as in a number of respects subversive of the established order. There was, for example, the Lockean prolegomenon to their case, already discussed.[6] A declaration of belief in the necessity of maintaining a distinction between ecclesiastical and civil allegiance was unlikely to provoke many. Yet the consistent application of this principle in the case of Ireland's Catholics would certainly have destroyed much of the structure of the country's *ancien régime*. The political turmoil of the latter part of the 1770s and the earlier part of the 1780s brought in its wake substantial measures of Catholic relief – as much as O'Conor and Curry had asked for. New demands were at once brought forward and, to support them, new arguments. The capacity of a Catholic agitation to undermine the social and political order, perceived by wary Protestants since mid-century, was now made very clear.

The persistence of a Catholic question after 1782 should not lead us to conclude, like many contemporary Protestants, that the moderation of the earlier proponents of Catholic relief had been no more than tactical. Such a view misrepresents the political environment of that earlier period. It disregards, firstly, the elitist character of the period's politics. The privilege of political participation may well have been regarded as hardly worth pursuit. It would have conferred certain benefits on individual Catholics; but in a nation – to use the word in the manner of contemporaries – as overwhelmingly Protestant as Ireland, corporately, they could have exerted but little influence. Further restraint on Catholic ambition came from the community's own political tradition. Even if they were by no means singular in their adherence to the doctrine of passive obedience, Irish Catholics no doubt felt a particular obligation to witness to it. Thus Curry reminded them that it was 'their Duty to bear with legal Punishments, *however unprovoked*; and that the severest often produce the *best Effect*, by improving the Piety, because they exercise the Patience, of Men'. He hoped that his co-religionists might

turn Repining into Gratitude, if it should happen that the civil Magistrate afforded a Protection, which *the Laws themselves deny*; or, if such

Compassion did not interpose, ...draw Consolations from the Merit of a State of Suffering, (often the most salutary State that a Christian can fall into).[7]

Sentiments of this sort were not confined to public statements. In private correspondence, O'Conor expressed his own acceptance of the 'rank' he filled, 'that of a Roman Catholic in a Protestant country, that of one in a low way, obnoxious to the laws' and urged his son to cultivate a similar disposition.[8] This was at a time, in the 1750s, at which there was but small hope of change. However, the advances his cause made in the latter years of his life do not appear to have altered his views. When, in the 1780s, the participation of the Catholics in political affairs was being solicited, O'Conor marked out the path he thought proper for them. It was to 'acquiesce in the operation of laws which forbid our taking an active part in any matter relative to legislation'. He went on:

This submission to *things* as they are is our duty and out of that no man or party of men I [presume] will attempt to persuade us. Let those who have an eligible right to sit in Parliament labour to reform what is amiss in our civil constitution. We who are excluded from such a right should avail ourselves of the negative right left us, that of being silent and passive.[9]

O'Conor's Catholic pamphlets, it has been suggested, were less than wholly honest, by virtue of their necessarily severe restraint in the expression of Irish Catholic identity and sentiment.[10] However, there is no reason to suspect O'Conor of any degree of duplicity in his statement of Catholic political objectives. He was equally sincere in the main arguments he used to advance their realisation. Undoubtedly O'Conor's abandonment of the argumentation used by previous Catholic apologists was primarily an adaptation in response to Protestant sensibilities. In constructing his new argumentation O'Conor constantly bore the Protestant viewpoint in mind. However, the task was not a difficult one. For, to a very considerable extent, his own thought was wholly in harmony with at least that section of Protestant opinion concerned with the diffusion of 'useful knowledge' as a preliminary to the reformation of Irish mores and institutions. In other words, the Catholic argumentation, as O'Conor moulded it, was the product of the Irish Enlightenment.

In view of the extent of Ireland's cultural integration with other parts of the Hanoverian empire, reference to an Irish Enlightenment is certainly problematic. Nevertheless, distinct Irish circumstances ensured a distinct Irish response to the intellectual movements of the time. At least Irish emphases were different. These are probably most clearly indicated by the importance, for anyone who aspires to speak of an Irish Enlightenment, of those societies which took it upon themselves to diffuse the new, and to use the contemporary term of approbation, useful knowledge in Ireland.[11] The most notable among them was the Dublin Society, founded in 1731 and the successor of a series of philosophical societies which flourished in the last years of the seventeenth and early years of the eighteenth centuries.[12] The Dublin Society for Improving Husbandry, Manufactures and other Useful Arts, to give the full title under which it was founded, in fact devoted by far the greater part of its attention to husbandry for most of its early history. Around 1770, however, there was some tendency to assert the importance of manufactures.[13] This brought complaint from Gorges Howard, whose acquaintance with the writings of the physiocrats had led him to a firm adherence to their doctrine of the primacy of agriculture in the national economy.[14] He reminded the Society of its public declarations of its 'primary, principal objects', 'the improvement of the vast tracts of uncultivated land and bog in the kingdom...and the further improvement of the cultivated lands' by, chiefly, converting them to tillage.[15]

Strictly practical, and particularly agricultural matters were never far from the minds of those Irishmen engaged in the enlightenment of their fellow countrymen. The Physico-Historical Society, founded in Dublin in 1744, set out 'to find means for the employment of Numbers of the Poor, for the Encouragement of Agriculture, by the discovery of Minerals or Materials for the manuring of land, etc'. This body, however, also sought

> to collect Materials, in order to publish the Ancient and Present State of the several Counties of Ireland, in Descriptions, natural, civil, ecclesiastical, historical, chronological, etc., to shew how we have been misrepresented by Writers of other Countries and their gross Mistakes in respect to the Ecclesiastical and Civil state of this Kingdom.[16]

Despite its universalist character and the cosmopolitanism of its proponents, Enlightenment thought contributed substantially, in many parts of Europe, to the development of national sentiment.[17] New methods of investigation were applied to the study of particular, local phenomena, renewing a sense of communal identity: and the universal lessons that were drawn urged a reform which was generally conceived in a national context. This was certainly true in Ireland.

O'Conor is remembered both as a Catholic champion and as 'the most valuable servant that Irish history had in the eighteenth century'.[18] These views may be convincingly merged, allowing the character of the defender of Catholic interests to dominate: for he retained that character as a historian.[19] However, there is a further unity in his work. This derives from his consistent wish at least to depict himself as one who wholly shared the concerns and convictions of the enlightened Irishmen who patronised such bodies as the Dublin Society and the Physico-Historical Society. O'Conor himself might well have chosen to represent his work as no more than an effort to advance the programme which these societies set.

When they moved beyond the preliminary matter of quietening Protestant fears of Catholicism and its Irish adherents, O'Conor's Catholic pamphlets, centrally, echoed and expounded the fashionable economic maxims of the day. The usual mercantilist themes – fears of a drain of population and of specie, anxiety about the use of foreign luxury goods, etc. – were all present. The application of such notions in the discussion of Irish affairs was already familiar from the works of such writers as Madden and Dobbs[20] and through the efforts of the Dublin Society, which they had helped to establish. On occasion, O'Conor used the popularly received mercantilist teachings quite directly in his pro-Catholic arguments. He argued in the 1750s, for example, that any new parliamentary measures which threatened serious damage to the Catholic Church would result in large-scale emigration among the better-off: 'And the Exiles, who have no other but a portable Property, would carry off a great part of the Specie yet left in our Hands'.[21] Generally, however, O'Conor's argumentation was more complex, making a more extensive use of reformist thinking. It asserted, fundamentally, the primacy of agriculture in economic life. The flourishing of the country's manufactures could do no more than give 'a florid Countenance to our Affairs and...flatter a decaying Body'.[22] Ireland's true need was for agricultural improvement and a reversal of the movement from tillage to pasture. From the abandonment of tillage came numerous evils, both economic and social. The worst consequence of the lack of an adequate native grain supply was the constant threat of famine; but there was too the expenditure of specie on imports. As to the practice of pastoral farming, that reduced the numbers employed on the land and thus increased the evils of vagrancy and emigration.[23] O'Conor had no doubt that the desired ends, both improvement and the increase of tillage, could be achieved through a general alteration of the terms on which land was held.

In proposing this as a remedy for them, O'Conor was not singular, any more than he was in his diagnosis of the country's ills. Both Madden and Dobbs, for example, had argued for longer leases, more advantageous to the tenant. This would 'breed yeomen'.[24] 'The Want of this Yeomanry', Dobbs observed, 'is the principal Evil to be removed from Ireland, from whence most of our Inconveniences flow'.[25] Both writers, too, had advocated such relaxation of the Popery laws as might be useful in this regard.[26]

What marked the views of O'Conor as economic reformer, was their reductionist character. Most agreed that Ireland's lack of prosperity sprang, primarily, from the condition of its agriculture. O'Conor, though he made passing complaints about the excessive importation of foreign luxuries and the stagnation of credit due to the insecurity of Catholic loans,[27] swept serious consideration of all non-agricultural matters aside. Many held that short, ungenerous leases encouraged the pursuit of quick returns from conversion to pasture and discouraged improvement. O'Conor, though he occasionally adverted briefly to the need to discourage absenteeism,[28] succeeded in depicting change in tenurial arrangements as a panacea for Irish agriculture. Few – particularly among those landlords who had the duty of legislating – could accept the points that were crucial for O'Conor: that it was the restriction of Catholic leases to a period of 31 years that accounted for the prevalence of short leases and that a restriction on the profitability of those leases was a further discouragement to agricultural enterprise. In fact, landlords possessed good reasons for offering only leases limited to 21 or 31 years and tenants good reasons for wanting them and neither would have been much influenced by a removal of the legal restriction to alter their practices. In addition, the statutory limitation of profitability was generally known to be enforceable.[29] Of course, O'Conor's Protestant opponents were not slow to point these things out.[30]

In truth, all of the important arguments advanced in the course of O'Conor's and Curry's pamphleteering campaign were less than persuasive. The assertions made about the beliefs entertained by Catholics in general lacked authoritative ecclesiastical confirmation.[31] With regard to Irish Catholics in particular, it was necessary to admit that loyalty to the Hanoverians was less than universal among them.[32] At best, O'Conor might hope that his own writings in particular – Curry's remained tinged with Jacobitism – were taken to represent a growing body of Catholic opinion. This, he frequently pointed out, might be added to if the ownership of real property made disaffection less attractive.[33] With his assertions about the dispositions of the Catholics rendered doubtful, a good deal rested on his economic arguments; but these too were far from satisfactory. He, however, undoubtedly believed them. This is clear from his correspondence with Curry. Anxiety about impending rural distress habitually led him to vent his indignation at the failure to tackle the problem at its root – the Popery laws.[34]

The weakness of their argumentation by no means rendered O'Conor's Catholic pamphlets valueless. The sustained moderation of these works, with their condemnations of religious extremism, declarations of loyalty and consistent depiction of Catholic relief as no more than an 'Agrarian law',[35] was valuable. It allowed discussion of the condition of the Catholics to be firmly placed within the legitimate political discourse of the period. As to the economic arguments in particular, they had just enough force to prevent them being dismissed entirely. The laws he sought to have repealed seemed certainly to be of no benefit to Irish economic life and, indeed, to have a capacity – albeit unrealised – to do harm. On the basis of these considerations, there was little reason for the Irish legislators to act; but there was a possibility of them doing so. In the late 1770s reason to act, in the form of the British government's perception of its military requirements, did emerge.[36] Then, the tendency to see the question of Catholic relief in association with tenurial reform, which O'Conor had so persistently developed, at least provided the Irish parliamentarians who took the government's side with some arguments and an obvious task to accomplish. The Act of 1778 was wholly concerned with landholding, its chief provision allowing Catholics to take leases of up to 999 years.

There are parallels between O'Conor's most fundamental assertion against confessionalism – that it was desirable to distinguish between civil and religious allegiance – and his assertions about economic matters. In both cases the real difficulty lay in persuading his readers that what was advanced should be applied in the discussion of the condition of the Catholics – in the first case because of their anti-Catholic beliefs and in the second because the connection O'Conor perceived between agrarian reform and Catholic relief did not in fact exist. In both cases the foundational assertions O'Conor adopted were not in serious dispute. Yet, in truth, these were very radical. As the consistent application of the Lockean principle of toleration would have destroyed confessionalism, so an effective tenurial reform would have at least radically mutated the Irish *ancien régime* in another of its aspects. As MacCurtain has pointed out, leases, as well as regulating much of the rural economy, regulated – often in considerable detail – the most important relationships of the social hierarchy.[37] What the proponents of tenurial reform sought, the strengthening, legally and numerically, of the most important intermediate group in the rural social hierarchy, the strong farmers, could not have been without far-reaching consequences for that system of relationships. In particular, it could not but have diminished both the power and influence of the landlords. Dobbs at least was aware that this, together with more material considerations, was among the most serious obstacles to the acceptance of his reform proposals and attempted to offer reassurance.[38] It was in vain, as all such reassurance would be until the Irish *ancien régime* came to an end.

O'Conor's writings divide conveniently into two categories: his Catholic
pamphlets and his historical studies dealing, for the most part, with pre-
Norman Ireland.[39] There is, in fact, a close relationship between the two
and neither can be well interpreted without reference to the other. This
point has not been noted. In so far as they have been examined, the
writings on ancient and early medieval history have received a simple
interpretation. They were, in the view of Catherine Sheehan, concerned
with the defence of 'Ireland as a nation'.[40] A more recent student of the
works has placed O'Conor in a tradition of writers who were concerned
with 'their... perceived situation as colonial subjects' and who were thus
anxious to refute the allegations of Irish barbarism which had served 'as a
justification for colonial policy'.[41] This inclination to find a place for
O'Conor in the history of Irish nationalism is not without some merit.
Certainly his insistence on the civility of the ancient Gael was congruent
with the views that would be developed by nineteenth-century nationalists.
Certainly, too, his writings found favourable reception among those
moved by the national sentiment which formed part of Irish Enlightenment
thought – as they were, no doubt, intended to do.[42] However, this characteristic should not be taken as the only key to their interpretation.

These works should be considered, firstly, as a distinctively Irish
response to the general historiographical trends of the eighteenth century.
With some of these O'Conor was somewhat at odds, by virtue of his
choice of pre-Norman Ireland as a field of study. An initial difficulty arose
with regard to sources. A historical pyrrhonism 'which had a curious
recrudescence at the end of the seventeenth century and the beginning of
the eighteenth'[43] continued to annoy Irish writers who had, perforce, to
make much use of the 'panegyrics of ancient bards'.[44] There was a body of
opinion which regarded the early history of Ireland as a 'great blank'.[45]
This was a problem addressed by the Anglican bishops Hutchinson (in his
Defence of the Ancient Historians) and Nicolson (in his *Irish Historical
Library*) in the early years of the century. O'Conor was more competent to
deal with the matter than these were. He possessed a far better knowledge
of the sources in question, as well as a developed understanding of how
they could be used in a discriminating way. It was precisely this more
critical attitude that was required, if objections were to be overcome.[46]
When the problem of sources was dealt with, yet another one remained.
The enlightened historian was expected to discuss the past in such a way
as to instruct his contemporaries in both their private and their political
conduct. Little by way of useful instruction was likely to be gleaned from
a study of the ages of barbarism.[47] Even if early Irish history could be
investigated, doubt remained about whether it was worth investigating.

Sheehan has remarked that 'Charles O'Conor thought of his own writing rather as a means of interesting others in writing history than as history itself.'[48] The point may be made differently. O'Conor's writing can be interpreted as constituting a prolegomenon to the study of ancient Irish history, made necessary by the eighteenth century's historiographical beliefs. That in his works which speaks of the civilised character of the ancient Gael and has been read as patriotic eulogy, may equally be taken as indicating the potential profitability of his field for the aspiring enlightened historian. Much of this assertion of the presence of civilisation, it may be added, is actually insistence on one point – the presence of literacy among the pre-Christian Irish. For if the earliest Irish preserved a written record, the Gaelic sources were soundly based.

O'Conor's only substantial work on ancient Ireland is his *Dissertations*. About two-thirds of it is taken up with arguments either demonstrating the early use of letters or relating directly to the reliability of Gaelic sources and with discussion of the characteristics of Gaelic civilisation in its various aspects.[49] In the remaining part of the work he offered only an 'Idea of the Scottish [i.e. Irish] History' of the early period.[50] Apart from the *Dissertations*, O'Conor published only half-a-dozen scholarly pieces. There was a letter to David Hume, the most celebrated of those who proclaimed the barbarism of the ancient Irish.[51] The rest were chiefly concerned with the matter of sources. The publication by James Macpherson in the early 1760s of three collections of poems, allegedly the work of a third-century Scottish bard, Ossian, provoked from O'Conor an essay published as an appendix to the 1766 edition of the *Dissertations* and another in the form of a preface to his edition of Roderick O'Flaherty's *The Ogygia Vindicated*. It has been uniformly remarked in discussions of O'Conor's participation in the Ossianic controversy that his interest was not with the poems as literature, but as purported history.[52] More precisely, his concern was historiographical. He objected to Macpherson's view of the Scottish and Irish past not merely because he regarded it as erroneous, but because it was that of Thomas Innes. This Scottish antiquarian

> To avoid historical credulity... fell into the opposite extreme of historical scepticism. By a number of negative arguments, plausible but unsatisfactory, he laboured to prove that the old senachies of *Ireland* were equally ignorant with [the Scottish historians] Fordun and Boece, relatively to the origin of their nation; and they had not the use of letters till introduced by the christian missionaries in the fifth century.[53]

Further encouragement for O'Conor to write came from the publication of opinions much more agreeable to him. These belonged to the Irish antiquarian, Charles Vallancey, who, with the aid of very bad linguistic arguments, had been able to attribute a Punic origin to the Gaels. O'Conor had long been anxious to find for the Gaelic invaders of Ireland a home-land where letters were known. In the *Dissertations*, following a very old Irish tradition, he had opted for Iberia.[54] However, mere propinquity to the Mediterranean provided a less than wholly satisfactory argument for liter-acy. The attribution of letters to the Phoenicians, however, was not to be contradicted. Hence, despite reservations about Vallancey's scholarship,[55] O'Conor gave a warm welcome to his theory in *The Ogygia Vindicated*[56] and contributed three pieces to his *Collectanea de Rebus Hibernicis*.

If O'Conor's scholarly work was a response to the problems raised for the study of ancient Ireland by Enlightenment historiography, this did not mean the exclusion of political statements. On the contrary, their presence was required. Examples of the practical wisdom to be gleaned from the experience of this civilised nation had to be given. Not surprisingly, some of these could be easily applied to the consideration of the Catholic question.[57] Most of O'Conor's political statements in the *Dissertations*, however, were of a rather commonplace kind. Chiefly, he was content simply to extol the balanced constitution, which, he maintained, had existed also in ancient Ireland.[58] When he went further, he suggested that it was not from the crown that the contemporary threat to the constitution's balance issued. The ancient Irish instructed the eighteenth century not only with their virtues and strengths, but also with their weakness. This 'arose from a Monarchy hurt in the Head and Feet, and too much controled [sic] by aristocratical Principles'.[59] Such remarks were, of course, in keeping with O'Conor's habitual political inclination – towards an attitude to the Patriots which lay between indifference and distrust. There was a good deal in O'Conor's historical writings that was capable of giving ideolo-gical support to Patriot politics. However, O'Conor hardly wrote with this in view. The national sentiment he encouraged could find expression in very different political views. For some, the interest they showed in Ireland's Celtic past was not an assertion of difference from England, but of identity with other parts of the Hanoverian empire.[60] O'Conor was rather more concerned about asserting Irish links with the dynasty itself. It was to do so that he undertook to edit O'Flaherty's *Ogygia Vindicated*. For this had been written to controvert the views of those Scottish historians, notably Sir George MacKenzie, who had sought to deny an Irish ancestry to their kings, whose 'posterity... reign at this day... in the person of his present Majesty'.[61] The opportunity which the new edition gave for attacking Innes and Macpherson, who by their rejection of the Gaelic sources also opposed the Irish claims, was perhaps incidental.

However, even if a belief in the need for a strong monarchy and a desire to assert loyalty to the dynasty were present in O'Conor's mind, they can scarcely be taken to have provided the political motivation for his historical writing. This may indeed be described as nationalist, provided the term is used with a degree of historical specificity. In other words, the peculiarly *ancien régime* character of his social and political beliefs must be emphasised. If it is not, then a description of him as a nationalist is considerably less than helpful. O'Conor declared himself to be concerned with 'the honour of our ancient race'.[62] By 'race', however, he seems to have meant no more than the members of 'some surviving noble and worthy Families'.[63] In describing a similar attitude among the Gaelic poets of the sixteenth and seventeenth centuries, Thomas Dunne observed that it 'was far more a matter of class than of nation'.[64] Speaking of O'Conor, it would be better to say that his concern was not with the Irish nation of his own era, which was Protestant; nor the Irish nation of a future period, which included the whole population; but with the Gaelic part at least of the Irish nation – an exclusively aristocratic and preponderantly Catholic one – of a previous era. As a service to this nation, O'Conor sought in his historical works to raise a 'funeral Pile' for its ancestors.[65] But he also sought to serve it as it endured into the late eighteenth century by agitating the only political matter which much concerned it – the matter of securing the privileges it had lost in the wake of the Protestant victory of 1691. This may be stated somewhat differently. O'Conor did indeed write with a consciousness that Ireland had endured colonisation. However, this did not lead him to the conviction that the existing relationship between Ireland and England ought to be weakened. The chief contemporary political lesson he wanted drawn was concerned not with this relationship at all, but with that which had arisen within Ireland itself – between those who looked on themselves as the heirs of the conquerors and those who were looked on as the heirs of the conquered . O'Conor's perception of contemporary England – or, more accurately, of the Hanoverian dynasty – was a positive one. It was from the king and his ministers that aid might come to correct the injustice which characterised the domestic relationship with which he was concerned.

The association of O'Conor with nationalism is defensible. It is also misleading, in view of the divergence between his beliefs and the beliefs of those identified as nationalists in the period after him. In fact, a more acceptable interpretative context for his historical writings can be readily provided by referring not to the works of later Irish writers, but to those of European contemporaries. Since O'Conor never concerned himself with any other political matter, a political *point de départ* for his work as a

historian is hardly to be sought anywhere else than in the Catholic question
– which is to say, in the question of the relationship between the *ancien
régime* elite and those who suffered what they considered to be unjust
exclusion from it. Such a question, it has already been pointed out, provoked activity among historians in many parts of contemporary Europe.[66]
For some, the origins myth of a conquest which supported elite racism and
thus privilege was to be re-expounded and elaborated to serve its conventional purpose. For others, it was to be reinterpreted to justify a process of
change.[67] Thus it was with O'Conor. His revisionism, however, was moderate. Only one part of the picture of the Irish past was redrawn. Pre-Norman
Ireland, though it suffered much for want of a strong monarchy, was not
sunk in barbarism. On the contrary, it was 'the Throne of *Liberty*, the
Emporium of *Literature*, and the Sanctuary of *Christianity*'.[68] But while
O'Conor was anxious to honour the ancestors of the dispossessed, he had
no desire, in the manner of some continental revisers of the origins myths,
to denigrate the invaders. This might have had an appearance of hostility to
England. Nor, for that matter, did he wish to express disapproval of the
invasion itself: that might have been taken as an expression of hostility to
monarchical power. In any case, not a few of the Irish Catholics were held
themselves to be of the 'Strongbonian race'. The coming of the Anglo-
Normans, O'Conor held, might well have been a blessing: they might have
extended their law to the whole island. He joined Sir John Davies, the early
seventeenth-century attorney-general who strove to make the Irish 'become
English', in bitterly regretting that no such development took place in the
High or late Middle Ages. For by this time, parts of the Gaelic legal corpus
were falling into disuse while others were becoming dysfunctional.[69] The
result was that 'Thro' the period from the conquest to James I the Irish
beyond the pale lived in the worst state of feudal anarchy; governed more
by customs than laws'.[70] It was because attention had been confined to this
period of decadence, that the accusations of barbarism made against the
native Irish had arisen.

O'Conor's revision of the context in which the Anglo-Norman invasion
was seen served good political purpose to whatever extent 'Gaelic' tended
to be read as 'Catholic'. But twelfth-century events were remote and identification with them hindered by the rather obviously tenuous nature of the
link between Anglo-Normans and eighteenth-century Protestants. Moreover, if Molyneux and the tradition of the Patriots was followed, what had
occurred in the twelfth century was no conquest, but merely a colonisation
and voluntary submission. The association of Ireland with the British
monarchy was the accomplishment of both Saxon and Gael.[71] In any case,
if Protestants wanted to reflect on the barbarous character of the Catholic

inhabitants of their country they were less likely to dwell on the peculiarities of brehon law than on that conduct exposed to them in vivid written narratives of the Rebellion of 1641 and in the sermons preached each twenty-third of October. In the ideology which sustained the Irish *ancien régime*, it was the Cromwellian conquest rather than the Anglo-Norman one which was truly important. This was the area of John Curry's expertise.

The main points of Curry's interpretation of the events of the 1640s were hardly his own. Archdekin, for example, had set out the bones of the case that he made with respect to the central topic, the Catholic rising of 1641.[72] Archdekin's purpose, however, was no more than to make plain the Catholics' fidelity to Charles I and consequently the injustice of the land settlement in the reign of his son, with a view to influencing a Stuart monarch and government. When he restated the arguments in his Jacobite pamphlet published in 1747 and in his work of 1758, Curry's object was hardly different – even if the Stuart regime did not, for the present, exist. However, by now, the significance of the dispute about the events of 1641 had changed. They were not merely the subject-matter of a political debate – one intended to influence government action. They had assumed a broader, ideological significance. They justified, or failed to justify, the political, economic and social relationships which had been brought into existence by the events of the mid- and late seventeenth century and which were confirmed and strengthened by the penal code. It was for this reason that they continued to be discussed, by Curry among several others, long after the hope of a Stuart restoration and a reversal of the land settlement had ceased to be entertained.[73] The Protestant accounts of 1641 derived their ideological effectiveness from one thing above all others – their depiction of Catholic moral depravity and barbarism. In other words, the chief task of Curry's argumentation, as it formed part of the debate on the Catholic question, was precisely the same as that of O'Conor's. If Protestant narratives referred to different conquests, their emphasis remained constant. That emphasis, on the vices of the conquered rather than the virtues of the conquerors, might be said to be the characteristic of the Irish elite's account of its beginnings. In the case of the account of the Cromwellian conquest, this was particularly advantageous. It did more than merely assert Protestant superiority over Catholics and in an area closely related to religion. It even suggested the appropriateness of reducing Catholics to a *status poenalis* – a status European *ancien régime* thought was inclined to ascribe to the lower ranks of the peasantry.[74]

The Protestant accounts of the Catholic insurrection raised a variety of points, though all pointing to the same interpretation of Catholic conduct.

In the first place, there were those relating to the cause of the revolt. This had to be shown to lie in nothing more than the propensity of Irish Catholics to engage in unnatural rebellion, springing either from racial and cultural traits[75] or from their subordination to an immoral ecclesiastical hierarchy. Curry was thus firstly obliged to refute the assertion 'that the State of their [the Catholics'] Affairs both spiritual and temporal, was *then* [in 1641], and for many Years before, as *quiet* and *happy* as they themselves could reasonably wish it'.[76] He went on to explain the immediate circumstances of the outbreak, bringing in the Haman figures, Parsons and Borlase, who, he maintained, deliberately provoked the taking-up of arms.[77] He was further obliged to deal with the question of the reputed clerical direction of the revolt.[78] However, what was crucially important in sustaining or refuting the accusations of Catholic depravity and barbarism was discussion of the 1641 massacres. Who had begun them?[79] How many had been killed in them?[80] Were they desired by the Catholic leaders or merely excesses of the rabble?[81] All of these were difficult points and Curry was often in error. Like the economic argumentation on behalf of the Catholics, this historical argumentation could hardly have been overwhelmingly convincing even to those well-disposed to their cause.

O'Conor and Curry's historical works formed part of their presentation of the Catholic case and, as such, shared the moderate character of that presentation as a whole. The arguments the two offered in their history as in their political tracts – though Curry was always less capable of adopting conciliatory positions than O'Conor was – constituted a serious effort to influence the mind of Irish Protestants. They sought to revise the Protestant view of the Irish past and not merely confront it with one in which Protestants were cast, as they were by MacGeoghegan, as alien tyrants.

It is true that, in some degree, O'Conor and Curry's historical arguments were less congruent with the thinking of their Protestant contemporaries than their economic ones. The latter were supported by a generally acceptable tradition of reformist writing, from which the Catholic apologists deviated not at all – except in applying it to the discussion of the condition of the Catholics. Their historical arguments certainly lacked this degree of support. Curry lacked any tradition of Protestant historiography on which to call for aid, short of returning to the more zealous royalist writers of the seventeenth century. O'Conor, however, was by no means so isolated. There was, as Hill has made clear, scholarly investigation of pre-Norman Ireland well before O'Conor began to write[82] and this was not without influence on those whose interests lay in other than scholarly matters. Ancient Irish history was, for example, an acceptable, if hardly popular source for the playwrights of the day to draw on.[83] The 'wave of enthusiasm for ancient Gaelic civilization' in the first half of the eighteenth century of which Hill speaks was not a powerful one; but it joined the other factors already mentioned to render the use of medieval history in anti-Catholic polemic less extensive than it would otherwise have been.[84] Moreover, this enthusiasm, in a considerable measure thanks to O'Conor's own endeavours, was to grow. Even the short period between the first and second editions of his *Dissertations* showed, O'Conor thought, most encouraging signs[85] and certainly later, in the last quarter of the century, interest in the Gaelic past did become widespread.[86] There was change too in regard to the matters which occupied Curry. This, though, had little to do with historical writing. It is true that the *History of Ireland* which Thomas Leland published in 1773 offered some modification of the traditional Protestant view of the outbreak of the warfare of the 1640s. But its challenge to anti-Catholic beliefs was hardly forceful. In any case, it was not an influential work.[87] More important than any revision of the historical facts was the growth of the conviction that they were not of great importance; that the sins of the fathers should not be visited on the children. In the 1770s such views were finding expression even in the major vehicle of the Protestant myth, the 1641 anniversary sermons.[88] But ideological change was overtaken by political events. After the sudden repeal of much of the penal code, the government no longer thought it appropriate to rehearse justifications for its existence and ceased its patronage of the twenty-third of October commemorations. Not all, however, were so minded: Dublin Corporation at least kept up the tradition.[89]

In their historical as in their political writings, therefore, O'Conor and Curry's ability to address the Protestant community effectively is apparent. They were able, quite consistently, to choose subject-matter that commanded Protestant interest and arguments that had already gained, or were at least capable of gaining the support of some significant section of the Protestant body. But – again as in the case of the political argumentation – this should not lead to the suggestion that what was advanced was harmless. In Ireland, as in the rest of Europe, the *ancien régime* elite was capable of producing or nurturing views which were highly subversive of the order which gave them their status. The myths constructed from the historical invasions, despite the acceptance of the undermining of them, were of considerable importance. Without them that peculiarly Irish elite which was constituted by the Protestant body as a whole could hardly have preserved its identity and coherence. If critiques such as those of O'Conor and Curry were accepted, it was because they were limited in their scope.

A revisionist interpretation of the Anglo-Norman conquest might be accepted while a traditional view of the Cromwellian era was preserved. When, in the final decades of the century, even this latter became unfashionable, much could still be made of the Williamite conquest. The application of any serious revisionism to the period of the Revolution still had something of the appearance of disloyalty.[90] Thus Dublin Corporation, in addressing the Protestants of Ireland in 1792, chose what was for the moment fairly safe ground when it looked no further to find a sword-right justification for their exclusive possession of political power.[91] 1798, when it had come and gone, might have provided another. Musgrave's *Rebellions*, with its insistence on perceiving 1798 as the renewal of the Popish barbarism and Protestant heroism of 1641, might well be seen as an attempt to make it do so.[92] But it was the Catholics who were to make the myths of the following century and 1798 was to be theirs.

Part IV

7 New Critiques

The Catholic argumentation of the decades after mid-century originated in the perception of the need for Catholics to abandon intransigence and make an effective approach to the Protestant body. It thus challenged Catholics considerably more than Protestants. In all the areas which were characteristically of central importance in *ancien régime* thought about the state – confessionalism, dynasticism, and the relationship between land and political power – the Catholics were obliged to make radical adjustments. Among Protestants, there were, of course, many who were very disturbed indeed by the emergence of a Catholic question; but it was the chief object of the Catholic apologists to reduce their fears to a minimum. Much reassurance was offered and few concrete concessions were requested. Furthermore, the supporting argumentation generally made use of trends that were already established in the thinking of the Protestant community. These, it is true, were frequently far from conducive to the maintenance of the established order; but, as they were familiar, the expression of them created little alarm.

The Catholic agitation of the last two decades of the century was to be much more disturbing for the upholders of the established order. To a considerable extent this was due to the changing political environment, within Ireland and without, in which it was conducted, rather than to the agitation itself. In the 1780s both England and Ireland witnessed challenges, albeit rather ineffective ones, to both its confessionalism and, with the calls for parliamentary reform, the political structure which was founded on it. In the 1790s anxieties about such things were quickly lost among the fears created by the universal threat now offered to the Christian order. Throughout the two decades, the events beyond Ireland, together with traditional anti–Catholicism, provided the not-altogether ill-fitting key for the interpretation of the domestic problem of insurrection – by the Rightboys, the Defenders and the United Irishmen. However, it was not merely English dissenters or French revolutionaries who were to be held responsible for having encouraged rebellion. The charge could also be made against a section of the Irish Protestant community itself and the imperial government, on account of the measures which had been accepted by the Irish parliament in the late 1770s and early 1780s. Enacted at a time when there was less fear of rebellion than there ever had been or ever was to be again in the eighteenth century, these quickly turned sour for many Protestants. Before the end of the decade the Catholics, who had received as much as their apologists had ever asked for in the Relief Acts of 1778 and 1782, were in revolt in Munster. The dissenters showed no more inclination to be reconciled to the existing order, but continued to harbour and propagate views that violently challenged orthodox Anglican political theology. This was despite, or perhaps because of the removal in 1780 of the sacramental test – an indulgence the English dissenters, though much less threatening to the Anglican establishment than their relatively more numerous brethren in Ireland, were very far from gaining. Now there was a political, or perhaps even insurrectionary alliance between Catholic and dissenter. A further cause for anxiety lay in the change in the relationship with England that had taken place. There was the possibility that the impending attack, whatever form it took, would have to be faced without English aid. Woodward, for example, perceived an alarming loosening, since the time of the constitutional changes, of what he pointed to as the chief bond between the sister kingdoms: Englishmen were losing their interest – in both senses of the word – in Irish land.[1] In short, within a few years there were excellent grounds for pointing out to those who had supported the measures that they had made a terrible mistake. What might have appeared to be an effort to unite Irishmen against a common adversary had turned out to be an encouragement of the Irish Protestants' implacable enemies which endangered their relationship with their truest friends. Further relief measures would now only be enacted by a parliament forced to accept them and it was indeed the government in London that pressed the bills of 1792 and 1793. But the inclination of so many leaders of the Protestant community thereafter to accommodate themselves to what had taken place greatly increased the sense of betrayal. Events beyond the shores or Ireland, the renewal of at least the threat of Catholic rebellion and the fear generated by the apparent wilful blindness in the face of danger of so many political leaders and other members of the Protestant body, each of these things individually and all together ensured that any Catholic claims, even if they were of the most moderate sort, would cause a degree of alarm not previously in evidence.

In fact, Catholic claims tended to become less and less moderate. Even if the Relief Acts were hardly responsible for the Rightboys and Defenders, they were inevitably an encouragement to politically conscious Catholics and their allies at least to hope for far more than they had previously sought. Again, even if the campaigns of dissenters against the Churches of England and Ireland, the campaigns for parliamentary reform and the French Revolution were not simply grist to the mill of Popish conspiracy, these movements and their associated ideological positions did exert considerable influence on many Irish Catholics. And even those

Catholics not so influenced were looked on as the natural allies of these movements in whatever degree they truly tended to the overthrow of the *ancien régime*. After all, it was no longer possible to contemplate a Catholic structure of king, lords and commons. Catholic politics, many assumed, would thus inevitably tend to anti-hierarchical modes of thought. Catholic political influence would inevitably be exercised in favour of that estate to which Catholics now, almost uniformly, belonged. From those Catholics who were content to be antagonists of their country's *ancien régime*, who welcomed new criticisms of the existing order and who were emboldened by the progress the Catholic cause had already made, new claims and new arguments to support them emerged whatever concessions were made. Together with this went a new boldness of action, culminating in the convention of 1792 and its decision to appeal directly to the king. Other Catholics faced difficult problems. Could a Catholic politics be pursued without the utilisation of argumentation repellent at least by virtue of its use in other contexts? More fundamentally, how could there be a challenge to the confessionalism which disadvantaged them without an undermining of the social and political structures which were interwoven with it? The difficulty which was encountered at the time of the quarterage dispute, of changing without destroying, now emerged as a much wider one. One writer, by no means hostile to the Catholics, put the point concisely when he warned them that 'it is only by making... [the constitution] a wreck... that your expectations can be pursued with any plausibility'.[2] Some solutions to these difficulties were found.[3] But, in a considerable degree, moderation was not possible for any Catholic political activist.

The fears of Protestants might not have been as widespread and as intense as they in fact were, had change not come upon them so unexpectedly in 1778 and the years immediately following. True, it was now almost three decades since a Catholic question had been raised and the Catholics had acquired a body of friends in parliament. These were capable of halting anti-Catholic measures and even of securing some very minor pro-Catholic ones. But that was all. The period just before 1778 was a depressing one for proponents of Catholic relief. In 1773 Bishop Burke explained to O'Conor why he had taken it upon himself to confirm anti-Catholic arguments by publishing the Roman condemnation of one of the texts of a proposed oath of allegiance.[4] It did not, in the bishop's view, set back the possibility of relief, since no such possibility existed. 'Members of both Houses...', he explained, 'gave me to understand very candidly, that we'l [sic] get no Favour from Parliament within a hundred Miles of repealing a Popery-Act'.[5] O'Conor was not mollified by this explanation. However, it was only in the previous year that he had indicated to Curry that he himself had come to much the same conclusion about the prospects for relief. The difficulty lay, he held, quite simply in the inclination of the legislators to put religious considerations before any others.[6] From time to time O'Conor was heartened. But only the year before the first major Relief Act he spoke again of his own despondency, that of his fellow Catholics and the view of their Protestant supporters, who 'think our cause too desperate'.[7]

O'Conor's observation about the cause of the apparent impasse – the preponderance of religious over more material concerns – was hardly justifiable. In fact, Protestants had been given little enough reason to believe that relief measures could be of any real benefit to more than a few Catholics. However, the observation does point accurately to the continuing strength of anti-Catholic belief. It would be wrong to suggest that there had been no diminution of this at all by the 1770s since O'Conor and Curry had begun to write.[8] However, what Protestants looked on as a generous and enlightened position was still very far away from that to which the Catholic apologists sought to bring them. The case of the historian Leland illustrates the point.[9] So does that of John Brett, the rector of Moynalty in County Meath. In 1769 Brett wrote to O'Conor informing him about his forthcoming book, the *Judgment of Truth*, which, he said, was intended to aid the Catholic cause in the approaching parliamentary session.[10] It is true that this work displayed some marked changes in Brett's views of a decade before, when his anti-Catholic preaching had provoked a reply from Curry.[11] Nevertheless, all the important elements of the anti-Catholic ideology which supported confessionalism were articulated forcefully and at length. Popery remained '*an idolatrous form of worship*', which the magistrate had a duty to contain, the more so since it concealed a conspiracy to impose a dreadful tyranny.[12] All that commended leniency was the fact that Rome, though unchanged in nature, was now diminished in her powers and unable to control her subjects effectively. The force of interest might induce them, even in Ireland, to loyalty.[13] In brief, Catholics might be indulged to the extent that they gave up their religion, at least as Protestants perceived it.

Whatever the Irish Protestant community thought on the subject of Catholicism and the Catholics, by 1782 it found that its representatives had legalised the religion and all but admitted its adherents to the political nation. Initially, the impetus for change came not from any Irish circumstances, but from the Empire's need for Catholic troops for the American war and the ensuing struggle with France. The need was considered great enough for Lord North and the Irish government to press on with a relief measure in the face of stiff opposition from Irish legislators. These gained some small restriction of the government's generosity, but were unable to prevent the destruction of a great deal of the penal code as it related to landowning.[14] This attack on the Protestant interest and humiliation of the Irish parliament added to the political excitement which the overseas conflicts had already triggered. However, if anti-Catholic sentiment added fuel to the agitation for first the removal of trade restrictions and then legislative independence, the passion ultimately aroused diminished its importance. For the moment, the Catholics were looked on less as a subject of dispute than as an element to be taken into account by those concerned with the strategy of the all-absorbing conflict with England. As the climax approached, the Patriots were anxious to give the government a clear demonstration that they were no longer subject to that fear which bound them to England: they would dare to act. Perhaps some even hoped that they might by generosity remove the Catholic hostility which was the cause of that fear. Inevitably, when the Patriot party addressed its suit to the Catholics, the government was willing to offer itself as a rival. Thus came Gardiner's Relief Act of 1782, removing most of the remaining restrictions on Catholic landholding and substantially ending the law's hostility to the Catholic clergy. Like relief measures before and after it, it was a response to the pressing needs of the moment, far more than any change of mind or heart in response to the Catholic case.[15]

Of course, both the rivals for the affections of the Catholics had their supporters within the Catholic body and this division continued in the years immediately following 1782. Looking to the government for further relief was the party associated with the name of Lord Kenmare; while looking to the proponents of change and, in particular, parliamentary reform, was the party whose best-known leader was the wealthy Dubliner, John Keogh. Between these two parties stood those members of the Catholic Committee who considered that there might well be profit to be derived from the courting of both the government and the reformers. This situation did not last beyond the middle of the decade. For the campaign for electoral reform came to nothing, in a considerable measure precisely because Catholics were prominently involved in it. Though the government was not at this point well-disposed to the Catholics either, there was nothing else but to turn to them.[16] Nevertheless, if conflict among Catholic activists subsided for a time, it soon reappeared. In early 1792 there was the celebrated Kenmare schism, when, alarmed at the refusal by the Catholic Committee to disown those who embraced the opinions of the United Irishmen,

Kenmare led a group out of it. Unity was re-established before the convention which led to the Relief Act of the following year. However, the continuing tendency of the Committee to represent 'the democracy of the Catholics' ensured that some of its members were not at all unhappy that the Convention Act forced it to dissolve itself.[17] That, of course, did not end the conflict. Men such as Keogh, Lewins and McNeven took the dissolution as the opportunity to mix 'their grievances [as Catholics] with those of the country' – or, more accurately, of the United Irishmen.[18]

This was a quarrel that grew as the years passed. In the 1780s it still had something of the appearance of merely being about tactics. There was good reason for making it appear so. A united Catholic front had to be kept up. In any case, an alliance with dissenters – whatever fears existed in the Protestant community – was still far from being a matter of practical politics. Thus little was to be gained from a militant display of the ideological positions which would support it. Yet those positions were being taken and provoking much unease. There were Catholics prepared to accept the arguments now being propounded among the dissenters and merge them with their own. The result was the abandonment of one of the foundations of the Catholic case as it had been put forward since mid-century: that Catholics might be accommodated within the existing order without destroying or radically mutating it. In brief, some Catholic argumentation now became a very plain assault indeed on the Irish *ancien régime* as a whole. The point is well illustrated by the first piece of writing by Theobald McKenna, the young man whose next pamphleteering effort was to be the immediate occasion of the Kenmare schism. The earlier work, *A Review of Some Interesting Periods of Irish History*, was perhaps less offensive by virtue of its slightly scholarly appearance. In fact, most of the historical information in it was made up of acknowledged borrowings from Curry.[19] However, the observations on events which McKenna made in the manner of a philosophical historian were very far from reflecting the mind of the earlier Catholic champion.

Almost at the beginning of McKenna's tract stood a plain declaration of hostility to Anglican confessionalism and indeed – though here he was a little hesitant – to confessionalism of any kind. This was a root-and-branch opposition. He complained not merely of the consequences of confessionalism for those who did not adhere to the establishment, but of any connection between the Irish state and Anglicanism.[20] Perhaps more alarming was the argument with which he advanced this view. In effect, he commended doctrinal indifferentism.[21] Such religious argumentation, of a very different kind from that used by the Catholics in the earlier part of the eighteenth century, appealed to the young McKenna chiefly, no doubt, because it seemed to cut the Gordian knot of the Catholic question. For he never, in a writing career spanning twenty years, showed any interest in any issue other than those that affected the Catholics. However, this argumentation also had the advantage of identifying him with contemporary radicalism, which, at least frequently and possibly uniformly, rested on religious dissent. With McKenna's adoption of radicalism's fundamental mode of thinking, there came a variety of fashionable doctrines – or at least, since this was no very profound work, shibboleths. The enthusiasm which he expressed for 'the freedom of religious judgment',[22] tended to lead among heterodox dissenters to assertions about natural rights. These generally included extensive political rights: it was difficult to escape confessionalist modes of thought, even when attacking confessionalism.[23] This, apparently, was McKenna's path too. He was less than explicit about what rights he wished to see universally possessed. However, they certainly included whatever had been or still was denied to Catholics by the penal laws.[24] Even if the argument was not developed, the message was clear. No elite, however constituted, possessed an exclusive claim to political power.

Those zealous for the cause of the established order had little reason to worry about the publication of a set of opinions like that of McKenna. The Catholic grouping which he aspired to represent was, for the present, sub-stantially impotent, isolated by a lack of response from both the Protestant community and the lower ranks of the Catholics. The Dublin mob showed a rather different attitude from that of McKenna towards dissenters: its reaction to the Gordon riots was to threaten to destroy their meeting houses in the city.[25] Under these circumstances, Catholic activists were unlikely to be won over in any number by arguments like those of McKenna. How-ever, if his views as a whole were far from generally acceptable, indi-vidually they found at least echoes in more respectable contexts; and other views were in circulation, which, if they were not so obviously pro-vocative, tended nevertheless to a subversion of the Irish *ancien régime*.

The Franciscan Arthur O'Leary was respectable enough to be spoken of in parliament as a proof of the loyalty and useful character of the regular clergy.[26] Both his writings and those of Edmund Burke on the Catholic question – even in the 1780s these latter were influential despite their slight bulk[27] – tended to display the similarities between Catholicism and Protes-tantism. In Burke, the fundamental identity of the two religions was generally a matter of assumption, rather than of explicit statement. How-ever, the assumption became clear enough, for example, in the comparisons he made as occasion required.[28] O'Leary utilised the theme much more directly and frequently, with the result that he earned the disapproval of some of his fellow priests zealous in the cause of orthodoxy. In fact he was careful enough when he came close to 'admitting the famous distinction between fundamentals and non-fundamentals' and certainly did not preach indifferentism – though he felt obliged to utter an explicit denial that he did so.[29] Moreover, O'Leary's motive for adopting the position he did was quite different from McKenna's. O'Leary wanted to see the ecclesiastical establishment modified in such a way that Catholics might be accommodated within it. He had no wish to see it overthrown. Nevertheless, to some it may have appeared that the difference between O'Leary and McKenna was but one of degree.

Again, McKenna was not singular in speaking of natural rights. O'Conor had done so, though for him these did not include civil rights. Indeed, the terms 'natural rights' and 'civil rights' were used for mutual definition.[30] Burke too mentioned 'the rights of human nature' when he spoke of the Catholic question; but his sense was the same as that of O'Conor. He was thinking, in this context, chiefly of rights relating to property.[31] However, if Burke did not use the concept of natural rights, except in relation to the matters dealt with by the early relief measures, he certainly used the concept of natural justice. In the famous speech to the electors of Bristol it went under the name of 'common justice... [and] and common honesty' – substantially the only grounds which that speech used to commend relief.[32]

This line of argument took its place with others of a similar nature. Together they display a new approach to the Catholic question adopted in the 1780s. O'Conor and Curry had pleaded for Catholic relief on the grounds of its public utility. Arguments of this sort were not entirely dropped; but the specific ones used by the earlier writers were no longer serviceable, as the measures they had advocated – relating to property rights – had been passed. Now relief was sought as a matter of justice. However, the argument was not always precisely the same as that used by Burke in 1780. Arthur Browne, Dublin University's representative in parliament, drew attention to the reappearance of a Catholic argument which seemed to him novel. He considered it necessary

> to examine the truth of an opinion which as far as my observation extends, very generally pervaded the nation, that the Penal Laws were a breach of public faith; and that the abolition of them is not so much to be considered in the light of bounty as of just restitution of the privileges set forth in the Treaty of Limerick; which privileges seem to be almost universally supposed to have been very nearly equal to those of his Majesty's Protestant subjects of the Established Church.[33]

It was in the 1780s too that the Harringtonian dictum that power must follow property came to be used on behalf of the Catholics.[34] Another

Protestant writer complained that it was being stated that 'the Roman Catholics... are now... enabled to acquire landed estates... [and political] power is the concomitant of dominion over the lands'.[35]

These new arguments were alarming enough to many Protestants; but they did not threaten, as McKenna's did, a general overthrow of hierarchical order. Burke's 'common justice' was such an imprecise concept that it was meaningless unless restricted to the discussion of a particular body of persons. The number of those who might benefit from an appeal to the articles of Limerick was, of course, even more restricted. And certainly use of the Harringtonian dictum indicated belief in hierarchy – of a kind.

In brief, the Catholic argumentation of the 1780s did not contain a great deal to alarm those concerned about emerging democratic ideas. True, some advocates of the Catholic cause, such as McKenna, could be singled out as holding dangerous opinions. Others were guilty of no more than rhetorical exuberance or of entertaining views which, if of doubtful tendency when considered in isolation, were substantially neutralised by their contexts. Burke, for example, certainly showed an inclination to reckon by numbers when he spoke of the Irish nation as Catholic.[36] Still, if the Catholic argumentation was not, on the whole, the vehicle of the most extreme views of the period, it can, nevertheless, be seen as genuinely subversive of the Hanoverian *ancien régime* as it existed in Ireland. Obviously, any pro-Catholic argumentation, in any part of the Hanoverian Empire, weakened the state's confessionalist ideology by seeking to exscind what was still, in the popular mind at any rate, its most important element – its anti-Catholicism. In Ireland, anti-Catholicism not only provided a part of the state's *raison d'être*, but also, alone or in union with other sets of beliefs, a basis for the hierarchical ordering of society. The Catholic agitation did not attack all hierarchies. However, it did attack the one which was of primary importance to many, that based on religious affiliation alone. Indeed, since its inception it had done so. But now, in the 1780s, the conflict was becoming fiercer. A rather wider section of the population was being politicised. Combatants were increasing. And the Catholic claims – increased in number – were being made far more assertively and with far more hope of success.

The 1790s saw no fundamental change, but only an intensification of these trends. Similarly, no very remarkable innovation was displayed in the argumentation used. Perhaps chief among the causes of this was the feeling that debate was becoming futile. Points were not being taken on either side. For what divided the disputants was no longer mere politics. There was now a divergence of moral judgement about what constituted a just and reasonable basis for the ordering of society, which, everywhere in Europe, heralded the challenge to the *ancien régime*.[37] Attempts to persuade thus gave way to expressions of moral outrage – a marked characteristic of the Catholic debate as the century drew towards its end. However, there were apologists for the Catholics who continued to seek points of contact with the Irish Protestant body: and from this and other circumstances in the 1790s a few new lines of argumentation did emerge.

The legislation of the early 1790s did not immediately open new areas for discussion as that of a decade before had. The issue before its enactment had been political rights for Catholics and that remained the issue afterwards. At least, that was the matter most easily debated. Slowly, but increasingly, it became understood, by some anyway, that mere legislative action would always be insufficient to resolve Ireland's Catholic question. As Theobald McKenna, who had now renounced his adherence to the United Irishmen to become the leading pamphleteer of the aristocratic party, remarked: 'Repeal the distinguishing laws; good, but you cannot by your act of parliament reach the spirit of distinction'.[38] The penal code had been substantially repealed; but the ideology, from which it had derived its true importance, remained. Certainly the merely permissive Acts of the 1790s had not been capable of destroying it. It continued to exist in a symbiotic relationship with continuing *ancien régime* institutions, such as the urban corporations, and to influence social intercourse in innumerable ways at all levels of society. As McKenna concisely put it, the heart of the problem lay in 'the practice and manners of the country'.[39] However, if the Catholic question was not to be solved entirely by political action, this did not render such action unimportant. The chief practical conclusion that McKenna drew from his reflection on past legislation's lack of efficacy was that future legislation should be more wide-ranging. What was required was change in a measure beyond the ability of the existing constitution to achieve. It was therefore with much enthusiasm that he greeted the proposed new, unionist constitution. Under this, he declared, 'All the bearings and relations of authority are to be varied: civil society itself is to be new-modelled.'[40]

If Catholic opinion of consequence tended to favour the Union,[41] this should not be thought of as merely the consequence of the promise of a relief act. There was a belief in the measure for its own sake, wholly congruent with the tradition of seeking sympathy from the king in London rather than his parliament in Dublin.[42] Indeed, this had previously given rise to expressions of unionist sentiment, albeit muted when national sentiment ran high.[43] In short, once again the agitation of the Catholic question induced, among some considerable part of the Catholic community at any rate, the adoption of characteristically modern political attitudes. *Ancien régime* particularism was rejected in favour of a centralising tendency, which had been present indeed within the spectrum of opinion which characterised *ancien régime* politics, but the triumph of which was central to the emergence of the modern state. An enthusiasm for distinct Irish institutions, most notably an Irish parliament, which could be unequivocally linked to a modern politics, had to await the further development of nationalism.

Endorsement of the Union constituted a new approach to the Catholic question. It was also a point of contact with Protestant opinion or, at least, that part of it which supported a Union as other than primarily a security against the Catholics. However, in this respect it was weak. Some Protestants may have taken enthusiasm among Catholics for integration into a state in which their influence was likely to be diminished as a more genuine indication than had hitherto been given of acceptance of the existing order; some may have acknowledged a degree of unity of interest with Catholics. But this was incidental. Catholic pro-Union declarations were an attempt to assist in the creation of institutions in which Irish Protestant opinion would be of less importance. They were not, as all previous public argumentation on behalf of the Catholics had been, primarily an attempt to alter that body of opinion. The 1790s' most notable effort in this respect undoubtedly came from Burke. In 1792, as a result of the acclaim which he had received for his anti-Jacobin writings, his capacity to influence consideration of the Catholic question was at its zenith. Of this circumstance he made excellent use with his long *Letter to Sir Hercules Langrishe*. As a hostile observer remarked some years later to Chief Secretary Pelham:

> The republican reveries of Paine shedding disastrous influence over the Empire in all its dependencies, have been far less mischievous in this Island, than the insidious arguments of Burke in support of papal claims [contained in the letter to Langrishe].[44]

In fact, the latter part of this *Letter*, though it contained considerable originality of expression, displayed little real profundity of thought. There was not much more than the old argument, put forward now with reference to the threat that the opinions of Protestant dissenters offered, that Catholic discontent was dangerous and easily removed.[45] However, this argument from political prudence was prefixed by a constitutional argument which was altogether more novel and more provocative. If this latter argument was read as a whole, the degree of provocation it offered was reduced. Burke asserted that to attempt to defend the constitution with anti-Catholic measures was to defend it with principles that were alien and dangerous to it. 'Our constitution', he argued at some length, 'is not made for great, general, and proscriptive exclusions; sooner or later it will destroy them, or they will destroy the constitution'.[46] This much he might have maintained without giving a great deal of provocation. However, he went on: it was, in particular, improper to exclude Catholics. The law, Burke pointed out, knew nothing of Protestantism in general, but only of Christianity and the religion of the Churches of England, Ireland and Scotland. Such an argument, in other hands, might have served as an appeal for the restoration of a strict Anglican confessionalism which excluded Protestant dissenters. But Burke laid emphasis on the fact that Britain – and thus Ireland – was a Christian state. It was so essentially; but it was a Protestant state only accidentally, in that the form of Christianity established by existing law happened to be Protestant. In the Middle Ages, he pointed out, it happened to be Catholic. In short, Burke was denying that there was any constitutional basis for a belief in Protestant – as opposed to Anglican – confessionalism, the emphasis on which gave to the Irish *ancien régime* much of its distinctive character.[47] Since the *Letter* also contained a very forceful denunciation of the theory of elite composition which emerged from this emphasis,[48] it can be seen as a particularly thorough attack on the deviance of the Irish *ancien régime* from its English model. As such, it should perhaps be taken as a key to understanding Burke's habitual approach to Irish affairs.

Coming from the pen of the great anti-revolutionary champion and constructed to a large extent as a constitutional argument, Burke's *Letter* was undoubtedly an effective, if far from universally acceptable address to Irish Protestants. It was also fresh. The same may be said of the argumentation of the Catholic Unionists, such as McKenna, a few years later. In contrast, the writings of those who sought to subsume the Catholic campaign under a broader assault on the country's *ancien régime*, as had the McKenna of the 1780s and early 1790s, showed very few signs of innovative thinking. Perhaps the best-known pamphlet of the 1790s on the Catholic question was Wolfe Tone's *Argument on Behalf of the Catholics of Ireland*. Tone might have taken Charles O'Conor's pamphlets of upwards of twenty years before as his models. Like O'Conor, he asserted that his fundamental concern was with Ireland's economic condition[49] and insisted that the key to its amelioration was Catholic relief. O'Conor argued that Catholic relief was necessary if the economic panacea of tenurial reform was to be effective, Tone that Catholic relief was necessary if his panacea of parliamentary reform was to work.[50] There was nothing else in Tone's tract, except a repetition of conventional replies to assertions of Catholic disloyalty and espousal of dangerous beliefs.[51] That the Catholics had a claim on the basis of right was hardly more than adverted to.[52]

In truth, Tone's arguments were just as questionable and unconvincing as O'Conor's had been. There was no more basis than there had been previously for making authoritative statements about those Catholic doctrines which Protestants found disturbing. No doubt most were prepared to accept Tone's assurance that the Irish Catholics were no longer Jacobites; but it was not Jacobitism that was arousing concern. The assertion that parliamentary reform was necessary to deliver Ireland from economic distress was the commonplace of oppositionist rhetoric. Tone was answered in the usual way: Ireland was prosperous – a clear proof that it was already well-governed.[53] The assertion that the concession of the franchise to Catholics was necessary to a general parliamentary reform was also easily denied.[54] Indeed, Tone had offered no very convincing justification of this.[55] In fact, the assertion was justifiable, but only if 'parliamentary reform' was given a meaning much more alarming than that which it usually possessed.

For most of Tone's contemporaries 'parliamentary reform' retained its usual eighteenth-century meaning: the removal of corruption from the existing system. How, one critic of Tone asked, would concessions to Catholics ensure that the country was governed by more virtuous men?[56] Why should Catholics be any more committed than others to such an objective? For some, however, the phrase was coming to betoken something else – a very radical alteration of the governmental system and indeed the social order. To this, Catholics, by virtue of the alienation which confessionalism imposed on them, might very well become committed. Since it was with this latter understanding of reform that Tone wrote, his argument, if hardly likely to gain general approval, did make sense.

It should also be taken as a wholly honest disclosure of his thinking. O'Conor had urged the Protestants of Ireland to grant Catholic relief since this would benefit the country. He appears to have at least come to believe that this was the case; but it is hardly to be believed that a zeal for agrarian reform was the real motive force of the campaign which he conducted with Curry. Similarly, it appears probable that the primary commitment of McKenna, as he wrote in the 1780s, was to the Catholic cause. This at least is what his later career suggests. However, the assertion made by Tone, that Catholic relief was merely a means to a greater end, should undoubtedly be taken at face value. Such an approach was quite characteristic of the United Irishmen and in this lies, no doubt, the explanation of their failure, despite very active participation, to contribute anything of originality to the discussion of the Catholic question. Creatures of the Enlightenment, their thought simplistic and universalist, their political creed had to be a panacea and one that needed but little local adaptation to ensure effectiveness. When their greater hopes were fulfilled, the Catholic question would, they presumed, disappear. The presumption displayed a remarkable blindness to Irish history and contemporary social reality. In their defence it can only be said that a similar unwillingness to come to terms with the primacy of religion was shared by other political figures of the period. Grattan's petulant reaction to the call for support for Protestant ascendancy in 1792, his assertion that this was a mere distraction from his own political programme, illustrates the point.[57] If the political and historical significance of an individual indeed hinges on a capacity to sense and relate to the most potent emergent forces of the time, the reputations of both Tone and Grattan stand in need of reassessment. Neither could have related well to the predominantly sectarian politics of the succeeding era.[58]

8 The Meaning of Gallicanism

The difficulty faced by those Catholic activists of the late eighteenth century who were less than well disposed to being cast as challengers of the established order has received little attention. It was they, however, who constituted, at least in the 1780s and perhaps in the following decade, the bulk of Catholic opinion. They resented the restrictions that Irish confessionalism placed on them; but for them, as for most other Irishmen, anything other than a confessional state, despite the American experiment, was difficult to conceive. They were excluded from attaining higher rank in the existing social hierarchy; but that did not lead them to question the concept of hierarchy. It might be suspected that such an unwillingness to challenge fundamentals could only lead to a restricted and ineffective politics. This was not the case. The 1780s saw the emergence of a new approach to the difficulties of Catholics – one which combined an ability to advance their cause and respect for their conservative beliefs. This is generally adverted to as 'Gallicanism'.

The term 'Gallican' is used to refer to phenomena scattered over a period from the reign of Philippe le Bel almost to the present and over a number of European countries. Further, it is used to refer to both intellectual and political activity. In the eighteenth century Gallican views tended to be merged with most of the not-very-clearly distinguished streams of reformist thought flowing through the Catholic church. These the Roman authorities, for want of any more accurate or opprobrious term, tended to designate as 'Jansenist'.[1] These views could be used politically to support a considerable variety of interests. Thus, for example, in speaking of France it is customary to distinguish between royal Gallicanism, episcopal Gallicanism and the Gallicanism of the lower clergy, known as Richerism. Then again, there was the Gallicanism of the *parlements*, engaged in a Jansenist-inspired struggle against both the Jesuits, as agents of Ultramontanism (or perhaps merely obscurantism), and royal absolutism. In general, it appears, the complex of Gallican and allied views had a particular appeal, in some countries at any rate, to those somewhat below the highest levels of society.[2]

In view of this complexity, when, in 1782, we find the bishop of Ossory, John Troy, describing Archbishop Butler of Cashel and most of his suffragans as 'i Capi Gallicani', it is not at once clear precisely what attitudes and opinions he was mentally ascribing to them.[3] In clarifying this it is of help to explain the immediate political conflicts in which the bishops were engaged.[4] It may be said that the Gallicans were simply those Catholics, clerical and lay, who had, despite Roman disapproval, accepted the oath by which the Act of 1774 had enabled them to testify their loyalty and were now less than wholehearted in their opposition to a parliamentary assault on the regular clergy. Other issues would soon arise. Most notably, a proposal to limit or remove the rights of the Holy See in the nomination of Irish bishops would make its appearance among parliamentarians. In short, Gallicans were those prepared to make generous concessions to parliamentary opinion in order to ensure the passage of relief measures – perhaps because they were not altogether displeased at the prospect of the Holy See and the religious orders being discomfited.[5] However, to state a party's stance on particular issues in this way is not to explain, but only to suggest, what its beliefs were and why they were held. The impression is left that Gallicanism was little more than a tactic, developed in response to immediate political needs, clothed in language borrowed from the European mainland. It would certainly be foolish to suggest that Irish Gallicanism possessed either the social and political significance or the intellectual sophistication of related movements elsewhere – late Jansenism, Josephinism, Febronianism, the Catholic Enlightenment, etc. – which lent it credibility. However, it would also be wrong to perceive it as merely the insubstantial product of ephemeral political debate.

At first glance, it may appear somewhat odd that Gallicanism was spoken of at all in early- or mid-eighteenth-century Ireland. After all, the Hanoverian state generally directed no official attention – except a hostile one – towards the Catholic church in its territories: it was not therefore in competition with Rome for influence over it. Equally, there was little to encourage the development of episcopal Gallicanism or Richerism. The matter which was to provide occasion for the expression of these forms of Gallicanism in the early nineteenth century, the nomination of bishops, was uncontentious: James III made the nominations.

Yet Gallicanism was indeed discussed: for it was perceived, by Protestants, as dealing with matter which was central to the doctrinal conflict between Protestantism and Catholicism. The whole Protestant apologetical tradition, after all, derived from an assertion that all the distinctive features of Catholicism had sprung from the papal claim to a *potestas jurisdictionis* that rightly belonged to Christian princes.[6] Central to Anglican confessionalism was the doctrine of royal supremacy which countered this claim. Thus from a Protestant viewpoint, acceptance by the

Papists of a Gallican view – if it was pressed to its conclusion – would turn them, potentially, into Protestants. They would at least have destroyed the foundation on which their false beliefs were built and shown understanding of a characteristically Anglican position. It was their pattern of thought which had led the archbishop of Canterbury, William Wake, to respond enthusiastically to proposals made by some French ecclesiastics, overexcited by the conflicts which followed the issuing of the anti-Jansenist bull *Unigenitus*, for a union of the Gallican and Anglican churches. These discussions inevitably came to nothing. They were founded on mutual misunderstanding, the French churchmen believing that disputed high-church positions were those of the Church of England as a whole, Wake believing that a hostility to Rome involved an inclination to reject Tridentine Catholicism. In any case, neither Wake nor his Gallican correspondents really represented anyone.[7] However, an interest in Jansenist-inspired Gallicanism endured in England throughout the eighteenth century.[8]

The view which sustained Archbishop Wake's interpretation – or rather misinterpretation – of Gallicanism appeared frequently in Irish writings on the Catholics. It was succinctly stated by Stephen Radcliffe in his attack on whig notions about religious toleration.[9] In abjuring 'the Pope's Supremacy' the Catholics would be renouncing 'the Fundamental Principle of their Religion'. They would thereby 'cease to be Papists and... easily be brought to Uniformity'.[10] Radcliffe did not think this possible. His opponent, Edward Synge, was, in truth, probably of the same mind; but for the purpose of his reply asserted that, in some degree, it might be. In the degree that the Catholics did display their adherence to Gallican principles concessions to them could be considered.[11] For most Irish Protestants this remained the limit of the practical implications of Gallicanism throughout the eighteenth century. Gallicanism might allow concessions, in that its theologians opposed those doctrines which rendered Catholics a menace to a Protestant state; it did not augur reconciliation. On this basis, Protestants remained willing to respond to Gallicanism throughout the century. However, they also remained very doubtful about its widespread existence. It was perhaps right, Bishop Woodward observed in the 1780s, to distinguish 'between Papists and Roman Catholics of the Gallican Church ... But what proportion of Popish inhabitants of this Kingdom would know, what is meant by the *Gallican Church*?'[12]

For themselves, Catholics were inclined to look on questions about the relationship of the church to the secular order as of secondary importance. However, if the issues Gallicanism dealt with were so important to

Protestants, they did require attention. In the first place, to whatever extent Catholics sought reconciliation, or at least a *modus vivendi*, with the Protestant state in which they lived, they were and always had been obliged to adopt a stance which may be described as Gallican. The first important signs of Catholic desire for such reconciliation came from the Appellant party in the English archpriest controversy late in the reign of Queen Elizabeth. The Appellants perceived that in order to declare their loyalty, it was necessary for them to draw a clearer distinction between the spiritual and temporal spheres by a denial of papal rights – particularly the right to depose heretical princes – in the latter.[13] The tradition that stemmed from the Appellants was represented in Ireland notably by the supporters of the remonstrance advocated by the Franciscan priest, Peter Walsh, in the 1660s.[14] This was the Gallicanism espoused by O'Conor and Curry. Their position was stated without subtlety. They did little more than draw a coarse distinction between the spiritual and the temporal spheres and then proceed, in general terms, to exclude the pope from the latter.[15] In fact, it was not in dispute that the pope's proper sphere was the spiritual. What was disputed was the extent of the so-called indirect power which he might exercise in the temporal sphere.[16] But then, it was only political pamphlets, not works of theology, that O'Conor and Curry produced. True, those conclusions of the Gallican theologians about specific papal powers which worried Protestants were stated clearly enough.[17] But for all that this offended sections of clerical opinion, it can hardly be said to have been an extreme variety of Gallicanism that was being advanced. It pertained only to powers which the Holy See claimed, not which it actually exercised: the days of king-deposing popes were gone. When a right which Rome might have exercised and indeed came to exercise – that of nominating Irish bishops – was in question, O'Conor was willing to argue the Roman case.[18] This Gallicanism was not motivated by any antipathy to Rome founded on theological conviction of the sort that was present in Catholic states. The early agitators of the Catholic question, like the Appellants and Remonstrants before them.[19] adopted a Gallican stance chiefly because they sought greater toleration. Such a stance gratified Protestants and made them amenable to persuasion. More theoretically, Gallicanism had the appearance of being a parallel in Catholic thought to the Lockean separation of civil and ecclesiastical allegiance – the foundation of the pamphleteers' case. In other words, Gallicanism, at this point, had the character of a criticism of *ancient régime* confessionalism.

Irish Gallicanism – and for that matter the corresponding English phenomenon[20] – was chiefly, but not merely, a commendation of relief legislation. More generally, it sought to commend the Catholic community and the Catholic religion. It was essentially for this reason – rather than for the reasons that the same circumstance prevailed in Catholic Europe – that it was associated with reformist trends. For these trends too were at least thought to enhance the appearance of Catholicism in the eyes of enlightened Protestants. When an Irish Catholic pastor attempted to suppress manifestations of what he considered superstitious beliefs or prevent abuse of orthodox practices, it was always at least partly with a view to how Catholic religious behaviour might be construed by Protestants. As one bishop put it: their 'prejudices required that the doctrine of the Catholic Church ... should be put in the clearest light'[21] The adoption of reformist views, with Gallicanism at their centre, would perhaps soften Protestant hostility; and this might pave the way not merely for relief, but for conversion. O'Conor entertained a high opinion of the capacity of Gallicanism in particular to win Protestants over to the Catholic faith. If indeed the matter of papal power was so important to Protestants, might a more moderate assertion and a more restricted exercise of it not do much to dislodge them from their position?[22] This was by no means a singular view. It was one which constantly influenced Catholic apologists who dealt with British Protestantism.[23] Thus, to both Protestants and Catholics alike Gallicanism could have the appearance of a bridge which spanned the doctrinal division between them – a bridge over which the other side might well march to surrender. That such a prospect of an end to religious division existed in the minds of some should not be forgotten when the civil and ecclesiastical politics of the 1780s are considered.

In the 1780s Irish Catholics had some reason to think that the policy of seeking rapprochement with the Protestant society around them was highly successful. It seemed – though a *post hoc ergo propter hoc* fallacy was involved – that the declaration of loyalty they proffered in 1774 had brought almost instant and unexpectedly large gains. Certainly further relief measures could be expected; but there were hopes for more than that. In large measure these hopes derived from the change in the content of the Gallicanism which was so crucial to the policy of rapprochement. Gallicanism was no longer about rights that the Holy See claimed but did not expect to exercise. It was now about the acquisition of rights, which most certainly would be exercised, by the Irish authorities. The debates which took place at the time of the 1782 Relief Act in particular, and, to a certain extent, the Act itself had suggested the possibility of an Irish church under a control which would be very effective indeed. Government involvement in episcopal nominations would allow a very direct influence over that section of the clergy which looked for preferment. Others would at least be subject to an indirect influence, exercised through the newly reliable bishops. Clerical education might be closely supervised.[24] The number of regulars in the country might be reduced. Now a law to this effect would be enforceable, since the clergy were registered.[25] Extensive control of the church by the government had been proposed before, most notably by Viscount Limerick in the 1750s. In the 1780s, however, since they came with relief measures, such proposals did not have to be interpreted as threatening to Catholicism. Instead, they could be understood positively as promises of a grant of a subordinate establishment status for it and thus welcomed.

It is a noteworthy feature of the history of the European *anciens régimes* in the period before the revolutionary assault that those who felt most the effects of the exclusive character of the existing structures displayed little inclination to declare their hostility to them. They may have entertained notions that were in fact subversive of those structures. However, an elite cultural hegemony ensured that they continued to seek admission to them and not their destruction. If this was so with regard to the members of the French *bourgeoisie* and the second estate,[26] it was equally true with regard to Irish Catholics and the ecclesiastical establishment. Given the encouragement of proposals for close association between their church and the state – whatever the purposes of the framers of those proposals may have been – it was not long before some Catholics began to speak of themselves quite explicitly as part of an establishment. Thus perceiving themselves, they became the defenders of establishment in general. The Catholic case as it had been presented before the 1780s certainly had the appearance of offering no threat to the established order. However, this appearance was deceptive. Its arguments were selected only from those which commanded widespread approval, though, in truth, this was far from ensuring that views which might reasonably be called radical were avoided. The Catholics were loud, if generally unconvincing, in their protestations of loyalty; but they could speak this way only by adopting a Lockean – or Gallican – position which in fact undermined the confessionalist principles on which the state rested. Now, however, in the 1780s, a new Gallicanism offered the possibility that Catholics would be able to declare their loyalty not only to their country's civil, but also to its ecclesiastical constitution. A genuine Catholic conservatism became possible. It is true certainly that some Catholic argumentation in the 1780s constituted a very plain assault on the Irish *ancien régime*. At the same time, however, there was much that constituted a genuine defence of it.

The man whom Bishop Troy identified as the leader of the Irish Gallicans in the 1780s, Archbishop Butler, needed little encouragement to adopt conservative stances. He came from a very wealthy gentry family, which had provided the two previous archbishops of Cashel. In the 1770s he had assisted in organising against the Whiteboys, who, he believed, 'would fain bring down to their own level all superior ranks of people, would crush them if they could, and give the law to those whom the Almighty has thought proper to place above them'.[27] His activity had resulted in the so-called battle of Ballyragget, which was fought around the house of his brother and caused the deaths of some of the insurgents. It may be that in 1782 Butler had much to do with the emergence of the proposal to allow government involvement in the nomination of bishops.[28] However this may be, in the course of the 1780s he certainly displayed a strong inclination to be seen as a prelate of an established church. When Bishop Woodward raised the cry against the Popish conspiracy he believed the Rightboy disturbances revealed,[29] Butler produced a very conciliatory reply. He rallied to the support of the Established Church, attacking its critics among the Cork gentry – Woodward's political enemies – with the accusation that it was they who had fomented the disorder.[30] He went on to express his sympathy for 'the *persecuted* [Anglican] *clergy*' in their '*grievous situation*', as they struggled against this anti-tithe campaign. However, his own particular duty was to point out that Catholic clergy had suffered too. For the insurgents had attacked 'the ecclesiastics of both establishments'.[31]

That there were not a few Catholics who shared the archbishop's optimistic view of what extensive government control of their church might mean, need occasion little surprise. Confessionalist attitudes prevailed among Catholics and Protestants alike. Since religious dissent was at best an anomaly and recognition of it as a permanent phenomenon was given most unwillingly, a positive interpretation of the proposals for control sprang readily to mind. If Catholicism would not go away – and Catholics knew it would not – then it would have to be made part of the establishment. A predisposition to accept the new Gallicanism of the 1780s came also from specifically Catholic modes of thought. Irish Catholics never forgot that their religion had once been the established one[32] – a position it had come close to recovering in the days of King James. They were conscious too that it still fulfilled some of the functions of an establishment. Catholicism took its place in the combat with the 'religious Infidelity [which] is Gaining Grounds in these Islands, by hasty and large Strides'.[33] Again, it was the Catholic church which, of necessity, bore the burden of impressing on the people 'the Obedience they owed to the Government' and checking 'Tumults, Riots, or popular Intemperance'.[34] In the tasks it carried out it was already associated with the Church of Ireland. Why should this association not be recognised and developed by the law? There may indeed have been Catholics who looked further still. Even as they had engaged in polemic against it, Catholic controversial divines had always made clear that Anglicanism, in particular the variety of it espoused by old-fashioned high-churchmen, had doctrinal links with Catholicism which were not possessed by other sects.[35] Was there a limit to the extent to which these might be increased and strengthened in the climate created by Gallicanism?

As a party, the Irish Gallicans faced considerable difficulties in advancing their views. Those who were its leading members were not free to declare clearly their position on the matters which were of central concern to it. The activity and statements of bishops were under Roman observation. More important was the desire of all to preserve a united Catholic front. And if some Catholics welcomed the suggestion that the government might assume extensive powers over their ecclesiastical affairs, others were alarmed by it. For the government, in dealing with those affairs at a local level, would be likely to take advice from the Protestant notables of the district, who would thus obtain an influence in an area Catholics had been able to regard as exclusively their own.[36] Those who were thus alarmed found an able presenter of their case in Burke.[37] Later, however, in the 1790s, Burke wrote a good deal that was supportive of a Gallican position – though repeating his condemnation of the specific suggestion that the government might become involved in episcopal appointments. In his polemic against the Revolution he pointed out that the conflicts generated by the old supra-national ideologies, Catholicism and Protestantism, were 'now extinguished'. Loyalty ought now to return to its proper locus – patriotism.[38] If Burke did not draw the conclusion that a comprehensive national church was now possible and desirable, particularly in view of the existing threat to all forms of Christianity, others may have. Again, there was the *Letter to Sir Hercules Langrishe*. Though Burke certainly did not state that Catholicism ought to be established, he did make it clear that it could be.[39] A few years later he put the matter more clearly.

> Therefore my humble and decided opinion is, that all the three religions [Anglicanism, Presbyterianism and Catholicism], prevalent more or less in various parts of these islands, ought all, in subordination to the legal establishments, as they stand in the several countries, to be countenanced, protected, and cherished; and that in Ireland... the Roman Catholic religion should be upheld in high respect and veneration; and should be, in its place, provided with all the means of making it a blessing to the people who profess it; that it ought to be cherished as a good,... and not tolerated as an inevitable evil.[40]

If a summary of Burke's view on this topic is required, it is probably best to say that while, in principle, he would have welcomed a Catholic establishment in Ireland, he did not believe that, in practice, it would be advantageous to Catholicism. Establishment would make it vulnerable to manifestations of Protestant zealotry in high places.[41]

Those Catholics who were sympathetic to the legislative proposals that were being made in the 1780s had difficulty in arguing for them. Burke was hostile to them, but nevertheless gave support to views that can easily be construed as Gallican. Such circumstances serve as a warning against focusing too narrowly on those proposals in considering the nature of Irish Gallicanism in this period. If one wishes to understand the phenomenon, the literature of the Catholic question in general should be looked at.

Particularly revealing is the work of Arthur O'Leary, the Cork friar who, by the 1780s, had become the approved pamphleteer of the Catholic Committee.[42] His various tracts reveal very clearly indeed the Catholic urge, which underlay Gallican opinion, to be accommodated within the framework of *ancien régime* confessionalism. O'Leary may be regarded as the successor of O'Conor and Curry – the chief Catholic advocate. However, his writings were quite different from theirs in form. He rarely – and never at length – simply stated a case for relief. Instead, he wrote pieces of religious controversy and commentary on such current affairs as touched on the condition of Irish Catholics. But though their subject-matter is diverse, from these writings a coherent and consistent approach to the question of the place of Catholics and, more especially, Catholicism in Irish society is readily discernible.

There is a good deal in O'Leary's work, as it related to matters strictly religious, which might be put down simply to an Enlightenment-inspired eirenicism. He argued that what should mostly be heard from Catholic and Anglican pulpits were the tenets of a universally accepted natural religion.[43] As to controverted points of revealed religion, of which indeed he was a zealous defender,[44] he urged, by example, a moderate and conciliatory mode of presentation.[45] Yet, in truth, this was more than mere eirenicism, intended to induce a more favourable treatment of Catholics. O'Leary was less interested in commending Catholics as reliable fellow-subjects, than in commending Catholicism as a suitable partner for Anglicanism. Catholicism was no mere dissenting sect, like those on which he poured scorn.[46] It was, he pointed out, endowed with almost all of the characteristics proper to an establishment. Catholicism was 'the religion of the greatest monarchs, and the creed of flourishing universities'. In Ireland it had votaries who had every claim to be considered gentlemen, by virtue of their blood and military valour[47] – men who were showing themselves most zealous in assisting their clergy to preserve the social fabric threatened by plebeian disorder.[48] In view of circumstances such as these, it was objectionable that Catholicism was not already, in everyday practice, treated as the equal of Anglicanism – for example, in the laws relating to marriage.[49]

However, O'Leary sought to display more than the mere respectability of Catholicism. What really commended Catholicism to Anglicans as a partner in establishment, O'Leary cleary believed, was its character as an orthodox Trinitarian form of Christianity. Possessing this character, it would take its place in the combat against those religionists who, by rejecting the fundamental beliefs held by Catholics and Protestants alike, would have undermined the existing social and political order. O'Leary's first pamphlet and its history are indicative of the chief tendency of his entire pamphleteering career.[50] This first effort was a reply to a tract by a Cork physician named Blair, who though using 'Michael Servetus' as a pen-name, went considerably beyond the unfortunate Spaniard in his opinions. O'Leary was not content with the thought of the approval which his defence of the divinity of Christ and the immortality of the soul would earn from orthodox Anglicans. He wanted the approval registered. Thus, before undertaking his work he sought the blessing of Isaac Mann, the Protestant bishop of Cork – a cleric certainly not known for his pro-Catholic sympathies.[51] Mann readily gave it, observing that Blair's work was not part of 'a doctrinal controversy between religious churches, but an attempt to subvert the great and important truths, in which the advocates of every church were agreed'.[52]

Competent enough as his reply to Blair was, O'Leary's forte was not the learned defence of fundamental Christian doctrines. He continued his writing career with works which dealt with less profound matters. Nevertheless, he did not cease to demonstrate his goodwill towards orthodox Anglicans[53] or his own zeal and that of his church in opposing the common enemy. Such zeal was equally in evidence whether it was the religious substructure or the political superstructure of the state that was under assault. At times, it may well have seemed excessive or even alarming to more timid spirits. There was, for example, his suggestion that adherence to certain heresies might be dealt with by means of capital punishment.[54] Such remarks were perhaps less than prudent for a Catholic priest. His opinions about monarchical government were equally strong. His enthusiastic assertion of divine right on Catholic principles and fervent condemnation of any belief in a right of resistance,[55] showed O'Leary wholly in sympathy with that revival of monarchist thought which was characteristic of the period.[56]

The French Revolution gave the Hanoverian Empire and Catholicism a common enemy and both the British government and the Holy See became concerned about the cultivation of a closer relationship – a circumstance which was bound to have consequences in Ireland. Rome, for its part, urged the Irish church to act zealously in defence of the established order; or, in other words, to assume more clearly the role of an establishment. That such a development was not unwelcome to those in authority, was signalled by the state's endowment of the new Catholic seminary at Maynooth.[57] It is true that the party within the Catholic body which was well-disposed to such trends fared badly in the earlier years of the 1790s. It now faced, at times, defeat and, always, stronger opposition and the need to compromise. But the degree of adversity it suffered should not be exaggerated. If indeed – and the assertion is very doubtful – the Kenmare schism marked 'the emergence of the catholic middle classes... as an unmistakable and potent force in Irish public life',[58] its consequence was certainly not the immediate eclipse of aristocratic and gentry leadership. The United Irishmen still found it very necessary in the following years to engage in polemic against the Catholic 'leaders, who were men of the first lordly and landed interest in Ireland, and who shamelessly and meanly deserted the people'.[59] As it happened, the decade ended with apparent triumph for these leaders. After 1798 the politics of their opponents was in eclipse. They stood on the side of the victors in the dispute over the Union and expected to reap the rewards. In this position, their bishops stood with them. With the promise of relief measures as part of a new unionist order, the prelates at last agreed to both a government veto on episcopal appointments and payment of the clergy.

It may well be true that the hopes that were entertained by late-eighteenth-century Catholics for the integration of their church into the confessionalist structures of the Irish *ancien régime* were, in a considerable measure, the product of a wilful misunderstanding. If Protestants sought government control of the Catholic church, it was chiefly because they feared it and not because they desired to favour it. Such control would at least give a sense of security and at most increase the hope that Protestantism would, as Grattan bluntly put it, 'become the religion of the Catholics'.[60] Yet, for all that, the position taken by the Gallicans cannot be said to have been a foolish one. A campaign for the modification of confessionalist structures was far more credible politically than a struggle against them. And what matter if the Protestants acted from the wrong motives? By granting an establishment status to Catholicism, they would still be acting wisely.

Efforts to obtain establishment status for the Catholic church in Ireland came to an end only in 1869, when Gladstone, under the influence of English dissenters more anxious to attack Anglicanism than ensure a religious settlement for Ireland, rebuffed them.[61] Until then, the possibility of a plural establishment remained, though both any British government and any Irish episcopal bench would have had to contend with much deep-seated prejudice, not least among their own members, to turn possibility into reality. However, only in the 1780s and in the years immediately after 1798 could the acceptance of such an arrangement have profoundly altered the course of Irish history. In the 1780s the Irish Catholics stood between Jacobitism and Jacobinism. In the years after 1798 the Irish form of the latter had been substantially eradicated. In these periods the British monarchy lacked any real rival as a focus of loyalty. Had the order which existed under it been adapted to allow a place for Catholics and their church, no such rival need have appeared. Irish nationality would, no doubt, have offered itself in this role. But in the development of the sense of nationality which the nineteenth century actually saw, sectarian conflict played certainly a large, even, it may be argued, the most important part. Had the state in that era undertaken the support of both Protestantism and Catholicism, this conflict might have been much reduced. At least, the policy actually followed, of undermining the Anglican establishment while showing no particular favour to Catholicism, appears to have done much to stimulate the fear which made conflict unavoidable.

Conclusion

It has not been the purpose of this study to offer criticism of any existing general understandings of modern Irish history. If nationalist historiography is little more than a tradition to be reacted against by present-day historical scholarship, this is regrettable. For it will report well on the past, at least to the extent to which Irishmen have indeed been motivated by nationalist beliefs and, more generally, a sense of national identity. If any general view of the Irish past has replaced that once provided by nationalist historiography (though the two may not be readily distinguishable in the popular mind), it is that offered by those who have spoken of Ireland's colonial experience. This too, corresponding with a consciousness which indeed existed, should not be slighted. Many who settled in Ireland in the sixteenth and seventeenth centuries were self-consciously colonists. In the eighteenth century and indeed beyond many spoke of England as the mother country and Ireland as a colony, though rather more used images which indicated equality between the two kingdoms.

When those concerned to speak of Ireland as a nation or of Ireland as a colony go beyond the self-consciousness of the past, they are drawing analogies, at least implicitly, with other countries – and *omnis analogia claudicat*. They should thus be supplemented with further analogies, in the hope that more of the Irish phenomena can be comprehended. Such analogies should be sought primarily in Europe, rather than elsewhere – as is suggested by referring to Ireland as a colony. For, certainly after the fall of the Gaelic order, there were few aspects of Irish life which displayed very marked deviation from contemporary European norms. It is this which has suggested the appropriateness of the consistent application of the idea of *ancien régime* to the study of eighteenth-century Ireland. The suggestion has been elaborated in the early part of this study.

A particularly strong argument in favour of reading the history of eighteenth-century Ireland as that of an *ancien régime* lies in the importance in that history of one of the chief marks of an *ancien régime*, namely confessionalism. The central chapters of this study have offered an explanation of the importance of this Protestant – as opposed to specifically Anglican – confessionalism in itself. But they have also illustrated how it supported and was supported by characteristically *ancien régime* modes of thought and characteristically *ancien régime* social and political structures.

At first it would seem easy to explain the relationship of the case for the Catholics of Ireland that began to be put forward in the middle of the eighteenth century to the country's *ancien régime*: inevitably the former constituted a critique of the latter. This statement of the relationship should not be contradicted. However, as the chapters of the final part of the study have shown, there is a good deal more to be said. In the first place, the new Catholic argumentation was more effective and radical in its critique of the *ancien régime* as Catholics would have wished it to be than in its critique of the *ancien régime* as it actually was. This argumentation's primary challenge was to the dynasticism, confessionalism and estimation of the importance of landed property entertained among Catholics as the basis of their political hopes. As to the *ancien régime* as it existed, the challenge offered was, ostensibly, a very moderate one, reflecting the weakened political condition of the Catholic community. However, if the pro-Catholic writers generally confined themselves to arguments already commonly received among Protestants and therefore scarcely alarming, this did not mean that their views were harmless. It was characteristic of *ancien régime* elites to sire and nurture notions that in fact undermined their own position. Such notions could come from nowhere else.

The political developments of the late 1770s and early 1780s produced two divergent trends in pro-Catholic argumentation. Some Catholic argumentation became a defence as well as a critique of the Irish *ancien régime*. There was now the prospect of integration within the existing order for Catholics and, it was hoped, integration within its confessionalist structures for their church. Some were quick to respond with a display of conservatism which was in many ways natural to them as Catholics. Other Catholics preferred to identify with those who were radically critical of the established order and this trend too was reflected in the literature. However, even those Catholics who were most decidedly inclined towards a conservative position could not simply accept the Irish *ancien régime* as it was. Catholics could accept and in some cases zealously defend many of the principles which governed the existing distribution of privilege. They could accept that if these prevailed, Ireland would remain a Protestant nation. What they could not accept was the inclination of the Irish *ancien régime* to distribute privilege on the grounds of the mere profession of Protestantism without reference to other factors. And indulgence of this inclination was becoming more marked as the defenders of Protestant ascendancy sought allies among those of their co-religionists who had previously been regarded as little qualified for extensive privilege. Thus, all Catholic argumentation, whatever shade of opinion within the Catholic body it represented, reflected at least some degree of hostility to the *ancien régime*.

The Irish *ancien régime* is worthy of more exploration than this study, concerned only with its confessionalist aspect, has allowed. This is true, it may be finally pointed out, not only for the student of the eighteenth century. After all, late-eighteenth-century Ireland, unlike much of Europe, experienced no even temporarily successful attack on the established order. Its *ancien régime* survived. However, even had it not done so, reflection on its nature would still be of importance to those concerned to understand nineteenth-century Ireland.

Everywhere in Europe, nineteenth-century political conflict was fundamentally determined by variant views of the continent's *anciens régimes* and the assaults that had, since 1789, been made on them. To the degree they endured, the conflict was the more bitter. To understand this together with what has been pointed to in this study – the importance of the confessionalism of the *ancien régime* which existed in Ireland – is to understand the fundamental structure of the country's nineteenth-century politics. To observers from the European mainland this was very strange indeed.[1] It was not merely that Irish politics were sectarian. All Europeans were familiar with the power which religion – or irreligion – exercised in the formation of political loyalties. What was striking about Ireland was the nature of the loyalty religion encouraged. In Ireland Catholicism had entered into an alliance with liberalism. Indeed the word 'alliance', suggesting an arrangement such as that made in Belgium in the 1820s,[2] seems inappropriate. Catholicism and liberalism had become, politically, one force. There was no need, however, for astonishment on the part of foreign observers. What response to Ireland's Protestant *ancien régime* could have been more natural?

In other words, the political spectrum of nineteenth-century Ireland was, like the political spectrum of eighteenth-century Ireland, recognisably that of contemporary Europe: it was created by positive and negative responses to the *ancien régime* and the forces which had attacked or were attacking it. The deviation of politics in Ireland from European norms was the consequence of the peculiar nature of the *ancien régime* which had existed and in a degree continued to exist there. It was this which ensured that Catholicism as well as liberalism was its enemy. Irish conservatism was thus checked: it could never flourish while Catholicism was obliged to be its enemy. The Gallicans of the late eighteenth century had proposed a more hopeful strategy for conservatism, involving the comprehension of Catholicism. But this was doomed to come at length to nothing – the victim of Protestant intransigence and the rise of a far more assertive Catholicism backed by a developing Ultramontanist ideology.[3]

However, if the development of Irish conservatism was checked by the confessionalist emphasis of the country's *ancien régime*, Irish liberalism was no less checked. True, it was checked also by its association with nationalism. This it had in common with other European liberalisms, which, unable to divest themselves of their early nineteenth-century association with nationalism, were compromised and debilitated when the authentic voices of nationalism were those of Bismark and Napoleon III. In Ireland, however, nationalism – Irish and British – took second place to or served as vehicle for the expression of a politics founded on religious identification. For at least half of the nineteenth century, for the first three decades of the century and again in the decades after the death of O'Connell, the dominant questions in Irish politics related to the relationship of Catholics *qua* Catholics to the British state. And it takes little ingenuity to see the O'Connellite politics of Repeal and whig alliance as variations on the same theme. Reduced to jostling with nationalism for the status of an ideological adjunct of an increasingly powerful Catholicism – thereby ultimately alienating potential Protestant support – Irish liberalism could never have been anything other than a stunted growth.

Notes

1 Unimportance and Importance

1. McDowell, *Irish Public Opinion 1750–1800*, p. 10.
2. Reynolds, *Catholic Emancipation Crisis*. See especially Chapter 5. A similar view is taken in a more recent work. Its author refers to the 'change in the content of "Emancipation" ... wrought by O'Connell in Ireland – from an upper-class quest for equal access to privilege to one for the liberation of the Irish people from their manifold grievances'. See O'Ferrall, *Catholic Emancipation*, p. 40.
3. See, for example, *Queries Humbly Proposed to the Consideration of the Public*, pp. 3–4.
4. This, of course, did not prevent many members of the Catholic lower orders seeing the Pretender and his sometime allies, the French, in a messianic light. The view found frequent expression in Gaelic poetry. It remained common until the end of the century and, losing what was specifically Jacobite in it, beyond. See, for example, O'Leary, *Essays on the Kingdom of Ireland*, pp. 1–15.
5. See, for example, [O'Conor], *Protestant Interest*, pp. i–v.
6. See below, p. 117.
7. [Brooke], *Essay on the State of Ireland*, p. 58. The conventional attribution of this work has been challenged only by C. C. and R. E. Ward in their edition of the *Letters of Charles O'Conor*, I, p. 300. Their attribution to O'Conor is inexplicable.
8. At least one line of anti-relief argumentation made this point explicit in debate. It was argued that the Catholic peasantry required protection from their avaricious co-religionists, who were, in the event of relief, likely to become their landlords. See, for example, *Dublin Evening Post*, 13 August 1778 (Brady [ed.], *Catholics and Catholicism*, p. 191).
9. Cullen, *Emergence of Modern Ireland*, p. 99. David Dickson, in his *New Foundations*, p. 99, speaks of the middlemen 'enjoying genteel status as *tiarnaí beaga* [little lords]'. See also below, p. 9.
10. Quoted by Coombes in *John O'Brien*, p. 16.
11. Wall, *Catholic Ireland*, pp. 78–82. See also Corish, *Irish Catholic Experience*, p. 152.
12. For a discussion of the quarterage dispute, see below, Chapter 4. While the quarterage dispute was, obviously, a part of the Catholic question, it was not, strictly speaking, a matter of Catholics seeking relief from the legislature. The law was already on the side of the Catholics: the point was ascertained in the courts. It was the Protestant guildsmen who sought a change in the law. See Wall, *Catholic Ireland*, pp. 66–71.
13. See, for example, Kevin Whelan's observations on the lists of those who took the oaths of allegiance in Co. Tipperary in 1775 and 1793 in his 'Catholic Church in County Tipperary', pp. 219, 221, 223 and 225.

14.   Connolly, 'Religion and history'.
15.   Wall, *Catholic Ireland*, pp. 9–18.
16.   Brady and Corish, *Church under the Penal Code*. For the references to religious, see pp. 12–14, 35–7.
17.   Fenning, *Undoing of the Friars*.
18.   Descriptions of urban Catholic life can be found, for example, in Burke, 'A hidden church?' and in Corish, 'Diocese of Ferns', pp. 10–11. This might be compared with what is to learned about Catholic life at mid-century in north-east Munster, an area in which generally the Catholics encountered no more hostility than did their co-religionists in the towns, from O'Dwyer, (ed.), 'Archbishop Butler's visitation book'. This source is used by Whelan in his 'Catholic Church in County Tipperary'. See especially pp. 225–7.
19.   McCracken, 'Ecclesiastical structure', pp. 87–8.
20.   Wall, *Catholic Ireland*, pp. 20–25.
21.   Bartlett, *Fall and Rise*, p. 46.
22.   Cullen, 'Catholics under the penal laws', p. 29.
23.   The case for placing a convert interest on the Catholic side of Ireland's religious divide is stated by Power in 'Converts'. The suggestion has merit, in view of previous contrary assumptions. Some converts undoubtedly did retain a sympathetic attitude towards Catholics and Catholicism. This did not go unnoticed by their new co-religionists. However, it is unsafe to generalise about a diverse group of individuals, with diverse attitudes to religion, politics, kin and friends.
24.   Cullen, 'Catholics under the penal laws', p. 24.
25.   The point made here would presumably be accepted by Professor Cullen. See his 'Catholic social classes', p. 57.
26.   An illustrative account of gentry survival is given in Harvey, 'Family experience'.
27.   O'Neill, 'Discoverers and discoveries'.
28.   Dickson, 'Middlemen', pp. 171–3.
29.   Whelan, 'Regional impact', pp. 257–8. More detail and background is offered in Cullen, 'Catholic social classes'. For local exemplification see Whelan, 'Catholic Church in County Tipperary', pp. 215–17 and 'Catholic community in County Wexford', pp. 131–48.
30.   Dickson, 'Catholics and trade'. Louis Cullen offers a study of a city in which the Catholic interest was dominant in his 'Galway merchants'.
31.   Wyse, *Historical Sketch of the Catholic Association*, I, Chapter 2.
32.   Burke's incomplete *Tract on the Popery Laws* was probably written in the latter part of 1761, but not published until after his death. See Mahony, *Edmund Burke and Ireland*, p. 15.
33.   Bartlett, *Fall and Rise*, pp. 60–5.
34.   See, for example, O'Conor to Curry, 4 January, 23 June 1758, Ward (eds), *Letters of Charles O'Conor*, I, pp. 53–4 and 57–8 and Curry to O'Conor, [March 1760], Dublin, Royal Irish Academy, O'Conor Correspondence, BI1.
35.   Curry to O'Conor, 19 November 1771, Dublin, Royal Irish Academy, O'Conor Correspondence, BI2.
36.   Wyse, *Historical Sketch of the Catholic Association*, I, pp. 31–2.
37.   Whelan, 'Catholic Church in County Tipperary', p. 216, 'Regional impact', pp. 257–8 and Cullen, 'Catholics under the penal laws', pp. 26–7.
38.   Ward, 'Catholic pamphlets of Charles O'Conor', pp. 259–60. The blunt

assertion here that O'Conor ran a great risk by publishing on the Catholic question cannot be sustained. It is true that a few of the pamphlets of both O'Conor and Curry produced in the 1750s and 1760s do not bear a publisher's name. However, in each case the fact that the pamphlet either was, or might have been taken to be, concerned with more than the Catholic question accounts for the caution. See, for example, the remarks on O'Conor's *Counter-appeal to the People of Ireland* in O'Conor, 'Early life of Charles O'Conor', Dublin, National Library of Ireland, IR 92 o162, pp. 35–41.

39. See below, p. 91.
40. See below, pp. 113–14.
41. See, for example, Harris, *Fiction Unmasked* pp. 10–11.
42. [O'Conor], *Danger of Popery*, p. 23.
43. [McKenna], *Interesting Periods of Irish History*, p. 7.
44. Brady, 'Proposals to register Irish priests'.
45. See, for example, Archbishop John Carpenter to Propaganda, 20 May 1772 and 4 April 1774, Dublin Diocesan Archive, Clonliffe College, Linegar, Lincoln, Fitzsimon and Carpenter Papers, 116/2/85 and 116/2/125.
46. See, for example, Harris, *Fiction Unmasked*, p. 18.
47. Loftis, *Politics of Drama*, pp. 145–51. See also Greene, *Politics of Samuel Johnson*, pp. 99–105. Greene's observations on the political tendency of the play are very misleading. The text supports the view of Jonathan Clark that the play's politics are those of the opposition that looked to Leicester House. See Clark, *English Society*, pp. 179–80. As Clark indicates, this would not exclude the possibility of expressions of Jacobite sympathies, which do indeed seem to be present. See, for example, the fairly obvious reference to Scottish support for the Jacobite cause in the prologue. Brooke, *Gustavus Vasa*, p. ix.
48. O'Conor, 'Early life of Charles O'Conor', Dublin, National Library of Ireland, IR 92 o162, p 23.
49. See below, pp. 101 and 102.
50. [Brooke], *Farmer's Case of the Roman Catholics*, II, pp. 12–22.
51. Brooke, *Trial of the Cause of the Roman Catholics*, pp. 219–21.
52. [Brooke], *Case of the Roman Catholics*, pp. 6 and 8–14 and [Brooke], *Farmer's Case of the Roman Catholics*, III, 16–22 and IV, passim.
53. [Brooke], *Essay on the State of Ireland*, pp. 6–27. This section shows heavy dependence on O'Conor's *Dissertations on the Ancient History of Ireland*.
54. [Brooke], *Essay on the State of Ireland*, pp. 5–6.
55. Ibid., p. 58.
56. Ibid., pp. 53–6 and 61–2.
57. Ibid., pp. 49–50 and 62–6.
58. Howard, *Laws Against the Further Growth of Popery*, p. vi.
59. *Some Observations and Queries on the Present Laws relative to Papists*, p. 3.
60. See, for example, Jephson, *Speech Delivered on 11 February 1774*, pp. 13–16.
61. The connection is emphasised by Bartlett in his *Fall and Rise*, Chapters 3 and 4.
62. Cullen, 'Catholics under the penal laws', pp. 24 and 25. Cf. Harvey, 'Family experience', p. 171.

63. See below, pp. 91–3.
64. See below, pp. 65 and 134–5.
65. Rogers, *Irish Volunteers and Catholic Emancipation*, p. xi.
66. Connolly, 'Religion and history', p. 79.
67. Cullen, 'Catholics under the penal laws', p. 25. See also Power, 'Converts', pp. 119–20.
68. Clark, *English Society*. See especially Chapter 6.
69. Ibid., pp. 353 and 358.
70. Some remarks on the question of nationalist sentiment and the writings of Charles O'Conor are made below. See pp. 119 and 121–2.
71. For critical reviews of Clark's positions see, for example, Innes, 'Jonathan Clark, social history and England's "ancien regime"' and J. G. A. Pocock, '1660 and all that'. For a reply by Clark to the former see his 'On hitting the buffers'.
72. Ibid., pp. 199 and 200.
73. R. Mousnier, *Institutions of France*, I, Chapter 1. Clark does, of course, offer evidence to show there was substantial correspondence between the ideology of which he speaks and the society it observed. On how successful he has been in this matter, or in justifying his ascription of hegemony to that ideology, it would be foolish for a non-English historian to give a judgement.

2   The Irish *Ancien Régime*

1. Doyle, *Ancien Régime*, Chapter 2, gives a conveniently brief survey of these varying emphases.
2. Cf. Cullen, 'Economic development 1750–1800', pp. 159–95 and Goubert, *Ancien Régime*, Chapters 2, 3 and 5.
3. P. Anderson, *Lineages of the Absolutist State*, Chapter 1.
4. M. MacCurtain, 'Rural society in post-Cromwellian Ireland', p. 135.
5. Lee, *Modernisation of Irish Society*, unpaginated preface.
6. Goubert, *Ancien Régime*, p. 51.
7. Connell, 'Land legislation', p. 1.
8. MacCurtain, 'Rural society in post-Cromwellian Ireland', p. 118.
9. See below, p. 40.
10. Clark, *English Society*. See especially Chapter 3 and pp. 201–16. The theme treated here is also treated, on the larger canvas of the seventeenth and eighteenth centuries but in less detail, in Clark's *Revolution and Rebellion*. See especially Chapter 5.
11. This continuance can be seen, for example, in the political thought of the most important of the philosophes. See Cranston, *Philosophers and Pamphleteers*, p. 2.
12. For the term 'corporative–representative' see Gagliardo, *From Pariah to Patriot*, p. 61. The term is not satisfactory, but is the most self-explanatory and least circumlocutionary that has been found.
13. For an extended discussion of this topic, see Kliger, *Goths in England*.
14. [Brooke], *Farmer's Letter[s] to the Protestants*, VI, p. 5.
15. See, for example, [Molesworth], *Account of Denmark*, [pp. 8–9 and 34–6 of] the preface.

16. Robbins, *Eighteenth-century Commonwealthman,* pp. 98–109.
17. For the historical circumstances Molesworth's work deals with and some comment on British attitudes to them, see Ekman, 'Danish royal law of 1665'.
18. Browning, *Court Whigs*, Chapter 5.
19. Clark, *Revolution and Rebellion*, pp. 88–91.
20. An investigation of what lies behind the statements made here should begin with the last part of Pocock's *Machiavellian Moment*, pp. 331–552. The limits of the truth of the statement, in other words the extent to which whigs and tories maintained their ideological integrity, can be judged by referring to (for the whigs) Robbins, *Eighteenth-century Commonwealthman* and (for the tories) Colley, *In Defiance of Oligarchy*, Chapter 4.
21. This point might be elaborated in different ways. See, for example, Monod's references to extreme manifestations of this phenomenon in his *Jacobitism and the English People*, pp. 15–44. Again, one might advert to the practical cooperation which corresponded to the ideological coalescence. For an example of this at a local level see N. Rogers, 'Aristocratic clientage'.
22. Browning, *Court Whigs*, pp. 21–2.
23. A brief survey of recent writing on this topic can be found in Thomas, 'Party politics in eighteenth-century Britain'.
24. Robbins, *Eighteenth-century Commonwealthman*, p. 5. Robbins' teleological view of the early eighteenth-century Commonwealthman is modified a little later in her work when she refuses them the title of 'radicals', pointing out that their mind was closer to that of the seventeenth century than to that of the nineteenth. Ibid., p. 7.
25. [Molesworth], *Account of Denmark*, Chapters 7, 8 and 9.
26. Ibid., pp. 73–4, 79.
27. Browning, *Court Whigs*, p. 25.
28. See, for example, the views of Fénelon quoted by Chaussinand-Nogaret in *French Nobility*, p. 16.
29. McCartney, *Democracy and its Nineteenth-Century Irish Critics,* pp. 9–12 and 15–23.
30. Ives, *Enlightenment and National Revival*, p. 58. Section 5 of this work illustrates what is spoken of in this paragraph from Hungarian history. For a further example from the European mainland, see Kossmann's discussion of the Dutch Patriot party in his *Low Countries*, pp. 39–47.
31. Robbins, *Eighteenth-century Commonwealthman*, pp. 9–10 and Browning, *Court Whigs*, pp. 169–73.
32. Robbins, *Eighteenth-century Commonwealthman*, pp. 137–43. For a longer treatment of Molyneux see Simms, *William Molyneux*. See especially Chapters 7 and 8.
33. Robbins, *Eighteenth-century Commonwealthman*, pp. 153–5. For a longer treatment of Lucas, see Murphy, 'Lucas affair'. See also below, Chapter 4.
34. Robbins, *Eighteenth-century Commonwealthman*, pp. 147–52 and 157–8. Simms, 'Establishment of Protestant ascendancy', p. 7.
35. O'Malley, 'Patrick Darcy'.
36. See, for example, Declan O'Donovan's study of 'The Money Bill dispute of 1753'. O'Donovan's study depicts the conflict as one between Dublin Castle, as the instrument of the king and his ministers, and their opponents in the

Irish parliament. This contrasts with the older view of J. L. McCracken, who regarded the dispute as an internal Irish one. See McCracken, 'Conflict between the Irish administration and parliament'.

37.   For this latter see Király, *Hungary in the Late Eighteenth Century*. See especially pp. 170–87.

38.   See below, pp. 55–8 and 104–5.

39.   [Michael Reilly] to Charles O'Conor, 3 October 1755, Dublin, Royal Irish Academy, O'Conor Correspondence, BI1. The printed passage referred to in this letter is in O'Conor's *Vindication of 'The Case of the Roman Catholics'*, pp. 32–4.

40.   See, for example, *London Evening Post*, XIV (27–30 August 1763), p. 203. This piece has been ascribed to Charles O'Conor. See Ward (eds), *Letters of Charles O'Conor*, I, p. 301. However, the intemperate language used is quite uncharacteristic of O'Conor when speaking on this topic. It may well be the work of his brother, Daniel, who had some literary pretensions and was in London about the time the piece was published. See the copy of the text filed in Dublin, Royal Irish Academy, O'Conor Correspondence, BI1. See also Daniel O'Conor to Charles O'Conor, 7 April 1763, in the same file.

41.   See below, pp. 134–5.

42.   O'Conor to Charles Ryan, [late 1777], Ward (eds), *Letters of Charles O'Conor*, II, pp. 109–10. In view of the anti-Americanism expressed by O'Conor here and elsewhere, the attribution to him by Catherine and Robert Ward of a pro-American pamphlet, *Reflections on Our Present Critical Situation*, is inexplicable. For the attitude of other prominent Catholics see Bartlett, *Fall and Rise*, pp. 85 and 98.

43.   It seems that O'Conor too joined in the rejoicing. 'To the lords and gentlemen of the Volunteer associations of Ireland', the dedication of Thomas Sheridan's *Dictionary*, has been ascribed to him. See Ward (eds), *Letters of Charles O'Conor*, I, p. 300.

44.   See below, pp. 140–1.

45.   In this notion of elite hegemony, especially elite cultural hegemony, lies the explanation of the description of *ancien régime* society as a society with only one class. See Laslett, *World We Have Lost*, Chapter 2. Laslett's concern is with Tudor and Stuart England. However, what is said provides a substantially reliable guide to the social structure of Hanoverian England. Laslett himself suggests that the beginnings of the demise of the single-class society he speaks of are to be observed in the 1760s. If nothing else could be objected, such dating is certainly too precise.

46.   Chaussinand-Nogaret, *French Nobility*, Chapter 2.

47.   Mousnier, *Institutions of France*, I, Chapter 1. See p. 6 for his definition of the *société d'ordres*. See also Behrens, *Society, Government and the Enlightenment*, pp. 7–23.

48.   Richet, 'Origines idéologiques', p. 23.

49.   For a description of the character of the English elite, see Clark, *English Society*, pp. 93–118. For the most part, this description is applicable in speaking of contemporary Ireland.

50.   Sutherland, *France 1789–1815*, p. 14.

51.   Mackrell, *Attack on 'Feudalism'*, pp. 85–100.

52.   Davies, 'Military traditions of the Polish *szlachta*' and Kramár, 'Military

ethos of the Hungarian nobility'. For the *pospolite ruszenie*, see also
Fedorowicz *et al.* (eds), *A Republic of Nobles*, p. xv.

53.   As Reed Browning has concisely remarked: 'The pulpit was as important as
      the bookstall in the political wars of the eighteenth century.' See his *Court
      Whigs*, p. 90.

54.   Charles O'Conor, when called upon to give advice on the writing of a
      history of Kerry, indicated that he required little more of such a history than
      'an interesting account of the great and good family of the O'Sullivans
      More, and Bear, O'Donaghoes, O'Mahonys, Fitzgeralds of Desmond, and
      the knights of the Glin, etc.' He did, however, caution against overloading
      the work with genealogies and advocated selectivity in the presentation of
      'heroes'. See Charles O'Conor to Bryan O'Conor [c. 1754], Ward (eds),
      Letters of Charles O'Conor, I, pp. 8–9.

55.   The term 'myth' seems appropriate here. What is referred to is a narrative of
      'events alleged to have taken place long ago', which is used to regulate
      behaviour, especially social behaviour. It is possible so to use it by virtue of
      the fact that it is in fact timeless: it explains the present and the future as
      much as the past. See Lévi-Strauss, *Structural Anthropology*, p. 209.

56.   Greengrass, 'Conquest and coalescence', pp. 7–10.

57.   Chaussinand-Nogaret, *French Nobility*, p. 17.

58.   Macartney, 'Hungary'.

59.   Bilmanis, *Latvia*, pp. 214–17.

60.   See, for example, Chaussinand-Nogaret, *French Nobility*, pp. 1–2.

61.   Gasiorowski, 'The "conquest" theory'.

62.   See, for example, Woodward, *Present State of the Church of Ireland*, pp.
      32–4.

63.   Leighton, 'Theobald McKenna', pp. 224–31. See also Leighton, *Irish
      Manufacture Movement*, pp. 21 and 31–2.

64.   McCormack, *Ascendancy and Tradition*, pp. 61–96. McCormack's error in
      asserting that the phrase does not appear before the early 1790s was
      corrected in his 'Study of Irish parliamentary rhetoric'. See especially p. 17.
      James Kelly, in 'The genesis of "Protestant ascendancy"' and in 'Eighteenth-
      century ascendancy', has argued for its importance in the 1780s in devel-
      oping a resurgent conservative ideology. Jacqueline Hill, in 'The meaning of
      "Protestant ascendancy"', also holds its use in the 1780s to be significant, but
      as a manifestation of a confessionalist consensus, accepted by Protestant dis-
      senters and Catholics.

65.   Burke, *Works*, III, pp. 303–5.

66.   Bush, *Noble Privilege*, pp. 206–7.

67.   Though it substantially confines its attention to Scotland, John Robertson's
      Scottish Enlightenment and the Militia Issue conveys the importance of this
      tradition in eighteenth-century British politics. The origins of the tradition
      are traced at length in Pocock's *Machiavellian Moment*, passim.

68.   Campaigns of opposition to army augmentation, the most notable of which
      was at the beginning of the Townshend viceroyalty, in 1767, were, of
      course, in part motivated simply by hostility to increased taxation. It ought
      to be emphasised though, as Townshend himself made clear, that hostility to
      a peacetime standing army and enthusiasm for a militia force were equally
      important in fomenting opposition. See McDowell, 'Colonial nationalism',

pp. 205–6. These motives were certainly emphasised in such guides to public opinion as the newspapers and the resolutions of the Dublin guilds. For the former see, for example, the views of the *Freeman's Journal*, reported by McDowell in his *Ireland in the Age of Imperialism and Revolution*, p. 222. For the latter see, for example, Transactions of the Guild of Cutlers, etc., Dublin, National Library of Ireland, MS 12125, p. 32; or, Records of the Guild of Merchants, etc., London, British Library, Egerton MS 1765, fols 71b, 72b and 75a.

69.   Brooke's Farmer's *Letter[s] to the Protestants*, written during the Jacobite rising of 1745, offers an excellent example of the union of pro-militia and anti-Catholic rhetoric.

70.   During the Seven Years War, for example, the viceroy, the duke of Bedford, decided that it was necessary to leave the garrisons that would have borne the brunt of a French attack undermanned, in order to guard against a Catholic uprising. See Bedford to [George Stone], archbishop of Armagh, 22 May 1759, *Correspondence of [the] Duke of Bedford*, II, pp. 373–7.

71.   See below, p. 79.

72.   [Henry], *Appeal to the People of Ireland*, p. 9. This pamphlet has been attributed to Sir Richard Cox. See O'Conor, 'Early Life of Charles O'Conor', Dublin, National Library of Ireland, IR 92 o162, pp. 35–47. While the work is obviously on Cox's side in his conflict with Charles Lucas, internal evidence supports the attribution to Dr William Henry.

73.   [Henry], *Appeal to the People of Ireland*, pp. 11–12.

74.   The notion that the Protestant conquerors of Ireland were aided by divine providence was emphasised in a number of ways. For example, accounts of the 1641 rebellion frequently included a number of supernatural events, which testified to the righteousness of the slaughtered Protestants and thus, of course, the justice of the cause of the Cromwellians who avenged them. See, for example, [Curry], *Brief Account of the Irish Rebellion*, pp. 59–62.

75.   Arthur Young adverts to a practice among late eighteenth-century Catholics of passing on to their heirs the title to land which had been confiscated from their ancestors. See Young, *Tour in Ireland*, II, pp. 59–60. This remark should not be dismissed as testimony merely to Protestant anxiety. Catholics may well have cherished land claims, albeit that they existed chiefly in the genealogical and narrative forms that had been adequate under the Gaelic order. See Cunningham and Gillespie, 'The purposes of patronage'.

76.   Burke, *Works*, III, p. 308.

77.   Leighton, 'Theobald McKenna', pp. 189–203.

78.   See, for example, Duigenan, *Fair Representation of the State of Ireland*, pp. 48–50.

79.   See below, pp. 49–51.

80.   The definition as well as dating of the term 'Protestant ascendancy' is extensively discussed in the book and articles cited in note 64 above.

81.   The most important of these latter commemorations were in early July, the commemorations of the battle of the Boyne and of the battle of Aughrim, and in early November, the commemoration of King William's birthday and the discovery of the gunpowder plot. These celebrations were exceedingly popular and tended to last for days on end. See, for example, *Public Journal*, 1–3, 8–10, 13–15 July 1772. Also important was the annual commemoration, on

23 October, of the outbreak of the rebellion of 1641. This too had a popular character. See O'Conor to Curry, 23 October 1758, Ward (eds), *Letters of Charles O'Conor*, I, pp. 66–7. Apart from these great feasts, there were numerous lesser ones. Dublin was, for example, still annually celebrating the battle of Culloden in the 1770s. See *Public Journal*, 17–20 April 1772.

82. Swift, *History of the Dublin Bakers*, p. 134. In the following pages Swift gives an interesting account of this splendid annual event which, the Dublin press boasted, surpassed London's Lord Mayor's Show, Paris's Corpus Christi procession and Venice's Wedding of the Sea. Providing an appropriate bezel for this attraction were the festivities organised by individual guilds.

83. A starting-point for such an examination has been offered by the study of the closely-related calendar of early modern England by David Cressy. See his *Bonfires and Bells*.

84. The qualification made here is made necessary by the inclination of some historians of early nineteenth-century France to stress the continuities between the pre-revolutionary period and their own. See, for example, Ellis, 'Rhine and Loire'. Apart from this moderate revisionism, there exists a much more sweeping claim, which may be adverted to here, that the term *ancien régime* may be as well applied in discussing the nineteenth century as in discussing the eighteenth. See Mayer, *Persistence of the Old Regime*. In brief, one cannot speak of a consensus of opinion about when the *ancien régime* came to an end, even if it is only France that is under discussion. Of course, this matter was always problematic when the historian's scope extended to Europe as a whole.

85. Goubert, for example, adopts this as an initial approach to the question of definition. See his *Ancien Régime*, pp. 1–15.

86. The history of this representation of society is discussed by Georges Duby in his *Three Orders*. The early pages of the work refer to the persistence of the concept in the early modern period and beyond.

87. For an example of an explicit defence of the three orders in the literature dealt with here, see O'Conor, *Dissertations* (1766 edn), p. 56, where it is argued that 'the Expedient of three Orders of Government' was a well-nigh universal response to the 'Experience of the Ways of Mankind'.

88. The inclusion of a fourth order, the sovereign, among the estates is justified at least by the English whig tradition. See Dunn, *Beyond Liberty and Property*, Chapter 4.

89. It is primarily to Clark's *English Society* that reference is being made. It should be noted that Clark himself explicitly eschews extensive discussion of definition of the *ancien régime*. See his 'On hitting the buffers', pp. 198–9.

90. It is not, however, suggested that all of the Catholic literature can be considered unequivocally hostile to the country's *ancien régime*. This qualification is elaborated particularly in the final chapter of the study.

3   The Catholic Question and the Irish Confessional State

1. See above, p. 21.
2. For some brief indication of the extent of the social and economic changes

associated with the political upheavals of this period, studied in this case from a local perspective, see Gillespie, 'Lords and commons'.

3. For such an approach see, for example, Gerhard, *Old Europe*. Whether or not continuity is regarded as an essential element in definition, the notion is frequently integrated into discussions of the character of the *ancien régime*. See, for example, Goubert, *Ancien Régime*, p. 17.

4. Even when they were dealing with strictly domestic matters, Irish pamphleteers frequently preferred to have their writings published in London. However, this was only partly because they hoped to influence English political opinion; a work which had managed to obtain a London imprint, it was thought, was more likely to get a favourable reception when it was eventually published in Ireland. See O'Conor to Curry, 17 September 1759, 31 October and 7 November 1766, Ward (eds), *Letters of Charles O'Conor*, I, pp. 76 and 206–9.

5. [O'Conor], *Seasonable Thoughts* (1753 edn), p. 25.

6. See, for example, Philemon, *Letter to Dr. James Butler*, p. 5.

7. A plain and brief statement of this frequently argued case can be seen in *Question Fairly Stated.*

8. Clark, *English Society*, pp. 137–41. The posthumous reputation of Hoadly is instructive. By the latter part of the century, it could be assumed that Anglicans as a whole were likely to lump him 'and his abettors' together with such notorious heretics as John Jones, Samuel Clarke and Robert Clayton. See Campbell, *Principles and Character of the Presbyterians*, p. 32. It seems that, in the end, the charge of heresy made by Hoadly's Nonjuring opponent William Law won the day in the court of public opinion. See Chapter 5, note 59.

9. The legal positions of English and Irish Protestant dissenters were very similar. In 1719 an Irish toleration act, substantially the same as the English one, came into existence. The sacramental test, which had been imposed in 1704, remained as a grievance. The campaign for its removal in the early 1730s triggered similar, and similarly unsuccessful, action in England. Thereafter there was a long cessation of agitation in both countries. Beckett's remark that this came about chiefly because the dissenters 'had little to complain of', though made in reference to Ireland, is applicable in speaking of England also. See Beckett, *Protestant Dissent*. See especially Chapter 9. See also Barlow, *Citizenship and Conscience*, Chapter 2 and 3.

10. Clark, 'On hitting the buffers', pp. 199–200.

11. It seems not unreasonable to ascribe Lockean origins to common eighteenth-century maxims justifying a tolerant treatment of dissenters. Recent re-evaluations of the eighteenth-century reception of Locke concede his importance in influencing thought on this matter. However, eighteenth-century writers themselves frequently preferred to cite less contentious authorities. See, for example, *Discourse Concerning the Laws Ecclesiastical and Civil*, pp. vi–vii, where the origins of eighteenth-century practice are traced to the political thought of the Restoration period.

12. 'When I mention religion, I mean the Christian religion; and not only the Christian religion, but the Protestant religion; and not only the Protestant religion, but the Church of England.' – *The History of Tom Jones*.

13. The point was made by the histories of some parts of the empire at a much

earlier date. For example, the Ministry Act of 1693 had given New York a Protestant establishment in which the Anglican church had no advantage over others. See Butler, *Awash in a Sea of Faith*, pp. 102–3. Again, there was the willingness, despite some misgivings, to accept a civil, without an ecclesiastical union with Scotland in 1707.

14.   This theme is a very common one in the writings of O'Conor. See, for example, his *Danger of Popery*, pp. 8–11 or his *Case of the Roman Catholics*, pp. 77–9.

15.   [Clayton], *A Few Plain Matters of Fact*, p. 23.

16.   The political character of the opposition to the Catholic claims, in this case in the early nineteenth century, is pointed out by G. F. A. Best, when he observes that the 'constitutional theory [of opponents of emancipation] was in practice supported by, although it was not dependent on, that hearty "No Popery" sentiment which seems to be a fundamental characteristic of the British Protestant'. See his 'Protestant constitution and its supporters', p. 109.

17.   The ways in which contemporary thought could be accommodated by eighteenth-century churchmen are discussed by Viner in *Role of Providence*. See especially pp. 8–17.

18.   See, for example, the account of the views of the mid-eighteenth-century archbishop of Canterbury, Thomas Herring, on Protestant dissent in Browning, *Court Whigs*, pp. 90–2. The view that the practice of toleration constituted a necessary mark of the true church is expounded, for example, by Thomas McDonnell in *The Spirit of Christianity and the Spirit of Popery Compared.*

19.   At least in Ireland, even the high church tradition could provide some support for the adoption of stances close to comprehensionism. See Bolton, *Caroline Tradition in the Church of Ireland*, pp. 72–8.

20.   Stromberg, *Religious Liberalism in Eighteenth-century England*, p. 5.

21.   Quoted in Kenyon, *Popish Plot*, p. 1.

22.   Skinner, *Foundations of Modern Political Thought*, II, pp. 10–15.

23.   By the late seventeenth century such argumentation had received unwelcome reinforcement from the extension of its use to assail all religion. See Popkin, 'Crisis of polytheism', pp. 9, 15 and 16–18.

24.   This and further quotations are from Hutchinson's *Sermon*, pp. 8–21.

25.   [Hutchinson], *Defence of the Ancient Historians*, pp. 122–49.

26.   For Luther's views on these topics see Tuveson, *Millennium and Utopia*, pp. 17 and 24–30. For Foxe's views see Olsen, *John Foxe and the Elizabethan Church*, Chapter 1. See especially p. 96. See also Haller, *Foxe's Book of Martyrs*, p. 141.

27.   Hutchinson, *Sermon*, pp. 25–6. In his reductionist representation of the apocalyptic tradition, Hutchinson should not be regarded as quite typical of his own period. Millenarian expectation remained widespread in the Anglican church during the intellectualy formative period of his life. It might be recalled that he was a student of Catherine Hall, Cambridge at precisely the time that Henry More, at Christ's, and Isaac Newton, at Trinity, were devoting so much of their time to the study of biblical prophecy. See Popkin, 'Spiritualistic cosmologies', pp. 106 and 108–112.

28.   See, for example, Brett, *Friendly Call*, pp. 1–2.

29.   These two themes were conveniently brought together in the popular accounts of Catholic practice in the matter of confession – a frequent topic in the popular anti-Catholicism of all periods. See, for example, ibid., pp. 12–16.

30.   The coalescence of Enlightenment and anti-Catholic thought in eighteenth-century Ireland is pointed out by Liechty in 'Testing the depth of Catholic/Protestant conflict', p. 23. See also Bartlett, *Fall and Rise*, pp. 68–9.

31.   *Protestant's Address*, p. 13. See also Curry to O'Conor, 24 October 1777, Dublin, Royal Irish Academy, O'Conor Correspondence, BI2.

32.   *Impartial Examiner*, pp. 33–8.

33.   See above, p. 17.

34.   See below, pp. 65 and 134–5.

35.   *Parliamentary Register*, VIII, pp. 216. However, Grattan drew a distinction between Popery and Catholicism and accepted the legitimacy of the latter as a religion. See, for example, ibid., VII, pp. 182–3.

36.   Jephson, *Speech Delivered on 11 February 1774*, pp. 21–4. For a further example, see *Some Observations and Queries on the Present Laws Relative to Papists*, pp. 8–11.

37.   See, for example, [O'Conor], *Danger of Popery*, pp. 23–4.

38.   ... to O'Conor, 2 November 1756, Dublin, Royal Irish Academy, O'Conor Correspondence, BII.

39.   Power, 'Converts', p. 105. See also McCracken, 'Social structure and social life', p. 38.

40.   Haller, Foxe's *Book of Martyrs*. See especially Chapter 7.

41.   Lamont, *Godly Rule*.

42.   Wiener, 'Beleaguered isle'.

43.   Lamont, *Godly Rule*, pp. 19–20.

44.   Maturin, *Sermon*, p. 13

45.   Wiener, 'Beleaguered isle', pp. 30–40 and 56. For the latter part of this period, see Clifton, 'Popular fear of Catholics', passim.

46.   *Admonition Critical and Friendly*. See especially pp. 3, 11 and 18.

47.   Black, *Eighteenth-century Europe*, p. 276.

48.   Sagarra, 'Frederick II in eighteenth-century Dublin'.

49.   O'Conor to Curry, 27 January and 17 February 1759, Ward (eds), *Letters of Charles O'Conor*, I, pp. 67–70.

50.   For Hume, see Hill, 'Popery and Protestantism, civil and religious liberty', p. 111. For Leland, see Liechty, 'Testing the depth of Catholic/Protestant conflict'.

51.   There is a case for accepting this perception as well-founded, at least at an intellectual level. It is put most profoundly, it has been argued, in the writings of John Henry Newman, where concern with Arianism and its consequences constitutes a central and even perhaps the dominant theme. See Pattison, *The Great Dissent*, passim, but see especially Chapter 3.

52.   See above, p. 33–9.

53.   See below, Chapter 4.

54.   See, for example, Wall, *Catholic Ireland*, p. 108. Discussion of the motivations for the enactment of the code have also failed to direct attention to the topic of Protestant anxiety about the insecurity of the state. See Connolly, 'Religion and history', which reviews such discussion.

55. Black, *Eighteenth-century Europe*, p. 180.
56. McCracken, 'Protestant ascendancy and the rise of colonial nationalism', p. 109.
57. See, for example, Corish, *Irish Catholic Experience*, p. 137. This conventional view receives some support from what is almost the only published study dealing with Ireland and Jacobitism in its later phase, McLynn's '"Good behaviour"'. However, this piece, which attempts to explain why 'not a flicker of support for the House of Stuart was discernible in Ireland during the rising', is necessarily, in view of 'the almost total lack of evidence on Catholics in Ireland at this time', a highly speculative one.
58. Ó Tuama (ed.), *An Duanaire*, pp. xxii–xxiii and xxvi–xxix. For examples of the poetry referred to, see pp. 152–67.
59. See, for example, de Rís (ed.), Peadar Ó Doirnín, pp. xxxii–xxxiii.
60. McLynn, '"Good behaviour"', p. 56.
61. Clark, *Revolution and Rebellion*, p. 125. There is, however, no consensus among English historians on the matter. See ibid., appendix B, pp. 174–7, for a bibliographical guide to this debate.
62. Monod, *Jacobitism and the English People*, passim.
63. Cf. ibid., pp. 1–12.
64. See, for example, [Clayton], *A Few Plain Matters of Fact*, pp. 79–93 or *Axe Laid to the Root*.
65. Giblin, 'Stuart nomination of Irish bishops'.
66. See, for example, the Franciscan provincial's intimation that pro-Hanoverian views were uncommon among the clergy (in an expression of regret at their existence), referred to by McLynn in '"Good behaviour"', p. 58.
67. A concise account of such attempts is given in Wall, *Catholic Ireland*, pp. 107–14.
68. [O'Conor], *Principles of the Roman Catholics*, pp. 88–94.
69. O'Conor to Curry, 20 August 1756, Ward (eds), *Letters of Charles O'Conor*, I, pp. 20–2.
70. The Roman objection to the oath lay in the declaration made in it that the doctrine 'that princes excommunicated by pope may be deposed or murdered by their subjects' was detestable, 'pernicious and abominable'. This doctrine had been taught by the Holy See and it showed scant respect to denounce it in these terms. Thomas Burke, the bishop of Ossory, a man of strong Jacobite sympathies, had taken care to ensure that this Roman view was widely advertised in Ireland. See E. O'Flaherty, 'Ecclesiastical politics', pp. 35–6. See also McLynn, '"Good behaviour"', p. 58.
71. Furlong, 'Nicholas Sweetman', p. 16. See also Corish, 'Diocese of Ferns', p. 10.
72. O'Leary, *Miscellaneous Tracts*, pp. 63–76. This is a reprint of a collection of pieces made in 1781. The pamphlet dealing with the 1774 oath was originally published in 1777.
73. The celebrated divine, Archdeacon Paley, for example, expressed the view in 1785 that the legislation against Catholics remained justified on account of the Jacobitism which some of them professed. See Paley, *Works*, pp. 146–7.
74. See, for example, Butler, *Tenets of the Roman Catholic Religion*, p. 34.
75. Brady (ed.), *Catholics and Catholicism*, pp. 45–7.

76. See, for example, [Gorges Edmond] Howard, *Laws Relative to Papists*, pp. 6–9.
77. McLynn, "'Good behaviour'", pp. 50–1.
78. See below, pp. 100–2.
79. Ward, 'Ordeal', p. 11.
80. [Curry], *Brief Account of the Irish Rebellion*. See especially pp. 57–9. For the date of composition see p. 1.
81. Ibid. See especially pp. 64–8 and the fifth appendix, pp. 121–62. This appendix contains the Jacobite tract, *Galienus redivivus* – an account of the massacre of the Episcopalians of Glencoe and an attack on William III and 'the bigot *Presbyterian party* in Scotland' – by the distinguished Nonjuring divine, Charles Leslie.
82. See [Curry], *Essay Towards a New History of the Gun-powder Treason* and [Curry], *Candid Enquiry into the Late Riots*. See especially pp. 15–17. See also [Curry], *Second Appeal to the L[or]d P[rimat]e*, as cited below, p. 103. Reference here to the first and third pamphlets in this series is also relevant in this context.
83. The point is illustrated below. The proposals put forward by Viscount Limerick for the registration of the clergy might also be mentioned by way of example. These were inspired by the conviction 'That the Papists in Ireland are zealously attached to the Pretender... and that this zeal is fed and cherished by their priests'. Limerick believed that if some priests were indulged, their loyalty to the government might be secured. At the same time, those who refused to accept this indulgence by refusing an oath of allegiance would be isolated. See Clanbrassil to Bedford, 17 July 1757, *Bedford Correspondence*, II, pp. 263–5. That the proposals were not translated into statute was due, not to a failure of the parliament to share Limerick's objective, but to political chance and an unwillingness to grant any indulgence to Popery. See Brady, 'Proposals to register Irish priests', pp. 221–2.
84. [Duigenan], *Address to the Nobility and Gentry*, p. 31. This conventional theme of the anti-Catholic tradition not only found very frequent explicit statement in the writings of eighteenth-century Protestants, but also underlay almost all argumentation relating to Catholics.
85. Woodward, *Present State of the Church of Ireland*, pp. 7–21.
86. Two Arian Presbyterians, William Campbell, a minister in Armagh, and Samuel Barber, the minister in Rathfryland, were foremost in attacking Woodward's theoretical assertions. See Campbell's *Principles and Character of the Presbyterians*, his *Examination of the Bishop of Cloyne's Defence*, Barber's *Remarks on a Pamphlet* and his *Reply to the Reverend Mr Burrowes*'. A more moderate criticism of this part of Woodward's work is to be found in Thomas, *Observations on the Pamphlets*.
87. [Duigenan], *Address to the Nobility and Gentry*, p. 101. See also Woodward, *Present State of the Church of Ireland*, p. 81.
88. Kelly, 'Eighteenth-century ascendancy', p. 182.
89. Anglicans who entered the fray were, for example, Robert Burrowes, the author of *A Letter to the Rev. Samuel Barber*, and Edward Ryan, the author of *Remarks on the Pamphlet of Mr Barber*. The Catholics were represented by the archbishop of Cashel, James Butler, with his *Tenets of the Roman Catholic Religion* and *Letter to Viscount Kenmare*, and Arthur O'Leary, who produced a piece entitled *Mr O'Leary's Defence*. This piece contains

the assertion that Woodward's effort had been read even by the king. See p. 53. Presbyterian authors who replied to Woodward are mentioned in note 86 above.

90. The use of the name 'Rightboy' here follows modern convention. Woodward himself and others at the time were apt to prefer 'Whiteboy', a name now used to refer to earlier agrarian disturbances.

91. Bric, 'Priests, parsons and politics', pp. 168–72. See also Donnelly, 'Rightboy movement'. See especially pp. 139–40.

92. [Duigenan], *Address to the Nobility and Gentry*, p. 2.

93. Woodward, *Present State of the Church of Ireland*, p. 22.

94. For earlier use of the term see Kelly, 'Genesis of "Protestant ascendancy"', pp. 102–3, 'Eighteenth-century ascendancy', pp. 180–3 and McCormack, 'Study of Irish parliamentary rhetoric', pp. 15–16 and 20–7.

95. Kelly, 'Eighteenth-century ascendancy', p. 181. Cf. Hill, 'Meaning of "Protestant ascendancy"', pp. 11–12.

96. Woodward, *Present State of the Church of Ireland*, pp. 17 and 21–5.

97. Ibid., pp. 89–92. The scenario envisaged by Duigenan was but slightly different. See [Duigenan], *Address to the Nobility and Gentry*, pp. 102–9. Cf. also William O'Driscol, *Letter of the Rev. Doctor O'Leary*, pp. 13–14.

98. Woodward, *Present State of the Church of Ireland*, pp. 75–6.

99. Ibid., pp. 52–7.

100. Campbell, *Examination of the Bishop of Cloyne's Defence*, pp. 40–1. See also his *Principles and Character of the Presbyterians*, pp. 31–41 and 54–69.

101. Barber, *Remarks on a Pamphlet*, pp. 37–42.

102. Corish, *Irish Catholic Experience*, pp. 139–42.

103. See, for example, [Duigenan], *Address to the Nobility and Gentry*, p. 2. Cf. Bric, 'Priests, parsons and politics', pp. 174–5 and Donnelly, 'Rightboy movement', passim, but especially pp. 126–7. See also the latter's 'Irish agrarian rebellion', p. 331.

104. The point was particularly strongly made by Trant in his *Considerations on the Present Disturbances*. As a consequence, Trant fought and killed one of those most under suspicion of aiding the Rightboys, Sir John Colthurst, in a duel.

105. Clark argues the case that there was, in reality, a substantial identity between heterodox dissent and the radical politics of the 1770s and 1780s. See Clark, *English Society*, pp. 277–348. Here and below (pp. 131–2) it is merely argued that such an identity was, with at least some justification, perceived to exist. See also note 51 above.

106. Mentor, *Alarm*, p. 3.

107. Woodward, *Present State of the Church of Ireland*, pp. 26–7.

108. Woodward to Charles Broderick, 16 February 1787, Dublin, National Library of Ireland, MS 8870, file 1.

109. Bric, 'Priests, parsons and politics', pp. 187–8.

110. As one writer, Hardinge Giffard, began his account of Irish politics, written for the benefit of the new lord lieutenant, Fitzwilliam: 'The most obvious and the most unfortunate distinction of the people of Ireland is found in the diversity of religious opinions.' See his *Short Reply to Doctor Drennan's Letter*, pp. 13–20.

111. See, for example, Russell, *Letter to the People of Ireland*.

112. See, for example, [Tone], *Argument*.
113. The priority which Tone accorded to the Catholic question is emphasised, if in rather misleading terms derived from United Irishman propaganda, by Marianne Elliott in *Wolfe Tone*, p. 111.
114. Quoted by Madden in *United Irishmen*, II, pp. 568.
115. Clark, *English Society*, pp. 327–9.
116. The New Light movement arose from the first non-subscription controversy in the 1720s. This attempt to free the Presbyterian clergy from adherence to the Westminster Confession was an Irish manifestation of the assault on the use of credal statements as qualifications, i.e. on confessionalism, which the heterodox – Deist, Arian and Socinian – mounted in early Hanoverian Britain. Adherence to New Light principles did not necessarily mean adherence to Arianism, but it certainly strongly suggested it. See Ibid., pp. 300–7 and Reid, *Presbyterian Church*, III, Chapter 25.
117. Ibid., III, pp. 391, 392 and 397.
118. This was the view put forward by Samuel Barber, for example. See Stephen and Lee (eds), *Dictionary of National Biography*, I, p. 1070.
119. Miller, 'Presbyterianism and "modernization"', pp. 77–80. Miller's attempt to use this fact to demonstrate a lack of connection between the New Light movement and the United Irishmen is hardly acceptable. Ideological influence is not disproved by the unwillingness of some contemporaries to recognise it or to allow it to determine their political conduct.
120. Barkley, 'Arian Schism'.
121. Quoted from a statement of a Defender leader in County Meath by Marianne Elliott in *Partners in Revolution*, p. 43. See also pp. 42 and 45.
122. Cf. the remarks made below, pp. 94–5, about the development of a secular political discourse among Catholics.
123. Elliott, *Partners in Revolution*, Chapter 2.
124. Cf. Drennan, *Letter to Earl Fitzwilliam*, pp. 23–6 and [Giffard], *Short Reply to Doctor Drennan's Letter*, p. 8.
125. See, for example, Burke to Thomas Hussey, 4 February 1795, Copeland et al. (eds), *Correspondence of Edmund Burke*, VIII, pp. 136–46.
126. Musgrave, *Rebellions*, p. 153.
127. Ibid., p. 67.
128. Musgrave's desire to implicate the Catholic clergy in the rebellion is made plain more concisely than in his *Rebellions* in an earlier, much briefer work, his *Concise Account*.
129. Dickson, *New Foundations*, p. 179.
130. Musgrave, *Rebellions,* pp. v–vi

4   The Meaning of the Quarterage Dispute

1. Gilbert and Mulholland (eds), *Calendar of Ancient Records of Dublin*, XIV, pp. 284–7.
2. See above pp. 32–9. See especially p. 34.
3. This explains the significance of the protracted disputes about the role of the Presbyterians in the Williamite War mentioned by Beckett in *Protestant Dissent*, p. 27.

4. For an account of this movement see Maguire, 'Lord Donegall and the Hearts of Steel'. Though dated, Bigger's *The Ulster Land* War continues to provide useful information.

5. *Hibernian Journal*, 5–7 August 1772.

6. Barber, *Remarks on a Pamphlet*, p. 36.

7. Fagan, *Second City*, pp. 109–10.

8. See above, p. 26.

9. The presence of the third element mentioned here is not remarkable. Clark remarks in speaking of 'Wilkism': 'The urban disorder which Wilkes both exploited and fostered scarcely went beyond a popular cry for the restoration of traditional "rights" which people were brought to believe themselves robbed of: Wilkesite rioters were not proto-democrats.' Clark, *English Society*, p. 311. Similarly, at the heart of van der Capellen's campaigns was the desire to defend the old local rights, lost in consequence of the ascendancy of the stadhouder and his noble allies. See te Brake, *Regents and Rebels*, pp. 43–50.

10. The Committee's concerns are apparent from its earliest surviving minute book. Regrettably this does not cover the first decade of the Committee's existence. However, it seems most improbable that the Committee was any less preoccupied with quarterage in the 1760s, when the dispute over this matter was at its height, than it was in the 1770s. See Edwards (ed.), 'Minute book', pp. 3–45.

11. The history of the parliamentary careers of the quarterage bills is found in Day, 'Catholic question', pp. 43 and 55–105, passim.

12. In theory, the Committee consisted 'of every Roman catholic nobleman and gentleman of landed property' and representatives of the Dublin parishes and 'the several towns in this kingdom'. See Edwards (ed.), 'Minute book', pp. 50 and 88. In practice, it was always difficult to secure the involvement of members of the former group.

13. Wall, *Catholic Ireland*, pp. 61–5. Wall indicated, some years later, that she had altered her opinion, but did not elaborate on the matter. See ibid., p. 88. Day, writing later again, adopted the traditional view, stating that the Catholics believed that quarterage 'was levied only to penalize' them. See Day, 'Catholic question', pp. 55–6.

14. Wall was at first of the opinion that, since it was the guilds themselves which determined the amount each should pay in quarterage, the sums involved constantly rose, but, again, later altered her view. See Wall, *Catholic Ireland*, pp. 63–4 and 88. In view of the destruction of so many guild records, it is difficult to make an authoritative statement on this matter. However, there do not seem to be any grounds for believing that quarterage payments ever reached a level that could be objectively regarded as burdensome. The Guild of St Luke the Evangelist was probably not untypical. Its members were practitioners of very respectable trades, cutlers, painter-stainers and stationers. On the eve of the dispute, of the guild's 95 quarter brethren, only 22 paid more than 10/- p.a. The highest payment, £1.10s. p.a., was made by only three men. See Transactions of the Guild of Cutlers, etc., Dublin, National Library of Ireland, MS 12124, pp. 327–29.

15. For the most part, quarter brethren were integrated into the guild system only to the extent that was necessary for the effective control of trade. They

were fully subject to guild discipline. See, for example, Bye-laws of the Corporation of Sadlers, etc., Dublin, National Library of Ireland, MS 80, bye-laws 48 and 50 or Minute book of the Guild of Barbers, etc., Dublin, Trinity College MS 1447/8/2, fol. 25a. They were, however, debarred from office and most of the perquisites enjoyed by free brethren.

16. Webb must, for the most part, be followed in his confining of attention to Dublin. It appears that only one eighteenth-century manuscript of guild records from a town other than Dublin has survived.

17. Webb, *Guilds of Dublin*, Chapter 7. For a recent statement of this view see Murphy, 'Lucas affair', pp. 34–5.

18. See, for example, the study of the decline of the guild system in London by Kellett, 'Breakdown of gild and corporation control'.

19. Information about the survival and destruction of Dublin's guild records can be found in a collection of typescripts and off-prints of articles written or collected by H. S. Guinness, Dublin, National Library of Ireland, MS 680, passim. Lists of surviving records are to be found in Hayes (comp.), *Manuscript Sources*, V, pp. 428–9 and National Library of Ireland (comp.), *Manuscript Sources: First Supplement 1965–75*, II, pp. 148–9.

20. Minute book of the Guild of Masons, etc., Limerick, City Library, unnumbered MS, 16 June 1747.

21. Ibid., 16 July 1752.

22. Ibid., 11 May, 16 June 1747, 20 February and 6 June 1750.

23. See, for example, ibid., 7 February 1749 or 21 February 1750.

24. This was the case at least in the Guild of Cutlers. In 1765 attempts were made to change the mode of election of guild officers and increase the number of persons eligible for election. These attempts failed. However, when in 1767 the bye-laws were revised, the reforms proposed two years earlier were enshrined in them. See Transactions of the Guild of Cutlers, etc., Dublin, National Library of Ireland, MS 12124, pp. 405–9 and MS 12125, p. 11.

25. Ibid., pp. 6–8 and 10–13.

26. Transcripts from the transactions of the Corporation of Smiths, etc., Dublin, Public Record Office (Ireland), M 2925, 8 October 1768.

27. Bye-laws of the Corporation of Sadlers, etc., Dublin, National Library of Ireland, MS 80.

28. George, *London Life*, pp. 166–7 and 362.

29. Minute book of the Guild of Barbers, etc., Dublin, Trinity College, MS 1447/8/2, fols 25a–26a, 30b, 32b–33a and 34a. Cf. the remarks made by Kellett about the peruke-maker's trade in London in his 'Breakdown of gild and corporation control', p. 388.

30. Webb, *Guilds of Dublin*, p. 251.

31. See below, p. 76. For details of the Dublin guilds' constitutional role, see Murphy, 'Lucas affair', pp. 29–48.

32. See, for example, Records of the Guild of Merchants, etc., London, British Library, Egerton MS 1765, fol. 68b.

33. Minute book of the Guild of Barbers, etc., Dublin, Trinity College, MS 1447/8/2, fol. 79a.

34. Transactions of the Guild of Cutlers, etc., Dublin, National Library of Ireland, MS 12124, pp. 129–244.

35. Thus, for example, the Guild of Cutlers declared its support for the Patriots in the Money Bill dispute. However, it waited until 1755, by which time the government was making peace with its opponents, before doing so. See ibid., pp. 306 and 308.

36. Records of the Guild of Merchants, etc., London, British Library, Egerton MS 1765, fols 81b–83b.

37. For an account of the effects of this campaign in parliament see Day, 'Catholic question', pp. 77–9.

38. It may be, but probably is not significant that the petitions of some towns, including that of Dublin, followed a second pattern text, were much shorter and did not contain such claims. *Journals of the House of Commons*, VIII, pt 1, p. 81.

39. Ibid., VIII, pt. 1, p. 75.

40. Ibid., VIII, pt. 1, p.103.

41. Ibid., VIII, pt 1, p. 82.

42. A popular critique of the guild system can be found, for example, in the *Public Journal*, 13–16 March 1772.

43. See above, p. 69.

44. Transcript of a letter of Charles Lucas to the Guild of Merchants, 10 March 1768, London, British Library, Egerton MS 1765, fol. 75a. See also, for example, the freemen's petitions on quarterage, submitted in 1774, in *Journals of the House of Commons*, IX, pt 1, pp. 82 and 92.

45. This is the view taken, for example, in the article in the *Public Journal* cited above. See note 42. See also Howard, *Miscellaneous Works*, III, p. 231. The pamphlet cited here was originally published in 1774. See ibid., p. 225.

46. O'Halloran to O'Conor, 11 February 1766, Dublin, Royal Irish Academy, O'Conor Correspondence, BII.

47. *Journals of the House of Commons*, VIII, pt 1, p. 82.

48. Wall, *Catholic Ireland*, pp. 87–8.

49. See, for example, ibid., p. 86.

50. Such a gesture of good-will was made, for example, by the Dublin Guild of Feltmakers in 1764. See Transcripts of entries in the record book of the Guild of Feltmakers, Dublin, Public Record Office (Ireland), M 6118b, 1 August 1764.

51. Minute book of the Guild of Barbers, etc., Dublin, Trinity College, MS 1447/8/2, fol. 85a.

52. Lucas, *Liberties of Dublin*, p. 41 [recte p. 42].

53. '...freedom conceived of as a complex of freedoms, the meaning of which could be expressed in a number of rules, each valid within a restricted domain – rules which stated: "I am permitted to do what you are not permitted to do."' Quoted by J. J. Woltjer in 'Dutch privileges', p. 21.

54. This is the presupposition of almost all political thought throughout the century. Consequently, such statements of the view as are found were made only incidentally. See, for example, the remarks made by Molyneux about the origins of the 'people of Ireland', quoted by Simms in *William Molyneux*, p. 105, or, moving forward by a century, Duigenan, *State of Ireland*, p. 71.

55. Murphy, 'Lucas affair', p. 212. See also pp. viii and 153.

56. Lecky, *Ireland in the Eighteenth Century*, I, p. 461.

57. Murphy, 'Lucas affair', p. 212.
58. Ibid., pp. 138 and 165.
59. See above, pp. 23–4.
60. See above, p. 22.
61. See above, p. 27.
62. Dickson, *New Foundations*, p. 88.
63. See above, pp. 36–7.
64. For a full account of these disturbances, see Sheldon, *Thomas Sheridan of Smock-Alley,* Chapter 4.
65. These pamphlets are too numerous to list here. They are readily recognisable by title or date in the bibliography.
66. [Lucas], *Letter to the Free Citizens of Dublin*, p. 1.
67. Ibid., p. 5.
68. [Lucas], *Second Letter to the Free Citizens of Dublin*, p. 10.
69. [Lucas], *Third Letter to the Free Citizens of Dublin*, p. 15.
70. [Lucas] *Letter to the Free Citizens of Dublin*, pp. 1–2.
71. Murphy, 'Lucas affair', pp. 134, 150–1, 155 and 165–7.
72. Simms, *William Molyneux*, p. 105.
73. [Lucas], *Third Letter to the Free Citizens of Dublin*, p. 16.
74. See above, p. 31.
75. Murphy, 'Lucas affair', pp. 155 and 193.
76. See, for example, the dispute between Edward Synge and Stephen Radcliffe, discussed below, pp. 98–100.
77. Murphy, 'Lucas affair', p. 165.
78. See above, pp. 46–7.
79. Murphy, 'Lucas affair', p. 166.
80. See above, pp. 45–6.
81. McDowell, *Irish Public Opinion 1750–1800*, p. 11.
82. The major issues in the popular politics of the period are outlined in Cummins, 'Extra-parliamentary activity'.
83. It should be recalled that the Octennial Act of 1768 was commonly regarded as being, in part, an anti-Catholic measure. By virtue of the inability of constituents to exercise control over their representatives when it existed, 'a Standing or unlimitted Parliam[en]t', it was held, tended 'to discourage the Protestant religion'. Minute book of the Guild of Barbers, etc., Dublin, Trinity College, MS 1447/8/2, fol. 68a.
84. There was a second, enlarged edition of this work, *Liberties and Customs of Dublin*, published the following year.
85. Lucas, *Liberties of Dublin*, pp. 9–41. For the sake of accuracy, it might be noted that the pamphlet spends much time rehearsing the privileges of London also. Lucas considered that an examination of the privileges enjoyed by the capital of one kingdom would provide a good indication of what had at one time been proper to the capital of the other.
86. Woltjer, 'Dutch privileges', p. 34. Woltjer's reference is, in part, to the ideology of the Doelisten, whose movement was exactly contemporary with and notably paralleled that led by Lucas. See de Voogt, *Doelistenbeweging*.
87. Lucas, *Liberties of Dublin*, p. 8. This claim to prescription, it may be added, was motivated by more than a belief in the legitimising power of antiquity. It was also motivated by a desire to assert the historical independence of the

municipality from both crown and parliament. In this defence of local particularism, as much as in anything else adverted to in the present discussion, Lucas reveals his decidedly pre-modern cast of mind.

88. Ibid., p. 6.
89. That the eighteenth century very commonly regarded liberty as the possession of individuals, is made plain by Dickinson in *Liberty and Property*, passim. See also Browning, *Court Whigs*, pp. 48–54, 60–1 and 70–2.
90. There are a few very brief references to these themes. See Lucas, *Liberties of Dublin*, pp. 36–7 and 46–7.
91. See above, p. 74.
92. See above, p. 39.
93. Lucas, *Remonstrance Against Certain Infringements*, p. 5.
94. Ibid., pp. 7–15 passim.
95. Murphy, 'Lucas affair', Chapters 2 and 3 passim.
96. For the expression of Lucasite objectives in relation to municipal government in these terms see, for example, Minute book of the Guild of Barbers, etc., Dublin, Trinity College, MS 1447/8/2, fols 14a–14b.
97. Records of the Guild of Merchants, etc., London, British Library, Egerton MS 1765, fol. 77a.
98. Palmer, *Police and Protest*, pp. 71–3 and 92–104.
99. See, for example, Records of the Guild of Merchants, etc., London, British Library, Egerton MS 1765, fol. 77b.
100. Hill, 'Politics of privilege', p. 22.
101. Ibid., pp. 17 and 23–36.
102. Leighton, 'Theobald McKenna', pp. 226–8.
103. The nature of Protestant politics in Dublin in the years immediately after municipal reform is discussed in Hill, 'Protestant response to repeal'.

5 Questioning the Catholics

1. See above, Chapter 3.
2. See above, Chapter 4.
3. See below, Chapter 6.
4. See above, Chapter 3. See especially pp. 46–7.
5. See above, Chapter 4.
6. See below, Chapter 8.
7. See, for example, Ward, 'Catholic pamphlets of Charles O'Conor', p. 259.
8. Fagan, *Second City*, pp. 147–9 and below, pp. 97–8.
9. Robert and Catherine Ward, for example, make much of the contribution of Bishop Berkeley. See Ward, 'Catholic pamphlets of Charles O'Conor', passim. Cf. below, p. 98.
10. Fagan, *Second City*, Chapter 10. See especially pp. 135–42 and 149–52.
11. Coombes, *John O'Brien*, p. 22.
12. Fagan, *Second City*, pp. 121–2.
13. See, for example, the letter of [Edmund Gibson], bishop of London to his clergy, 17 December 1734 quoted from *Faulkner's Dublin Journal*, 7 January 1735 in Brady (ed.), *Catholics and Catholicism*, p. 54.
14. Cf. above, pp. 55–8.

15. *Impartial Examiner*, p. 8.
16. See above, pp. 6 and 7. The degree of confidence placed in the charter schools was considerable. See, for example, *Letter from a Noble Lord*.
17. For the beginnings of this, see Ford, *Protestant Reformation*, Chapter 9.
18. See above, p. 58.
19. Taaffe, *Observations on Affairs in Ireland*, p. 30.
20. Ibid., pp. 12–15.
21. *Lord Taaffe's Observations Examined and Confuted*, pp. 4–9.
22. [O'Conor], *Vindication of Lord Taaffe's Civil Principles*, p. 3.
23. *Reply to the 'Vindication of Lord Taaffe's Civil Principles'*, p. 4.
24. [O'Conor], *Principles of the Roman Catholics*, pp. 25–79.
25. Ibid., p. 25.
26. Cf. [O'Conor], *Case of the Roman Catholics*, pp. 71–3, where casual reference is made to the harmless character of certain Catholic doctrines, and *Remarks on a Late Pamphlet*, pp. 25–30, where that reference is taken up.
27. Butt, *Origin of Orangemen*, p. 20.
28. McKenna, *Essays*, pp. 12–13.
29. See above, pp. 49–51.
30. This latter point point came to be made with frequency as fear of Jacobites was being replaced by fear of Jacobins. The latter were tools of Rome as much as the former had been. See, for example, [Musgrave], *Observations on the Correspondence between Lord Redesdale and Fingall*, p. 37.
31. Cf. above, pp. 59–66.
32. [Archdekin], *Letter from an English Gentleman*. The date of composition is indicated on p. 18.
33. This work first appeared in 1695 and was republished under the original title in 1720. When it was issued again in London in 1744, together with other pieces of Catholic interest, it had become the *Impartial History*. It retained this title when it was published in London in 1754 and in Dublin, together with Burke's speech of 1780 to the electors of Bristol, in 1787. It appeared yet again in Dublin in 1799 under a third title, *The Genuine History of Ireland*. Its last appearance seems to have been in 1837. The volume published in 1744, which is cited here, was, in 1772, translated into Irish, a sure sign of popularity. See Reilly, *Stair fhír-cheart ar Eirinn*.
34. Reilly, *Impartial History*, p. 42.
35. Ibid., pp. 11–19. Cf. [Archdekin], *Letter from an English Gentleman*, p. 41.
36. Reilly, *Impartial History*, p. 41. Cf. [Archdekin], *Letter from an English Gentleman*, pp. 54–7.
37. Reilly, *Impartial History*, pp. 42–3, 62 and 63.
38. [Archdekin], *Letter from an English Gentleman*, pp. 6 and 72–85.
39. See, for example, Reilly, *Impartial History*, pp. 2–5, where a discussion of the reign of Elizabeth allows for an attack on the doctrines of the Reformation, the mode of their introduction to Ireland and Elizabeth herself, who 'was a notorious Bastard, and consequently had no right to the crown'. All this is in marked contrast to the views set out in Archdekin's *Letter*. Here it was said that the king had a duty to maintain the Protestant religion, which would not suffer loss as a result of the doing of justice to the Catholics. See pp. 30–3.

40. See, for example, Reilly, *Impartial History*, pp. 5–10, where the conduct of James I is discussed.

41. The edition of Nary's work used here is that produced in 1744 to accompany Reilly's *Impartial History*, under which title it will be cited.

42. For the attempt to impose the oath of abjuration in 1709, see J. G. Simms, 'Establishment of Protestant ascendancy', p. 18. For the terms of the Bill against which Nary wrote, see Reilly, *Impartial History*, p. 138.

43. Ibid., pp. 131 and 136–7.

44. Ibid., pp. 140–3.

45. Ibid., pp. 136 and 125–6.

46. Ibid., pp. 144–5.

47. Ibid., pp. 116 and 126–7.

48. See below, p. 116.

49. Berkeley, *Querist*, qq. 255–67, pp. 28–30. The tenor and content of these works are concisely described in Beckett 'Literature in English', pp. 460–1.

50. Synge, *Case of Toleration*, p. 41.

51. Radcliffe, *Letter to Edward Synge*, p. 38.

52. Synge, *Vindication of a Sermon*, pp. 45–7. Cf. Radcliffe, *Letter to Edward Synge*, pp. 23–4 and 27–8.

53. Synge, *Case of Toleration*, pp. 42 and 51–6 and *Vindication of a Sermon*, pp. 59–61 and 78.

54. Synge, *Case of Toleration*, pp. 46–7 and *Vindication of a Sermon*, pp. 73–7.

55. It is interesting to note that one of Primate Hugh Boulter's first responses to the raising of the Catholic question in the 1750s, was to commission a translation of the classical Anglican text on the subject of oaths. The work was by the seventeenth-century Oxford divine, Robert Sanderson and had been translated previously by the king-martyr himself. It appeared under the title *The Nature and Obligation of Oaths Explained*. See especially p. iii.

56. Clark, *Strangers and Sojourners*, Chapter 14.

57. Synge, *Case of Toleration*, pp. 64–5.

58. It may be noted that in later years Synge was not particularly known as a friend of the Catholics. O'Conor, who knew him quite well as bishop of Elphin, certainly did not so regard him. See O'Conor to Curry, 25 September 1759 and 3 October 1759 and O'Conor to Hugh Stafford, 3 October 1759, Ward (eds), *Letters of Charles O'Conor*, I, pp. 77–80.

59. While Synge's argument reflected the content of the case presented by Bishop Hoadly and his supporters in its most practical and immediately relevant aspect, the controversy as a whole raised wider questions. For concise accounts of some of the issues involved, see Barlow, *Citizenship and Conscience*, pp. 44–6; Rupp, *Religion in England*, pp. 88–101; and Walker, *William Law*, Chapter 2.

60. Synge, *Case of Toleration*, p. 29.

61. Radcliffe, *Serious and Humble Enquiry*, p. 8. When he entered into controversy, Radcliffe was already well-known for both his tory sentiments and his anti-Catholic zeal. For the former see his own *Sermon* and Weaver [pseud.], *Letter to Stephen Radcliffe*. For the latter see Fagan, *Second City*, p. 152.

62. Radcliffe, *Letter to Edward Synge*, p. 38.

63. He has been so regarded. See James, 'Church of Ireland in the early eighteenth century', p. 450.

64. See above, pp. 3–14.
65. Synge, *Vindication of a Sermon*, p. 79.
66. Ibid., p. 45.
67. It is on O'Conor's views that the remaining part of the present chapter chiefly focuses. The most important contribution of Curry to the Catholic argumentation was historiographical and is discussed below, pp. 124–5.
68. See above, p. 95.
69. O'Conor wrote in response to William Henry's *Appeal to the People of Ireland*. The quotation from this pamphlet given above will indicate its tenor. See p. 37.
70. O'Conor to [Michael Reilly], 28 October 1749, Ward (eds), *Letters of Charles O'Conor*, I, pp. 4–5.
71. [O'Conor], *Counter-appeal to the People of Ireland*, pp. 3–7 and 11–14.
72. [O'Conor], *Seasonable Thoughts*, pp. 26–51.
73. Ibid., pp. 14–23.
74. See, for example, the comments on monarchy, ibid., p. 9.
75. Ibid., p. 14.
76. O'Conor, 'Early life of Charles O'Conor', Dublin, National Library of Ireland, IR 92 o162, pp. 42 and 54.
77. Ibid., p. 46.
78. Monod, *Jacobitism and the English People*, pp. 38–44.
79. See above, p. 23.
80. Clark, *English Society*, p. 306.
81. See above, pp. 62–6 and below, pp. 135–7.
82. [O'Conor], *Case of the Roman Catholics*. Cf. pp. 45 and 75.
83. See below, p. 148.
84. See above, Chapter 3, note 70.
85. [Curry], *Appeal to the Lord P[rima]te*, p. 7.
86. See especially [Curry], *Third Appeal to the Lord Primate*, pp. 4–22.
87. [Curry], *Appeal to the Lord P[rima]te*, p. 22 and [Curry], *Second Appeal to the L[or]d P[rimat]e*, pp. 20–1.
88. See, for example, [O'Conor], *Danger of Popery*, pp. 14–15.
89. See above, p. 95.
90. See, for example, [O'Conor], *Danger of Popery*, pp. 15–16.
91. [O'Conor], *Case of the Roman Catholics*, p. 78.
92. [O'Conor], *Vindication of 'The Case of the Roman Catholics'*, p. 4.
93. [O'Conor], *Principles of the Roman Catholics*, p. 5.
94. See, for example, [O'Conor], 'Advertisement', pp. ix–xi or [O'Conor], *Danger of Popery*, pp. 8–11.
95. [O'Conor], *Case of the Roman Catholics*, p. 13.
96. See, for example, ibid., pp. 22–3 and 61–9 or [O'Conor], 'Advertisement', p. xvi.
97. See, for example, [O'Conor], *Case of the Roman Catholics*, pp. 31–2.
98. [O'Conor], *Vindication of 'The Case of the Roman Catholics'*, pp. 44–5.
99. [Curry and O'Conor], *Observations on the Popery Laws*, p. 19.
100. [O'Conor], *Vindication of 'The Case of the Roman Catholics'*. See especially p. 10.
101. [O'Conor], *Protestant Interest*, pp. v and vi.
102. [O'Conor], *Seasonable Thoughts*, pp. 26–8.

103. See, for example, [O'Conor], *Case of the Roman Catholics*, pp. 50 and 47.
104. See, for example, the use of Molyneux's arguments from the *Case of Ireland* effectively to justify Catholic rebellions of previous centuries in [O'Conor], 'Advertisement', pp. xvii–xix.
105. [O'Conor], *Danger of Popery*, pp. 9–10.
106. See, for example, [O'Conor], *Case of the Roman Catholics*, pp. 43–6 or [Curry and O'Conor], *Observations on the Popery Laws*, pp. 6–7 and 14–19.
107. See, for example, ibid., pp. 29–30. Cf. above, p. 14.
108. [O'Conor], *Protestant Interest*, pp. 14–15 [recte pp. 16–17] and [Curry and O'Conor], *Observations on the Popery Laws*, pp. 36–7.
109. Ibid., p. 9.
110. See below, pp. 114–18.
111. The justification of this remark must be sought in a perusal of O'Conor's works as a whole. The pamphlets, as popular writings, are certainly not well-provided with footnotes, though his *Case of the Roman Catholics* does contain references to such writers as Montesquieu, Voltaire and Warburton. Some indication of his personal taste in reading matter is given in his correspondence. See, for example, O'Conor to Curry, 22 August 1758, Ward (eds), *Letters of Charles O'Conor*, I, pp. 61–2.
112. [O'Conor], *Vindication of 'The Case of the Roman Catholics'*, p. 37.
113. O'Conor to Curry, 27 April 1757, Ward (eds), *Letters of Charles O'Conor*, I, pp. 29–30. With regard to the Catholic attitude to King William, it is worth remarking, in view of Jacqueline Hill's study of his cultus in eighteenth- and nineteenth-century Ireland, that while it is true that Catholics 'were prepared to invoke the memory of William', this was never much more than a tactical device. See Hill, 'National festivals'. Despite the lavish praise that had been heaped on King William in so many Catholic pamphlets for some decades, it could be remarked in 1786 that Catholics 'execrated his memory'. See [McKenna], *Interesting Periods of Irish History*, p. 34.
114. Only once did O'Conor venture into modern history in a scholarly fashion. In 1753 he had published his edition of the earl of Castlehaven's *Memoirs of the civil war in Ireland*. In the *Editor's Preface* (pp. iii–xii) he clearly indicated that he was less concerned to commit the era of the wars of religion firmly to the past, than to demonstrate that their outcome in Ireland had been the triumph of wrong over right. See especially p. iv.
115. See, for example, O'Conor to Curry. [January 1772], Ward, (eds), *Letters of Charles O'Conor*, II, pp. 3–5.
116. This attitude is clear from almost any part of the voluminous correspondence between the two men. For some instances of explicit expression of it, see O'Conor to Curry 3 December 1757, 27 January 1759 and 17 February 1759, ibid., I, pp. 52–3 and 67–70 or Curry to O'Conor, 27 July 1774, Dublin, Royal Irish Academy, O'Conor Correspondence, BI2.
117. See, for example, Curry to O'Conor, [March 1760], Dublin, Royal Irish Academy, O'Conor Correspondence, BII.
118. [Curry], *Historical Memoirs*, pp. 185–8.
119. See above, p. 58.
120. Ma-Geoghegan, *Histoire de l'Irlande*. The politics of the work is spoken of in Geoghegan, 'Jacobite history'. O'Conor, it should be noted, expressed

no disapproval of Ma-Geoghegan and, indeed, declared himself most willing to offer the abbé what assistance he could. See O'Conor to Curry, 3 October 1760, Ward, (eds), *Letters of Charles O'Conor*, I, pp. 98–100.
121.   See below, pp. 150–6.
122.   See above, pp. 62–4.
123.   O'Halloran, *Ierne Defended*, p. 4.
124.   O'Conor [of Stowe], *Memoirs of Charles O'Conor*, first pagination, p. ix.

6   Land and History

1.   See above, Chapter 5.
2.   See above, Chapter 4.
3.   See, for example, [O'Conor], *Danger of Popery*, pp. 27–32. This was so even when the proposals were being accepted in the 1770s. See [Curry and O'Conor], *Observations on the Popery Laws*, p. 41.
4.   [O'Conor], *Danger of Popery*, p. 12.
5.   See above, pp. 102–5.
6.   See above, pp. 45–8.
7.   [Curry], *Essay Towards a New History of the Gunpowder Treason*, p. iii.
8.   Charles O'Conor to Denis O'Conor, [17 November 1751] and Charles O'Conor to Daniel O'Conor, 3 March 1756, Ward (eds), *Letters of Charles O'Conor*, I, pp. 7–8 and 11–12.
9.   O'Conor to Thomas O'Gorman, 29 October 1784, ibid., II, pp. 219–20.
10.   See above, pp. 107–10.
11.   This statement may, if desired, be taken as an acknowledgement that in Ireland 'improvement' easily overshadowed 'enlightenment', two concepts which students of the period may prefer to keep separate. See, for example, Camic's study of eighteenth-century Scotland, *Experience and Enlightenment*, pp. 85–7.
12.   Luce, *Dublin Societies*.
13.   Meenan and Clarke, 'R.D.S. 1731–1981', pp. 1–30.
14.   Howard, Some *Scattered Pieces upon Agriculture*.
15.   Howard, *Miscellaneous Works*, III, pp. 259–60.
16.   Quoted by O'Conor in 'George Faulkner and Lord Chesterfield', p. 292. At a rather later date the Dublin Society 'appointed a *select committee* of their own body to inspect into the ancient state of literature and arts in Ireland'. See [O'Conor], 'Remarks on the "Essays on the antiquity of the Irish language"', p. 338.
17.   Ives, *Enlightenment and National Revival*, pp. 3–16.
18.   C. A. Sheehan, quoting the view of J. P. Kenny, in 'Charles O'Conor', p. iii.
19.   See below, pp. 122–3.
20.   See Madden's *Reflections and Resolutions* and Dobbs' *Essay on the Trade and Improvement of Ireland*.
21.   [O'Conor], *Principles of the Roman Catholics*, p. 87.
22.   [O'Conor], *Case of the Roman Catholics*, p. 54.
23.   These points are repeatedly made, in all O'Conor's writings on the Catholic question. For a statement of them in brief see, for example, [O'Conor], *Maxims,* pp. 11–12.

24.   Madden, *Reflections and Resolutions*, p. 40.

25.   Dobbs, *Essay on the Trade and Improvement of Ireland*, II, p. 77.

26.   Ibid., pp. 91–2 and Madden, *Reflections and Resolutions*, pp. 37–8.

27.   See, for example, [O'Conor], *Case of the Roman Catholics*, pp. 53–4.

28.   See, for example, [Curry and O'Conor], *Observations on the Popery Laws*, pp. 25–6.

29.   Cullen 'Economic development, 1750–1800', pp. 166–7. See also Cullen, *Economic History of Ireland*, pp. 78–9.

30.   See, for example, *Lord Taaffe's Observations Examined and Confuted*, pp. 9–10. In fact O'Conor's belief that the nature of Catholic tenures resulted in a disastrous movement from tillage to pasture was equally without foundation, though in this contemporary opinion generally supported him. See Cullen, *Economic History of Ireland*, pp. 67–8.

31.   See above, pp. 102–3.

32.   See above, pp. 104–5.

33.   See, for example, [O'Conor], *Principles of the Roman Catholics*, p. 102.

34.   See, for example, O'Conor to Curry, 22 January 1757, Ward, (eds), *Letters of Charles O'Conor*, I, pp. 26–8.

35.   [Curry and O'Conor], *Observations on the Popery Laws*, p. 34.

36.   See below, pp. 134–5.

37.   MacCurtain, 'Rural society in post-Cromwellian Ireland', pp. 135–6.

38.   Dobbs, *Essay on the Trade and Improvement of Ireland*, II, pp. 84–6.

39.   A few slight pieces, such as his *Statistical Account of the Parish of Kilronan*, fall into neither category.

40.   Sheehan, 'Charles O'Conor', p. 65.

41.   O'Halloran, 'Irish re-creations of the Gaelic past', p. 72.

42.   See above, pp. 25–6 and 27–8.

43.   Hay, *Annalists and Historians*, p. 170.

44.   [O'Conor], 'Remarks on the "Essay on the antiquity of the Irish language"', p. 337.

45.   O'Conor, 'Reflections on the times of heathenism', p. 219.

46.   Cf. Hutchinson's view of the work of one of the last great traditional historians, Geoffrey Keating, in [Hutchinson], *Defence of the Ancient Historians*, pp. 95–108 with O'Conor's, for which see O'Conor to Curry, [January 1772], Ward, (eds), *Letters of Charles O'Conor*, II, pp. 3–5.

47.   For explicit reference to this problem, see [Hutchinson], *Defence of the Ancient Historians*, pp. 54–69 and O'Conor, 'Third letter to Colonel Vallancey', p. 109.

48.   Sheehan, 'Charles O'Conor', p. 123.

49.   O'Conor, *Dissertations* (1766 edn), pp. iii–xx and 1–182.

50.   Ibid., p. 183.

51.   O'Conor, 'Letter to David Hume'.

52.   Sheehan, 'Charles O'Conor', pp. 108–21; Hill, 'Popery and Protestantism, civil and religious liberty', pp. 109–10; O'Halloran, 'Irish re-creations of the Gaelic past', pp. 75–8.

53.   O'Conor, 'Editor's preface' to O'Flaherty's *Ogygia Vindicated*, pp. viii–ix. Cf. Hill, 'Popery and Protestantism, civil and religious liberty', pp. 107–8.

54.   O'Conor, *Dissertations* (1766 edn), pp. 9–28.

55.   [O'Conor], 'Remarks on the "Essay on the antiquity of the Irish language"',
      p. 348.
56.   O'Conor, 'Editor's Preface' to O'Flaherty's *Ogygia Vindicated*, pp.
      xxx–xxxix.
57.   See, for example, O'Conor, *Dissertations* (1766 edn), pp. 63, 187, 194–5,
      212 and 219, where reference is made to the 'Boromean Tribute'. For an
      account of this by a modern scholar, see Byrne, *Irish Kings and High-kings*,
      pp. 144–6.
58.   See especially O'Conor, *Dissertations* (1766 edn), pp. 45–57.
59.   Ibid., p. 227.
60.   Hill, 'Popery and Protestantism, civil and religious liberty', p. 104.
61.   O'Conor, 'Editor's Preface' to O'Flaherty's *Ogygia Vindicated*, p. iv.
62.   Charles O'Conor to Bryan O'Conor, [c. 1754], Ward, (eds), *Letters of
      Charles O'Conor*, I, pp. 8–9. The quotation from this letter given above
      (Chapter 2, note 54) is relevant to the present point.
63.   Quoted by Sheehan in 'Charles O'Conor', p. 91.
64.   Dunne, 'Gaelic response to conquest and colonisation', p. 11.
65.   Quoted by Sheehan in 'Charles O'Conor', p. 91.
66.   See above, p. 32.
67.   See, for examples, the accounts of the writings of the comte de
      Boulainvilliers and of the Abbé Dubos on the Frankish conquest of Gaul in
      Mackrell, *Attack on 'feudalism'*, pp. 20–9.
68.   [O'Conor], *Counter-appeal to the People of Ireland*, p. 9.
69.   O'Conor, *Dissertations* (1766 edn), pp. 130–40.
70.   O'Conor's manuscript note in his copy of O'Halloran's *Ierne Defended*, p.
      6, Dublin, Royal Irish Academy, Tract Collection, box 254, no. 4.
71.   See above, p. 79.
72.   [Archdekin], *Letter from an English Gentleman*, pp. 36–44.
73.   See, for example, the account of the contemporary, and references to the
      continuing reaction to Thomas Leland's *History of Ireland* in Liechty
      'Testing the depth of Catholic/Protestant conflict'. See especially p. 27.
74.   See, for example, the views quoted in Király, Hungary in the *Late
      Eighteenth Century*, pp. 169–70.
75.   O'Conor sought to answer the Protestant belief that Irish Catholics were
      possessed of a 'peculiar Perverseness... and... Proneness to Rebellion above
      all other People' in the *Danger of Popery*, pp. 17–18.
76.   [Curry], *Historical Memoirs*, p. 38. For his argumentation on the point see
      pp. 40–8. For convenience, here and below only the work of 1758 is cited.
      For a much fuller treatment of the same subject-matter by Curry see his
      posthumous *Historical and Critical Review of the Civil Wars*, II, pp.
      57–268.
77.   [Curry], *Historical Memoirs*, pp. 59–76 and 100–35.
78.   Ibid., pp. 153–7.
79.   Ibid., pp. 145–53.
80.   Ibid., pp. 78–99.
81.   Ibid., pp. 139–44.
82.   Hill, 'Popery and Protestantism, civil and religious liberty', pp. 102–4.
83.   Beckett, 'Literature in English 1691–1800', p. 452.
84.   It may be noted that the most markedly anti-Catholic historian of the period,
      Walter Harris, argued that the centuries before the Norman invasion were

'Ages of Light and Learning'. Harris, *Hibernica*, pp. 271–2.

85. O'Conor, *Dissertations* (1766 edn), pp. xii–xvii. Cf. the 1753 edition, p. xl, where O'Conor declared himself to be 'alone in this Subject' of ancient Irish history.

86. Ó Cuív, 'Irish language and literature, 1691–1845', pp. 416–17.

87. Liechty, 'Testing the depth of Catholic/Protestant conflict', pp. 19–24.

88. Ibid., p. 17. See also Curry to O'Conor, 24 October 1777, Dublin, Royal Irish Academy, O'Conor Correspondence, BI2.

89. *Faulkner's Dublin Journal*, 23–25 October 1788.

90. There were some who disregarded this. They were disinclined to condemn the Revolution *tout court*, but pointed out that the blessings it conferred on Ireland were not unmixed. See, for example, [McKenna], *Interesting Periods of Irish History*, pp. 26–40. They received distinguished support from Burke in his *Letter to Sir Hercules Langrishe*. See Burke, *Works*, III, pp. 318–22. The Catholics acting as a body, however, were more restrained and avoided any attack on either the Revolution or its extension to Ireland. They merely made new use of Molyneux and denied this latter the character of a conquest, thus flatly contradicting Burke, who had condemned it as such. See Musgrave, *Rebellions*, p. 90.

91. See above, p. 67.

92. See above, pp. 65–6.

7 New Critiques

1. Woodward, *Present State of the Church of Ireland*, p. 77.

2. *Presbyterio-Catholicon*, p. 62.

3. See below, Chapter 8.

4. See above, Chapter 3, note 70.

5. Burke to O'Conor, 6 May 1773, Dublin, Royal Irish Academy, O'Conor Correspondence, BI1a.

6. O'Conor to Curry, [7 June 1772], Ward (eds), *Letters of Charles O'Conor*, II, pp. 25–6.

7. O'Conor to Charles Ryan, 15 October 1777, ibid., II, pp. 110–13.

8. For a brief discussion of the strength of anti-Catholicism over the whole of the later eighteenth century, see above, pp. 51–3.

9. See above, p. 126.

10. Brett to O'Conor, 22 May 1769, Dublin, Royal Irish Academy, O'Conor Correspondence, BI2.

11. [Curry], *Appeal to the Lord P[rima]te*, pp. 3–6 and 9–13.

12. Brett, *Judgement of Truth*. See especially pp. 52 and 72–132.

13. Ibid. See especially pp. 59–62 and pp. 133–63.

14. Donovan, 'Military origins of the relief programme' and Bartlett, *Fall and Rise*, pp. 82–92.

15. Ibid., pp. 92–102. See also Wall, *Catholic Ireland,* Chapter 9.

16. Ibid., Chapter 10.

17. McKenna, *Essays*, p. 213.

18. Burke to Thomas Hussey, 18 May 1795, Copeland *et al.* (eds), *Correspondence of Edmund Burke*, VIII, pp. 245–50.

19. [McKenna], *Interesting Periods of Irish History*, p. 40.

20. Ibid., pp. 5–7.
21. Ibid., pp. 11–12.
22. Ibid., p. 11.
23. See, for example, Clark's account of the thought of the Arian, Richard Price, in his *English Society*, pp. 330–2.
24. [McKenna], *Interesting Periods of Irish History*, p. 38.
25. Edwards (ed.), 'Minute book', pp. 47–8.
26. Wall, *Catholic Ireland*, p. 141.
27. See, for example, above, Chapter 5, note 33.
28. See, for example, his discussion of the education of the Catholic and Protestant clergy in his letter to Lord Kenmare or his passing reference to liturgy in his speech to the electors of Bristol. Burke, *Works*, II, p. 145 and III, pp. 289–93.
29. O'Leary, *Miscellaneous Tracts,* pp. 60–99.
30. [O'Conor], *Case of the Roman Catholics*, p. 66.
31. Burke, *Works*, III, pp. 288–9.
32. Ibid., II, pp. 145–6 and cf. ibid., III, p. 285.
33. Browne, *Articles of Limerick*, p. 4.
34. See above, pp. 37–8.
35. Mentor, *Alarm*, p. 19.
36. Burke, *Works*, II, p. 155.
37. See above, p. 29. Cf. Palmer's definition of a 'revolutionary situation' in his *Age of the Democratic Revolution*, p. 21.
38. McKenna, *Constitutional Objections*, p. 74.
39. McKenna, *Views of the Catholic Question*, p. 42.
40. McKenna, *Constitutional Objections*, p. 76. For further indication of the character of McKenna's unionism see his *Mémoire on the Projected Union*.
41. Bolton, *Irish Act of Union*, Chapter 5, passim. See especially pp. 154–5.
42. See above, pp. 27–8.
43. See, for example, the views of Bishop Delaney of Kildare and Leighlin cited in O'Donoghue, 'Catholic church and Ireland', p. 147.
44. Rev. Alexander Montgomery to Pelham, 1 July 1797, Dublin, State Paper Office (Ireland), Rebellion Papers, 620/31/186.
45. Burke, *Works*, III, pp. 326–44.
46. Ibid., III, p. 305.
47. Ibid., III, p. 308–18.
48. See above, pp. 32–9.
49. See [Tone], *Argument*, pp. 8–16 and above pp. 106 and 114–17.
50. [Tone], *Argument*, pp. 15 and 49.
51. Ibid., pp. 26–40.
52. Ibid., pp. 46–49.
53. *Argument on Behalf of the Romanists Reconsidered*, pp. 4–7. See also Elliott, *Wolfe Tone*, p. 82.
54. *Argument on Behalf of the Romanists Reconsidered*, pp. 10–15.
55. [Tone], *Argument*, pp. 21–5 and 50–1.
56. *Argument on Behalf of the Romanists Reconsidered*, pp. 10 and 14–15.
57. McCormack, *Ascendancy and Tradition*, pp. 84–5.
58. It is highly regrettable that the term 'sectarian' is, among many, opprobrious. There seems to be no better to describe what is here, without

moral disapprobation, referred to: simply the nineteenth century's use of denominational affiliation as the primary determinant of social and political identity.

8   The Meaning of Gallicanism

1.   Chadwick, *Popes*, Chapter 6.
2.   See, for example, Hersche, 'Der österreichische Spätjansenismus'.
3.   Troy to Cardinal Antonelli, 14 January 1782, Dublin Diocesan Archive, Carpenter and Troy Papers, 116/3/77.
4.   This has been done by O'Flaherty in 'Ecclesiastical politics'.
5.   It should be recalled that it was in the 1780s that 'Jansenist' views were given their clearest and boldest expression, notably at the synod of Pistoia. The issues which exercised the minds of those gathered there are conveniently summarised by FitzPatrick in his *Irish Wits and Worthies*, p. 48.
6.   See above p. 49.
7.   Adams (ed.), *Wake's Gallican Correspondence*. For a commentary on this, see Sykes, *Wake*, I, Chapter 4.
8.   Clark, *Strangers and Sojourners*, Chapter 18.
9.   See above, pp. 98–100.
10.   Radcliffe, *Letter to Edward Synge*, p. 34.
11.   Synge, *Vindication of a Sermon*, pp. 66–71.
12.   Woodward, *Present State of the Church of Ireland*, p. 30.
13.   Pritchard, *Catholic Loyalism*, Chapter 9.
14.   Simms, 'The restoration, 1660–85', pp. 429–30.
15.   See, for example, [O'Conor], *Principles of the Roman Catholics*, pp. 13–15.
16.   Ryan, 'Religion and state', p. 123.
17.   See above, pp. 102–4.
18.   [O'Conor], *Principles of the Roman Catholics*, pp. 20–1.
19.   Clark's *Strangers and Sojourners* makes clear the merely political nature of the Remonstrant campaign of the 1660s. See pp. 204–7.
20.   For a convenient survey of the content and fortunes of English Gallicanism, see Duffy, 'Ecclesiastical democracy detected'. For the points made here, see especially part 1.
21.   Pastoral letter of Bishop Bernard Dunne of Kildare and Leighlin, 1730, Dublin Diocesan Archive, Pre-1750 Papers, 116/1/82.
22.   O'Conor to his grandson, Charles O'Conor, 6 February 1782, Ward (eds), *Letters of Charles O'Conor*, II, pp. 174–5.
23.   Sharratt, '"Excellent professors and exact discipline"', pp. 119–20.
24.   Wall, *Catholic Ireland*, p. 143.
25.   Ibid., p. 146.
26.   Chaussinand-Nogaret, *French Nobility*, p. 1. See also Behrens, *Society, Government and the Enlightenment*, p. 9.
27.   Quoted in Donnelly, 'Irish agrarian rebellion', p. 323.
28.   O'Flaherty, 'Ecclesiastical politics', p. 48.
29.   See above, pp. 60–1.
30.   Butler, *Tenets of the Roman Catholic Religion*, pp. 19–21 Cf. above, p. 62.
31.   Butler, *Tenets of the Roman Catholic Religion*, pp. 21–7.

32.   See, for example, [O'Conor], *Danger of Popery*, p. 10.
33.   [O'Conor], *Vindication of 'The Case of the Roman Catholics'*, p. 30.
34.   Ibid., p. 35.
35.   See, for example, Gilley, 'Challoner as controversialist', p. 97
36.   Leighton, 'Gallicanism and the veto controversy', pp. 143–50. The remarks made here are about a somewhat later period, but are relevant to a discussion of the 1780s.
37.   Burke, *Works*, III, pp. 289–95.
38.   Ibid., III, pp. 350–1.
39.   See above, pp. 141–2.
40.   Burke, *Works*, VI, p. 53.
41.   Burke to Thomas Hussey, [*ante* 10 February 1795], Copeland *et al.* (eds), *Correspondence of Edmund Burke*, VIII, pp. 142–4.
42.   Edwards (ed.), 'Minute book', p. 60.
43.   O'L[early, *Essay towards the Reformation of Controversial Sermons*, pp. 14–16.
44.   See, for example, O'Leary, *Miscellaneous Tracts*, pp. 10–19.
45.   See, for example, his discussion of purgatory in ibid., pp 36–40 or cf. his treatment of Catholic teaching about the means of salvation in *Review of an Important Controversy [and] Letter from Candour*, pp. 29–55 with that of one of the most widely used Catholic apologists of the day, Bishop Challoner, as indicated by Gilley in 'Challoner as controversialist', pp. 94–5.
46.   See, for example, O'Leary, *Review of an Important Controversy [and] Letter from Candour*, pp. 15 and 83.
47.   O'Leary, *Defence*, pp. 85–6.
48.   Ibid., pp 25–46.
49.   O'Leary, *Review of an Important Controversy [and] Letter from Candour* pp. 81–3.
50.   Both the content and circumstances of the work are described in Buckley, *Arthur O'Leary*, pp 22–39. For a text, see O'Leary, *Miscellaneous Tracts*, pp. 1–56.
51.   See Mann's *Sermon*. This showed none of the tendency to dilute the anti-Catholicism of the aniversary sermon which was observable among other preachers of the period.
52.   Quoted in O'Leary, *Essays*, pp. iv–v.
53.   They, for example, were never attacked for their anti-Catholicism. This was uniformly depicted as a trait of the heterodox – or, with the Gordon riots in mind, of the rabble. See, for example, O'Leary, *Review of an Important Controversy [and] Letter from Candour*, p. 18 or O'Leary *Miscellaneous Tracts*, pp. iv–v.
54.   Ibid., pp. 77–80.
55.   Ibid., pp. 81–90.
56.   Clark, *English Society*, pp. 216–35.
57.   Buschkühl, *Great Britain and the Holy See*, Chapter 2.
58.   McDowell, *Ireland in the Age of Imperialism and Revolution*, p. 397.
59.   Russell, *Letter to the People of Ireland*, p. 2. See also pp. 1, 8 and 11–12.
60.   Quoted by Wall in *Catholic Ireland*, p. 139.
61.   Norman, *Catholic Church and Ireland*, pp. 301–19.

Conclusion

1. Kerr, *Peel, Priests and Politics*, pp. 4–5, 24–5 and 94–5.
2. Kossmann, *Low Countries*, pp. 138–150, 166 and 195–205.
3. Thus both Gallicanism and Ultramontanism played roles in the formation of nineteenth-century Irish politics which were the opposite of those which they commonly played in the formation of nineteenth-century European politics generally. Peter Hersche sees the origins of modern Austrian conservatism, for example, precisely in those groups most concerned to combat 'Spätjansenismus'. See his 'Der österreichische Spätjansenismus', p. 192.

Bibliography

I. MANUSCRIPT SOURCES

Dublin

Dublin Diocesan Archive, Holy Cross College, Clonliffe
116/1 Papers of the period prior to 1750 relating to the Catholic archdiocese of Dublin.
116/2–5 Papers of Archbishops John Linegar, Richard Lincoln, Patrick Fitzsimon, John Carpenter and John Troy.

National Library of Ireland
MS 801. Transcripts from records of the Guild of Merchant Tailors, Dublin (Guild of St John the Baptist).
MSS 2124–8. Transactions of the Guild of Cutlers, Painter–Stainers and Stationers, Dublin (Guild of St Luke the Evangelist).
MS 81. Bye-laws of the Corporation of Sadlers, Upholders, Coach Makers, etc., Dublin (Guild of the Blessed Virgin Mary).
MS 8870. Letters of Richard Woodward, bishop of Cloyne to Hon. Charles Broderick (afterwards archbishop of Cashel), 1787–94.
MS 680. A collection of typescripts and off-prints of articles relating to the trade guilds of Dublin, written and collected by Henry Seymour Guinness.

Public Record Office (Ireland)
M 6118a–b. Transcripts of entries in the record book of the Guild of Feltmakers, Dublin.
M 2925–7. Transcripts from a volume of the transactions of the Corporation of Smiths, Glaziers, Pinmakers, etc., Dublin (Guild of St Loy).

State Paper Office (Ireland)
Rebellion Papers.

Royal Irish Academy
BI1a, BI1 and BI2. O'Conor Correspondence (in the Stowe MSS).

Trinity College
MSS 1447/8/1–2. Minute books of the Guild of Barbers, Chirurgeons, Apothecaries and Periwig Makers, Dublin (Guild of St Mary Magdalene).

Limerick

Limerick City Library
Minute book of the Guild of Masons, Bricklayers, Slaters, Plasterers, etc., Limerick.

London

British Library
Egerton MS 1765. A transcription of records of the Guild of Merchants (Guild of the Holy Trinity) and other Dublin guilds.

II. MANUSCRIPT SOURCES (PUBLISHED)

Adams, L. (ed.), *William Wake's Gallican Correspondence and Related Documents, 1716–1731*. 3 vols. New York, 1988–9.
Correspondence of John, Fourth Duke of Beford: Selected from the originals at Woburn Abbey... 3 vols. London, 1842–6.
Copeland, T. W., *et al.* (eds), *The Correspondence of Edmund Burke*. 10 vols. Cambridge and Chicago, 1958–78.
Edwards, R. D. (ed.), 'The minute book of the Catholic Committee, 1773–92', *Archivium Hibernicum*, IX (1942), pp. 1–172.
Gilbert, J. T. and Mulholland, R. (eds), *Calendar of Ancient Records of Dublin in the Possession of the Municipal Corporation of that City*. 19 vols. Dublin, 1889–1944.
O'Dwyer, C. (ed.), 'Archbishop Butler's visitation book', *Archivium Hibernicum*, XXXIII (1975), pp. 1–90.
Ris, S. de (ed.), *Peadar Ó Doirnín: a bheatha agus a shaothar*. Dublin, 1969.
Ward, C. C. and R. E. (eds), The Letters of Charles O'Conor of Belanagare. 2 vols. Ann Arbor (Mich.), 1980.

III. NEWSPAPERS AND OTHER CONTEMPORARY PERIODICAL PUBLICATIONS

Faulkner's Dublin Journal
Hibernian Journal (Dublin)
London Chronicle
London Evening Post
Public Journal (Dublin)
See also Brady, J., (ed.), *Catholics and Catholicism in the Eighteenth-century Press*. Maynooth (Co. Kildare), 1965.

IV. WORKS BY CONTEMPORARIES

Note: Titles have frequently been abbreviated and their spelling and punctuation uniformly modernised. Anonymous and pseudonymous works have been listed by title or pseudonym respectively, unless the name of the true author is known.

Admonition Critical and Friendly to the Papists of Ireland. Dublin, 1759.

The Agonies of Ireland, both in Church and State: In a letter... to... the a[rch]b[isho]p of Ar[ma]gh. London, 1742.

[Archdekin, Richard], *A Letter from an English Gentleman... shewing the hardships, cruelties and severe usage with which the Irish nation has been treated...* London, 1751.

Argument on Behalf of the Romanists Reconsidered: Being observations on a pamphlet... signed 'A Northern Whig'. Dublin, 1792.

An Axe Laid to the Root: Or, reasons... for putting the Popish clergy in Ireland under some better regulation. Dublin, 1749.

Barber, Samuel, *Remarks on a Pamphlet Entitled 'The Present State of the Church of Ireland'...* Dublin, 1787.

Barber, Samuel, *A Reply to the Reverend Mr Burrowes' and the Reverend Mr Ryan's Remarks*, etc. Dublin, 1787.

Berkeley, George, *The Querist: Containing several queries proposed to the consideration of the public. To which is added... A word to the wise...* London, 1750.

Brett, John, *A Friendly Call to the People of the Roman Catholic Religion in Ireland: A sermon preached at the parish church of St Bridget, Dublin, on Sunday, 23 October 1757...* Dublin, 1757.

Brett, John, *The Judgement of Truth: Or, common sense and good nature, in behalf of Irish Catholics...* Dublin, 1770.

[Brooke, Henry], *The Case of the Roman Catholics of Ireland: In a course of letters from a member of the Protestant church in that kingdom to his friend in England. Letter I*. Dublin, 1760.

[Brooke, Henry], *An Essay on the Ancient and Modern State of Ireland...* London, 1760.

[Brooke, Henry], *The Farmer's Case of the Roman Catholics of Ireland: In a course of letters from a member of the Protestant church in that kingdom to his friend in England...* Letters II, III and IV. Dublin, 1760.

[Brooke, Henry], *The Farmer's Letter[s] to the Protestants of Ireland*. Letters I–VI. Dublin, 1745.

Brooke, Henry, *Gustavus Vasa...: A tragedy...* Dublin, 1739.

Brooke, [Henry], *The Trial of the Cause of the Roman Catholics: On a special commission directed to Lord Chief Justice Reason, Lord Chief Baron Interest and Mr Justice Clemency...* Dublin, 1761.

Browne, Arthur, *A Brief Review of the Question whether the Articles of Limerick have been Violated*. Dublin, 1788.

Burke, Edmund, *The Works of the Right Honourable...* London, 1876–7.

Burrowes, Robert, *A Letter to the Rev. Samuel Barber, Minister of the Presbyterian Congregation at Rathfryland...* Dublin, 1787.

Butler, James, *A Justification of the Tenets of the Roman Catholic Religion: And a refutation of the charges brought against its clergy by the... bishop of Cloyne*. Dublin, 1787.

Butler, James, *A Letter from... James Butler, Titular Archbishop of Cashel to... Viscount Kenmare*. Dublin, 1787.

Butt, John William, *The Origin of Orangemen, Completely Refuting all the Unfounded and Malicious Reports...* Cambridge, 1813.

Campbell, William, *An Examination of the Bishop of Cloyne's Defence of his Principles...* Dublin, 1788.

Campbell, William, *A Vindication of the Principles and Character of the Presbyterians of Ireland: Addressed to the bishop of Cloyne in answer to his book...* [Dublin], 1787.

[Clayton, Robert], *A Few Plain Matters of Fact Humbly Recommended to the Consideration of the Roman Catholics of Ireland.* Dublin, 1756.

[Curry, John], *An Appeal to... the Lord P[rima]te of All I[relan]d: Being a short vindication of the political principles of Roman Catholics..., [by] an honest free thinker.* Dublin, 1757.

[Curry, John], *A Brief Account from the Most Authentic Protestant Writers of the Causes, Motives and Mischiefs of the Irish Rebellion,... 1641...* London, 1747.

[Curry, John], *A Candid Enquiry into the Causes and Motives of the Late Riots in the Province of Munster...* 2nd edn. London, 1766.

[Curry, John], *An Essay towards a New History of the Gunpowder Treason: Wherein its origin, cause and design are candidly set forth...* London, 1765.

Curry, John, *A Historical and Critical Review of the Civil Wars in Ireland from the Reign of Queen Elizabeth to the Settlement under King William...* 2 vols. Dublin, 1786.

[Curry, John], *Historical Memoirs of the Irish Rebellion in the Year 1641: Extracted from parliamentary journals, state acts and the most eminent Protestant historians...* London, 1758.

[Curry, John], *A Parallel between the Pretended Plot in 1762 and the Forgery of Titus Oates in 1679: Being a sequel to the candid enquiry into the causes and motives of the late riots in the province of Munster...* Cork, 1767.

[Curry, John], *A Second Appeal to... the L[or]d P[rimat]e of All I[relan]d: In vindication of the political principles of Roman Catholics..., [by] an honest free thinker.* Dublin, 1758.

[Curry, John], *A Third appeal to... the Lord Primate of All I[relan]d: In vindication of the political principles of Roman Catholics, [by] an honest free thinker.* Dublin, 1760.

[Curry, John], *Occasional Remarks on Certain Passages in Dr Leland's 'History of Ireland' Relative to the Irish Rebellion in 1641...* London, 1773.

[Curry, John and O'Conor, Charles], *Observations on the Popery Laws.* 2nd edn. Dublin, 1774.

[Dennis, William], *Letter to the Town, [by] Brutus.* [Dublin], 1747.

Detector, *Observations on the Indecent and Illiberal Strictures against the... Bishop of Cloyne...* Dublin, 1787.

A Discourse Concerning the Laws Ecclesiastical and Civil made against Heretics by Popes, Emperors, etc.: Being a sensible demonstration of the falsehood of the religion of the Church of Rome... Cork, 1765.

Dobbs, Arthur, *An Essay on the Trade and Improvement of Ireland.* 2 vols. Dublin, 1729–31.

[Downes], Robert, *A Sermon Preached at Christ Church, Dublin, before the Lords Spiritual and Temporal... on Thursday, 5 November 1747...* Dublin, 1747.

Drennan, William, *A Letter to... Earl Fitzwilliam...* Dublin, 1795.

[Duigenan, Patrick], *An Address to the Nobility and Gentry of the Church of Ireland, as by Law Established..., [by] Theophilus.* Dublin, 1786.

Duigenan, Patrick, *A Fair Representation of the Present Political State of Ireland...* London, 1799.

An Epistle from Th[oma]s Sh[erida]n, Esq. to the 'Universal Advertiser'. [Dublin], 1747.

The Gentlemen: A heroic poem in two cantos. Dublin, 1747.

[Giffard, Ambrose Hardinge], *A Short Reply to Doctor Drennan's Letter, in Another Letter to... the Lord Lieutenant [by] an Irish Loyalist [or] Falkland.* Dublin, 1795.

Harris, Walter, *Fiction Unmasked: Or, an answer to a dialogue lately published by a Popish physician...* Dublin, 1752.

Harris, Walter, *Hibernica: Or, some ancient pieces relating to Ireland.* Dublin, 1770.

[Henry, William], *An Appeal to the People of Ireland: Occasioned by the Insinuations and Misrepresentations of the Author of a Weekly Paper..., by a Member of the Incorporated Society for Promoting English Protestant Schools in Ireland.* Dublin, 1749.

Howard, Gorges Edmond, *The Miscellaneous Works in Verse and Prose of...* 3 vols. Dublin, 1782.

Howard, Gorges Edmond, *Several Special Cases on the Laws against the Further Growth of Popery in Ireland.* Dublin, 1775.

Howard, [Gorges Edmond], *Some Observations and Queries on the Present Laws of this Kingdom relative to Papists.* Dublin, 1778.

Howard, Gorges Edmond, *Some Scattered Pieces upon Agriculture and the Improvement of Husbandry ...* Dublin, 1770.

A Humble Address to the Ladies of the City of Dublin, [by] a Plebeian. Dublin, 1747.

[Hutchinson], Francis, *A Defence of the Ancient Historians: With a particular application of it to the history of Ireland and Great Britain and other northern nations.* Dublin, 1734.

[Hutchinson], Francis, *A Sermon Preached in Christ Church, Dublin, on Friday, 5 November 1731... before... the Lords Spiritual and Temporal... Dublin, 1731.*

The Impartial Examiner: Or, the faithful representer of the various and manifold misrepresentations imposed on the Roman Catholics of Ireland ... Dublin, 1746.

Jackson, William, *Observations in Answer to Mr Thomas Paine's 'Age of Reason'.* Dublin, 1795.

Jephson, Robert, *The Speech Delivered by Robert Jephson, Esq. on 11 February 1774... on the... Heads of a Bill...* Dublin, 1774.

The Journals of the House of Commons of the Kingdom of Ireland... 19 vols. Dublin, 1796–9.

A Letter from a Noble Lord in Dublin to a Gentleman in the Country. 2nd edn. Dublin, 1740.

Lord Taaffe's Observations upon the Affairs of Ireland Examined and Confuted by an Impartial Hand. Dublin, 1767.

[Lucas, Charles], *A Letter to the Free Citizens of Dublin, [by] A. Freeman, Barber and Citizen.* 4th edn. Dublin, 1747.

Lucas, C[harles], *The Liberties and Customs of Dublin Asserted and Demonstrated upon the Principles of Law, Justice and Good Policy...* Dublin, 1768.

Lucas, C[harles], *The Liberties of Dublin Asserted and Demonstrated upon the Principles of Law, Justice and Good Policy...* Dublin, 1767.

Lucas, Charles, *A Remonstrance against Certain Infringements on the Rights and Liberties of the Commons and Citizens of Dublin...* Dublin, 1743.

[Lucas, Charles], *A Second Letter to the Free Citizens of Dublin, [by] A. F., Barber and Citizen.* Dublin, 1747.

[Lucas, Charles], *A Third Letter to the Free Citizens of Dublin, [by] A. F., Barber and Citizen.* Dublin, 1747.

McDonnell, Thomas, *The Spirit of Christianity and the Spirit of Popery Compared: A sermon preached before the... House of Commons in the parish church of St Andrew, Dublin, on Thursday, 5 November 1761.* Dublin, 1761.

Ma-Geoghegan, [James], *Histoire de l'Irlande ancienne et moderne tirée des monumens les plus authentiques.* 3 vols. Paris and [falsely] Amsterdam, 1758–63.

McKenna, Theobald, *Constitutional Objections to the Government of Ireland by a Separate Legislature...* Dublin, 1799.

McKenna, Theobald, *A Memoire on Some Questions Respecting the Projected Union of Great Britain and Ireland.* Dublin, 1799.

McKenna, Theobald, *Political Essays Relative to the Affairs of Ireland, in 1791, 1792 and 1793...* London, 1794.

[McKenna, Theobald], *A Review of Some Interesting Periods of Irish History, [by] T. M. K.* London, 1786.

McKenna, Theobald, *Views of the Catholic Question, Submitted to the Good Sense of the People of England.* London, 1808.

[Madden, Samuel], *Reflections and Resolutions proper to the Gentlemen of Ireland, as to their Conduct for the Service of their Country...* Dublin, 1738.

[Mann], Isaac, *A Sermon Preached at Christ Church, Dublin, before the Lords Spiritual and Temporal... on Sunday, 5 November 1775...* Dublin, 1775.

Maturin, Gabriel James, *A Sermon Preached at Christ Church on Sunday 3 November 1745.* Dublin, 1745.

Mentor, *The Alarm: Or, an address to the nobility, gentry and clergy of the Church of Ireland, as by law established.* Dublin, 1783.

Mr Francis Liberty, a freeman and citizen of Dublin, *A Letter of Thanks to the Barber for his Indefatigable Pains to Suppress the Horrid and Unnatural Rebellion, Lately Broke out...* Dublin, 1747.

[Molesworth, Robert], *An Account of Denmark, as it was in the year 1692.* London, 1694.

[Musgrave, Richard], *A Concise Account of the Material Events and Atrocities, which Occurred during the Present Rebellion...* Dublin, 1799.

Musgrave, Richard, *Memoirs of the Different Rebellions in Ireland from the Arrival of the English: With a particular detail of that which broke out 23 May 1798...* Dublin, 1801.

[Musgrave, Richard], *Observations on the Correspondence between Lords Redesdale and Fingall...* London, 1804.

[O'Conor, Charles], 'Advertisement', [Curry, John], *Historical Memoirs of the Irish Rebellion in the Year 1641: Extracted from parliamentary journals, state acts and the most eminent Protestant historians...* London, 1758, pp. ix–xxix.

[O'Conor, Charles], *The Case of the Roman Catholics of Ireland: Wherein the principles and conduct of that party are fully explained and vindicated.* Dublin, 1755.

[O'Conor, Charles], *A Cottager's Remarks on the Farmer's 'Spirit of Party'.* Dublin, 1754.

[O'Conor, Charles], *A Counter-appeal to the People of Ireland.* Dublin, 1749.

[O'Conor, Charles], *The Danger of Popery to the Present Government Examined...* Dublin, 1761.

[O'Conor, Charles], *A Dissertation on the First Migrations and Final Settlement of the Scots in North Britain: With occasional observations on the poems of Fingal and Temora.* Bound with, but paginated separately from, O'Conor, C[harles], *Dissertations on the History of Ireland...* Dublin, 1766.

O'Conor, Charles, 'A dissertation on the origin and antiquities of the ancient Scots of Ireland and Britain', O'Flaherty, Roderick, *The Ogygia Vindicated...* Ed. Charles O'Conor. Dublin, 1775, pp. xxv–xlviii.

[O'Conor, Charles], *Dissertations on the Ancient History of Ireland: Wherein an account is given of the origin, government, letters, science, religion, manners and customs of the ancient inhabitants.* Dublin, 1753.

O'Conor, C[harles], *Dissertations on the History of Ireland...* Dublin, 1766.

O'Conor, Charles, 'The editor's preface', O'Flaherty, Roderick, *The Ogygia Vindicated...* Dublin, 1775, pp. i–xxiii.

[O'Conor, Charles], 'The editor's preface' [Touchet, James], earl of Castlehaven, *Memoirs: Or, his review of the late wars in Ireland...* Waterford, 1753, pp. iii–xii.

O'Conor, Charles, 'A letter to David Hume, Esq. on some misrepresentations in his history of Great Britain', *Gentleman's Museum*, April–May 1763, pp. 55–64 and 65–78.

O'Conor, Charles, '[Letter to the publisher]', Jephson, Robert, *The Speech Delivered by Robert Jephson, Esq. on 11 February 1774... on the... Heads of a Bill...* Dublin, 1774, pp. iii–viii.

[O'Conor, Charles], *Maxims Relative to the Present State of Ireland, 1757: Humbly submitted to the consideration of the legislative powers.* Dublin, 1757.

[O'Conor, Charles], *The Principles of the Roman Catholics Exhibited in Some Useful Observations on a Pamphlet Intitled 'Plain Matters of Fact Humbly Recommended to the Consideration of the Roman Catholics of Ireland'.* Dublin, 1756.

[O'Conor, Charles], *Proposals for Printing by Subscription 'Ogygian Tales; Or, a curious collection of Irish fables, allegories and histories...'* Dublin, 1743.

[O'Conor, Charles], *The Protestant Interest Considered Relatively to the Operation of the Popery Acts in Ireland.* Dublin, 1757.

O'Conor, Charles, 'Reflections on the history of Ireland during the times of heathenism...: addressed to... Charles Vallancey', *Collectanea de rebus Hibernicis*, III (1782), pp. 211–46.

[O'Conor, Charles], 'Remarks on the "Essay on the antiquity of the Irish language"...' [by] Celticus, *Collectanea de rebus Hibernicis*, II (1781), pp. 337–48.

[O'Conor, Charles], *Seasonable Thoughts on our Civil and Ecclesiastical Constitution.* Dublin, 1753.

O'Conor, Charles, 'Second letter to Colonel Vallancey on the heathen state and ancient topography of Ireland', *Collectanea de rebus Hibernicis*, III (1783), pp. 647–77.

[O'Conor, Charles], *Some Seasonable Thoughts Relating to our Civil and Ecclesiastical Constitution: Wherein is occasionally considered the case of the professors of Popery.* Dublin, 1751.

O'Conor, Charles, *Statistical Account of the Parish of Kilronan in Ireland and of the Neighbouring District.* Edinburgh, 1798.

O'Conor, Charles, 'Third letter of Charles O'Conor, Esq. to Colonel Vallancey', *Collectanea de rebus Hibernicis,* IV (1784), 107–38.

[O'Conor, Charles], *A Vindication of a Pamphlet Lately Published Intituled 'The Case of the Roman Catholics of Ireland'.* Dublin, 1755.

[O'Conor, Charles], *A Vindication of Lord Taaffe's Civil Principles: In a letter to the author of a pamphlet entitled 'Lord Taaffe's Observations upon the Affairs of Ireland Examined and Confuted'.* Dublin, 1768.

O'Conor, Charles, [of Stowe], *Memoirs of the Late Charles O'Conor of Belanagare, Esq., M.R.I.A.* Dublin, 1796.

O'Driscol, William, [pseud.], *A Letter to the Rev. Dr O'Leary: Found on the Great Road Leading from the City of Cork to Cloughnakilty.* Dublin, 1787.

O'Flaherty, Roderick, *The Ogygia Vindicated...* Ed. Charles O'Conor. Dublin, 1775.

O'Halloran, [Sylvester], *Ierne Defended: Or, a candid refutation of such passages in the Rev. Dr Leland's, and the Rev. Mr Whitaker's works as seem to affect the authenticity and validity of ancient Irish history...* Dublin, 1774.

O'L[ear]y, A[rthu]r, *An Essay Towards the Reformation of Controversial and Recantation Sermons: Addressed to the Rev. Charles Farrel.* Dublin, 1778.

O'Leary, Arthur, *Essays by the Celebrated and Much Admired R[ev]. F[r] Arthur O'Leary on the Kingdom of Ireland...* London, 1782.

O'Leary, Arthur, *Miscellaneous Tracts.* Dublin, 1791.

O'Leary, [Arthur], *Mr O'Leary's Defence: Containing a vindication of his conduct and writing during the late disturbances in Munster...* 2nd edn. Dublin, 1787.

O'Leary, Arthur, *A Review of an Important Controversy between Dr Carroll and the Reverend Messrs Wharton and Hawkins... [and] A Letter from Candour to... Luke Gardiner...* London, 1786.

Paley, William, *The Works of..., Archdeacon of Carlisle.* Edinburgh, 1825.

Parliamentary Register: Or, History of the proceedings and debates of the House of Commons of Ireland. 17 vols. Dublin, 1784–1801.

Philemon, *A Letter to Dr James Butler of Ireland: Occasioned by his late publication entitled 'A Justification of the Tenets of the Roman Catholic Religion'.* Dublin, 1787.

Presbyterio-Catholicon: Or a refutation of the modern Catholic doctrines... in letter to the real Roman Catholics... Dublin, [1791].

A Protestant's Address to the Protestants of Ireland: Wherein some sure methods are laid down by which their number may be increased and that of the Papists diminished. Dublin, 1757.

Queries Humbly Proposed to the Consideration of the Public. Dublin, 1746.

The Question Fairly Stated, Whether it is Prudent to Repeal All the Popery Laws of this Kingdom: In a letter to Hibernicus, [by] a Protestant. Dublin, 1778.

Radcliffe, Stephen, *A Letter to the Reverend Mr Edward Synge...: Occasioned by a late sermon preached in St Andrew's, Dublin... before the... House of Commons, 23 October 1725...* 2nd edn. Dublin, 1725.

Radcliffe, Stephen, *A Serious and Humble Enquiry, Whether it be Lawful, Prudent or Convenient that a Toleration of Popery should be enacted by authority of parliament...* Dublin, 1727.

Radcliffe, Stephen, *A Sermon Preached at the Assizes... for the County of Kildare, 6 April 1714.* Dublin, 1714.

Reflections on Our Present Critical Situation: In a letter from a landed proprietor. London, 1777.

Reilly, Hugh, *The Impartial History of Ireland: Containing a summary account of all the battles, sieges, rebellions and massacres...* [and Cornelius] Nary, *The Case of the Roman Catholics of Ireland...* London, 1744.

Reilly, Hugh, *Stair fhír-cheart ar Eirinn... Uilliam O Murchadha do chuir i nGaedhilg...* Ed. Ní Shéaghdha, Nessa. Dublin, 1941.

Remarks on a Late Pamphlet Entituled 'The Case of the Roman Catholics of Ireland', by a Protestant. Dublin, 1755.

A Reply to the 'Vindication of Lord Taaffe's Civil Principles': In a letter to the author. Dublin, 1768.

Russell, Thomas, *A Letter to the People of Ireland, on the Present Situation of the Country.* Belfast, 1796.

Ryan, Edward, *Remarks on the Pamphlet of Mr Barber, Dissenting Minister of Rathfryland.* Dublin, 1787.

Sanderson, Robert, *The Nature and Obligation of Oaths Explained...* Translated and annotated by Thomas Dawson. Dublin, 1755.

A Serious Enquiry into the Cause of the Present Disorders in this City: Humbly offered to the consideration of the inhabitants. Dublin, 1747.

[Sheridan, Thomas], *A Faithful Narrative of What Happened at the Theatre on Monday, 19th. instant...* Dublin, [1747].

Sheridan, Thomas, *A Full Vindication of the Conduct of the Manager of the Theatre Royal: Written by himself.* Dublin, 1747.

Some Observations and Queries on the Present Laws of this Kingdom Relative to Papists, by a True Church of England Man. Dublin, 1761.

[Stone], George, *A Sermon Preached at Christ Church, Dublin, on Wednesday, 23 October 1751... before... the Lords Spiritual and Temporal...* 2nd edn. Dublin, 1751.

[Stone], George, *A Sermon Preached in Christ Church, Dublin... on Thursday, 5 November 1741... before... the Lords Spiritual and Temporal...* Dublin, 1741.

Story, [Joseph], *A Sermon Preached before the... House of Commons at St Andrew's Church on 5 November 1737...* Dublin, 1737.

Synge, Edward, *The Case of Toleration Considered with Respect Both to Religion and Civil Government: In a sermon preached in St Andrew's, Dublin, before the ... House of Commons on Saturday, 23 October 1725...* London, 1726.

Synge, Edward, *A Vindication of a Sermon Preached before the... House of Commons... on Saturday, 23 October 1725... in answer to the Revd Mr Radcliffe's letter.* Dublin, 1726.

Taaffe, Nicholas, *Observations on Affairs in Ireland from the Settlement in 1691 to the Present Time.* 3rd edn. Dublin, 1767.

Thomas, Daniel, *Observations on the Pamphlets Published by the Bishop of Cloyne, Mr Trant and Theophilus, on One Side, and Those by Mr O'Leary, Mr Barber and Doctor Campbell, on the Other...* Dublin, 1787.

'To the lords and gentlemen of the Volunteer associations of Ireland', Sheridan, Thomas, *A General Dictionary of the English Language...* [by Charles O'Conor?]. Dublin, 1784, pp. iii–iv.

[Tone, Theobald Wolfe], *An Argument on Behalf of the Catholics of Ireland. In which the present state of the country, and the necessity of a parliamentary reform are considered... [by] A Northern Whig.* Dublin, 1791.

Trant, Dominick, *Considerations on the Present Disturbances in the Province of Munster: Their causes, extent, probable consequences and remedies*. Dublin, 1787.

Weaver, R. M., [pseud.], *A Letter to the Revd Stephen Radcliffe...: Occasioned by a letter of his to the Revd Edward Synge...* Dublin, 1725.

[Woodward], Edward, *The Present State of the Church of Ireland: Containing a description of its precarious situation...* 7th edn. Dublin, 1787.

Young, Arthur, *Tour in Ireland (1776–1779).* Ed. and annotated by A. W. Hatton. 4th edn. 2 vols. London, 1892.

V. LATER WORKS

Anderson, P., *The Lineages of the Absolutist State*. London, 1974.

Barkley, J. M., 'The Arian Schism in Ireland, 1830', Baker, D., (ed.), *Schism, Heresy and Religious Protest: Papers read at the tenth summer meeting and the eleventh winter meeting of the Ecclesiastical History Society*. Studies in Church History, Vol. 9. Cambridge, 1972, pp. 323–29.

Barlow, R. B., *Citizenship and Conscience: A study in the theory and practice of religious toleration in England during the eighteenth century*. Philadelphia (Penn.), 1962.

Bartlett, T., *The Fall and Rise of the Irish Nation: The Catholic question 1690–1830*. Dublin, 1992.

Beckett, J. C., 'Literature in English 1691–1800', Moody, T. W., and Vaughan, W. E. (eds), *Eighteenth-century Ireland 1691–1800*. A New History of Ireland, Vol. 4. Oxford, 1986, pp. 424–70.

Beckett, J. C., *Protestant Dissent in Ireland*. London, 1948.

Behrens, C. B. A., *Society, Government and the Enlightenment: The experience of eighteenth-century France and Prussia*. London, 1985.

Best, G. F. A., 'The Protestant constitution and its supporters, 1800–1829'. *Transactions of the Royal Historical Society*, 5th series, VIII (1958), pp. 105–27.

Bigger, F. J., *The Ulster Land War of 1770: The Hearts of Steel*. Dublin, 1910.

Bilmanis, A., *A History of Latvia*. Princeton (NJ), 1951.

Black, J., *Eighteenth-century Europe 1700–1789*. New York, 1990.

Bolton, F. R., *The Caroline Tradition in the Church of Ireland: With particular reference to Bishop Jeremy Taylor*. London, 1958.

Bolton, G. C., *The Passing of the Irish Act of Union: A study in parliamentary politics*. Oxford, 1966.

Brady, J., 'Proposals to register Irish priests 1756–7', *Irish Ecclesiastical Record*, 5th series, XCVII (1962), pp. 209–22.

Brady, J., and Corish, P. J., *The Church under the Penal Code*. A History of Irish Catholicism, Vol. 4, fasc. 2. Dublin, 1971.

Brake, W. Ph. te, *Regents and Rebels: The revolutionary world of an eighteenth-century Dutch city*. Cambridge (Mass.) and Oxford, 1989.

Bric, M. J., 'Priests, parsons and politics: the Rightboy protest in County Cork, 1785–1788', Philpin, C. H. E. (ed.), *Nationalism and Popular Protest in Ireland*. Cambridge, 1987, pp. 163–90.

Browning, R., *Political and Constitutional Ideas of the Court Whigs*. Baton Rouge (La) and London, 1982.

Buckley, M. B., *The Life and Writings of the Rev. Arthur O'Leary*. Dublin, 1868.

Burke, N., 'A hidden church? The structure of Catholic Dublin in the mid-eighteenth century', *Archivium Hibernicum*, XXXII (1974), pp. 81–92.

Buschkühl, M., *Great Britain and the Holy See 1746–1870*. Blackrock (Co. Dublin), 1982.

Bush, M. L., *Noble Privilege*. The European Nobility, Vol. 1. Manchester, 1983.

Butler, J., *Awash in a Sea of Faith: Christianizing the American people*. Cambridge (Mass.) and London, 1990.

Byrne, F. J., *Irish Kings and High-kings*. 2nd edn. London, 1987.

Camic, C., *Experience and Enlightenment: Socialization for cultural change in eighteenth-century Scotland*. Chicago, 1983.

Chadwick, O., *The Popes and European Revolution*. Oxford History of the Christian Church. Oxford, 1981.

Chaussinand-Nogaret, G., *The French Nobility in the Eighteenth Century: From feudalism to enlightenment*. Translated by W. Doyle. Cambridge, 1985.

Clark, J. C. D., *English Society 1688–1832: Ideology, social structure and political practice during the ancien regime*. Cambridge, 1985.

Clark, J. C. D., 'On hitting the buffers: the historiography of England's ancien regime: a response', *Past and Present*, no. 117 (1987), pp. 195–207.

Clark, J. C. D., *Revolution and Rebellion: State and society in the seventeenth and eighteenth centuries*. Cambridge, 1986.

Clark, R., *Strangers and Sojourners at Port Royal: Being an account of the connections between the British Isles and the Jansenists of France and Holland*. Cambridge, 1932.

Clifton, R., 'The popular fear of Catholics during the English revolution', *Past and Present*, no. 52 (1971), pp. 23–55.

Colley, L., *In Defiance of Oligarchy: The Tory Party 1714–60*. 2nd edn. Cambridge, 1985.

Connell, K. H., 'Land legislation and Irish social life', *Economic History Review*, 2nd series, XI (1958), pp. 1–7.

Connolly, S. J., 'Religion and history', *Irish Economic and Social History*, X (1983), pp. 66–80.

Coombes, J., *A Bishop of the Penal Times: The life and times of John O'Brien, bishop of Cork and Ross, 1701–1769*. Cork, 1981.

Corish, P. J., 'The diocese of Ferns and the penal days', *The Past*, no. 8 (1970), pp 5–17.

Corish, P. J., *The Irish Catholic Experience: A historical survey*. Dublin, 1985.

Cranston, M., *Philosophers and Pamphleteers: Political theorists of the Enlightenment*. Oxford, 1986.

Cressy, D., *Bonfires and Bells: National memory and the Protestant calendar in Elizabethan and Stuart England*. Berkeley and Los Angeles, 1989.

Cullen, L. M., 'Catholic social classes under the penal laws', Power, T. P., and Whelan, K. (eds), *Endurance and Emergence: Catholics in Ireland in the eighteenth century*. Blackrock (Co. Dublin), 1990, pp. 57–84.

Cullen, L. [M.], 'Catholics under the penal laws', *Eighteenth-century Ireland: iris an dá chultúr*, I (1986), pp. 23–36.

Cullen L. M., 'Economic development, 1750–1800', Moody, T. W., and Vaughan,

W. E., (eds), *Eighteenth-century Ireland 1691–1800. A New History of Ireland.* Vol. 4. Oxford, 1986, pp. 159–95.

Cullen, L. M., *An Economic History of Ireland since 1660.* London, 1972.

Cullen, L. M., *The Emergence of Modern Ireland 1600–1900.* London, 1981.

Cullen, L. M., 'Galway merchants in the outside world, 1650–1800',Ó Cearbhail, D., (ed.), *Galway: Town and gown 1484–1984*, Dublin, 1984, pp. 63–89 and 287–93.

Cummins, S., 'Extra-parliamentary activity in Dublin in the 1760s', Comerford, R. V., *et al.* (eds), *Religion, Conflict and Coexistence: Essays presented to Monsignor Patrick J. Corish.* Dublin, 1990, pp. 118–34.

Cunningham, B., and Gillespie, R., 'The purposes of patronage: Brian Maguire of Knockninnny and his manuscripts', *Clogher Record*, XIII (1988), pp. 38–49.

Davies, N., 'The military traditions of the Polish *szlachta* 1700–1864', Király, B., and Rothenberg, G. E., (eds), *Special Topics and Generalizations on the 18th and 19th centuries.* War and Society in East Central Europe, Vol. 1. New York, 1979, pp. 37–46.

Dickinson, H. T., 'The eighteenth-century debate on the "glorious revolution"', *History*, LXI (1976), pp. 28–45.

Dickinson, H. T., *Liberty and Property: Political ideology in eighteenth-century Britain.* London, 1977.

Dickson, D. J. 'Catholics and trade in eighteenth-century Ireland: An old debate revisited'. Power, T. P., and Whelan, K. (eds), *Endurance and Emergence: Catholics in Ireland in the eighteenth century.* Blackrock (Co. Dublin), 1990, pp. 85–100.

Dickson, D. [J.], 'Middlemen', Bartlett, T., and Hayton, D. W. (eds), *Penal Era and Golden Age: Essays in Irish history, 1690–1800.* Belfast, 1979, pp. 162–85.

Dickson, D. [J], *New Foundations: Ireland 1660–1800.* Dublin, 1987.

Donnelly, J. S., 'Irish agrarian rebellion: the Whiteboys of 1769–76', *Proceedings of the Royal Irish Academy*, LXXXIII, C (1983), pp. 293–331.

Donnelly, J. S., 'The Rightboy movement 1785–8', *Studia Hibernica*, nos 17 and 18 (1977–8), pp. 120–202.

Donovan, R. K., 'The military origins of the Roman Catholic relief programme of 1778', *Historical Journal*, XXVIII (1985), pp. 79–102.

Doyle, W., *The Ancien Régime.* London, 1986.

Duby, G., *The Three Orders: Feudal society imagined.* Translated by A. Goldhammer. Chicago and London, 1982.

Duffy, E., 'Ecclesiastical democracy detected', *Recusant History*, X (1970), pp. 193–209 and 309–31; XVII (1975), pp. 123–48.

Dunn, J. A. W., *Beyond Liberty and Property: The process of self-recognition in eighteenth-century political thought.* Kingston (Ont.) and Montreal, 1883.

Dunne, T. J., 'The Gaelic response to conquest and colonisation: the evidence of the poetry', *Studia Hibernica*, no. 20 (1980), pp. 7–30.

Ekman, E. 'The Danish royal law of 1665', *Journal of Modern History*, XXIX (1957), pp. 102–7.

Elliott, M., *Partners in Revolution: The United Irishmen and France.* New Haven (Conn.) and London, 1982.

Elliot, M., *Wolfe Tone: Prophet of Irish independence.* New Haven (Conn.) and London, 1989.

Ellis, G., 'Rhine and Loire: Napoleonic elites and social order', Lewis, G., and

Lucas, C. (eds), *Beyond the Terror: Essays in French regional and social history, 1794–1815*. Cambridge, 1983, pp. 232–67.

Fagan, P., *The Second City: Portrait of Dublin 1700–1760*. Dublin, 1986.

Fedorowicz, J. K., *et al.* (eds), *A Republic of Nobles: Studies in Polish history to 1864*. Translated by J. K. Fedorowicz. Cambridge, 1982.

Fenning, H., *The Undoing of the Friars of Ireland: A study of the novitiate question in the eighteenth century*. Louvain, 1972.

FitzPatrick, W. J., *Irish Wits and Worthies: Including Dr Lanigan...* Dublin, 1873.

Ford, A., *The Protestant Reformation in Ireland, 1590–1641*. Studien zur interkulturellen Geschichte des Christentums, vol. 34. Frankfurt am Main, 1987.

Furlong, N., 'The times and life of Nicholas Sweetman, bishop of Ferns (1744–1786)', *Journal of the Wexford Historical Society*, no. 9 (1983–4), pp. 1–19.

Gagliardo, J. G., *From Pariah to Patriot: The changing image of the German peasant, 1770–1840*. Lexington (Ky), 1969.

Gasiorowski, Z. J., 'The "conquest" theory of the genesis of the Polish state', *Speculum*, XXX (1955), pp. 550–60.

Geoghegan, V., 'A Jacobite history: the Abbé MacGeoghegan's *History of Ireland*', *Eighteenth-century Ireland: iris an dá chultúr*, VI (1991), pp. 37–55.

George, M. D., *London Life in the Eighteenth Century*. 2nd ed. Harmondworth, 1966.

Gerhard, D., *Old Europe: A study of continuity, 1000–1800*. New York and London 1981.

Giblin, C., 'The Stuart nomination of Irish bishops, 1687–1765', *Irish Ecclesiastical Record*, 5th series, CV (1966), pp. 35–47.

Gillespie, R., 'Lords and commons in seventeenth century Mayo', Gillespie, R., and Moran, G. (eds), *'A Various Country': Essays in Mayo history 1500–1900*. Westport (Co. Mayo), 1987, pp. 44–66.

Gilley, S., 'Challoner as controversialist', Duffy, E. (ed.), *Challoner and His Church: A Catholic bishop in Georgian England*. London, 1981, pp. 90–111.

Goubert, P., *The Ancien Régime: French society 1600–1750*. Translated by S. Cox. London, 1973.

Greene, D. J., *The Politics of Samuel Johnson*. Port Washington (NY), 1973.

Greengrass, M., 'Conquest and coalescence', Greengrass, M. (ed.), *Conquest and Coalescence: The shaping of the state in early modern Europe*. London, 1991, pp. 1–24.

Haller, W., *Foxe's Book of Martyrs and the Elect Nation*. London, 1973.

Harvey, K. J., 'The family experience: the Bellews of Mount Bellew', Power, T. P., and Whelan, K. (eds), *Endurance and Emergence: Catholics in Ireland in the eighteenth century*. Blackrock (Co. Dublin), 1990, pp. 171–97.

Hay, D., *Annalists and Historians: Western historiography from the eighth to the eighteenth centuries*. London, 1977.

Hayes, R. J., (comp.), *Manuscript Sources for the History of Irish Civilisation*. 11 vols. Boston (Mass.), 1965.

Hersche, P., 'Der Österreichische Spätjansenismus: neue Thesen und Fragestellungen', Kovács, E. (ed.), *Katholische Aufklärung und Josephinismus*. Munich, 1979, pp. 180–93.

Hill, J. R., 'The meaning and significance of "Protestant ascendancy", 1787–1840',

Ireland after the Union: Proceedings of the second joint meeting of the Royal Irish Academy and the British Academy, London, 1986. Oxford, 1989.

Hill, J. R., 'National festivals, the state and "Protestant ascendancy" in Ireland, 1790–1829', *Irish Historical Studies*, XXIV (1984), pp. 30–51.

Hill, J. R., 'The Protestant response to repeal: the case of the Dublin working class', Lyons, F. S. L., and Hawkins, R. A. J. (eds), *Ireland under the Union: Varieties of tension: essays in honour of T. W. Moody*. Oxford, 1980, pp. 35–68.

Hill, J. R., 'Popery and Protestantism, civil and religious liberty: the disputed lessons of Irish history 1690–1812', *Past and Present*, no. 118 (1988), pp. 96–129.

Hill, J. R., 'The politics of privilege: Dublin corporation and the Catholic question', *Maynooth Review: Reiviú Mhá Nuad*, VII (1982), pp. 17–36.

Innes, J., 'Jonathan Clark, social history and England's "ancien regime"', *Past and Present*, no. 115 (1987), pp. 165–200.

Ives, M. C., *Enlightenment and National Revival: Patterns of interplay and paradox in late 18th century Hungary...* Ann Arbor (Mich.), 1979.

James, F. G., 'The Church of Ireland in the early eighteenth century', *Historical Magazine of the Protestant Episcopal Church*, XLVIII (1979), pp. 433–51.

Kellett, J. R., 'The breakdown of guild and corporation control over the handicraft and retail trade in London', *Economic History Review*, 2nd series, X (1958), pp. 381–94.

Kelly, J., 'Eighteenth-century ascendancy: a commentary', *Eighteenth-century Ireland: Iris an Dá Chultúr*, V (1990), pp. 173–87.

Kelly, J., 'The genesis of "Protestant ascendancy": the Rightboy disturbances of the 1780s and their impact upon Protestant opinion', O'Brien, G. (ed.), *Parliament, Politics and People: Essays in eighteenth-century Irish history*. Blackrock (Co. Dublin), 1989.

Kenyon, J., *The Popish Plot*. Harmondsworth, 1974.

Kerr, D. A., *Peel, Priests and Politics: Sir Robert Peel's administration and the Roman Catholic Church in Ireland*. Oxford, 1982.

Király, B., *Hungary in the late eighteenth century: the decline of enlightened despotism*. New York and London, 1969.

Kliger, S., *The Goths in England: A study in seventeenth and eighteenth century thought*. New York, 1972.

Kossmann, E. H., *The Low Countries 1780–1940*. Oxford, 1978.

Kramár, Z., 'The military ethos of the Hungarian nobility, 1700–1848', Király, B., and Rothenberg, G. E. (eds), *Special Topics and Generalizations on the 18th and 19th centuries*. War and Society in East Central Europe, Vol. 1. New York, 1979, pp. 67–79.

Lamont, W., *Godly Rule: Politics and religion, 1603–60*. London, 1969.

Laslett, P., *The World We Have Lost*. 2nd edn. London, 1971.

Lecky, W. E. H., *A History of Ireland in the Eighteenth Century*. 5 vols. London, 1913.

Lee, J., *The Modernisation of Irish Society 1848–1918*. Dublin, 1973.

Leighton, C. D. A., *The Irish Manufacture Movement, 1840–1843*. Maynooth (Co. Kildare), 1987.

Leighton, C. D. A., 'Gallicanism and the veto controversy: church, state and Catholic community in early nineteenth-century Ireland', Comerford, R. V., *et al.* (eds), *Religion, Conflict and Coexistence: Essays presented to Monsignor Patrick J. Corish.* Dublin, 1990, pp. 135–58.

Lévi-Strauss, C., *Structural Anthropology.* Translated by C. Jacobson and B. G. Schoepf. Harmondsworth, 1972.

Liechty, J., 'Testing the depth of Catholic/Protestant conflict: the case of Thomas Leland's "History of Ireland", 1773', *Archivium Hibernicum*, XLII (1987), pp. 13–28.

Loftis, J., *The Politics of Drama in Augustan England.* Oxford, 1963.

Luce, J. V., *Dublin Societies before the R. D. S.: A discourse delivered at a joint meeting of the Royal Dublin Society and the Dublin University Philosophical Society...on 10 December 1981.* [Dublin], n. d.

Macartney, C. A., 'Hungary', Goodwin, A. (ed.), *The European Nobility in the Eighteenth Century: Studies in the nobilities of the major European states in the pre-reform era.* London, 1953, pp. 118–35.

McCartney, D., *Democracy and its Nineteenth Century Irish Critics.* The O'Donnell Lectures, no. 22. Dublin, 1979.

McCormack, W. J., *Ascendancy and Tradition in Anglo-Irish Literary History from 1789 to 1939.* Oxford, 1985.

McCormack, W. J., 'Vision and revision in the study of eighteenth-century Irish parliamentary rhetoric' *Eighteenth-century Ireland: Iris an Dá Chultúr*, II (1987), pp. 7–35.

McCracken, J. L., The conflict between the Irish administration and parliament, 1753–6', *Irish Historical Studies*, III (1942), pp. 159–79.

McCracken, J. L., 'The ecclesiastical structure, 1714–60', Moody, T. W., and Vaughan, W. E. (eds), *Eighteenth-century Ireland 1691–1800. A New History of Ireland*, Vol. 4. Oxford, 1986, pp. 84–104.

McCracken, J. L., 'Protestant ascendancy and the rise of colonial nationalism, 1714–60', Moody, T. W., and Vaughan, W. E. (eds), *Eighteenth-century Ireland 1691–1800. A New History of Ireland*, Vol. 4. Oxford, 1986, pp. 105–22.

McCracken, J. L., 'The social structure and social life, 1714–60', Moody, T. W., and Vaughan, W. E. (eds), *Eighteenth-century Ireland 1691–1800. A New History of Ireland*, Vol. 4. Oxford, 1986, pp. 31–56.

MacCurtain, M., 'Rural society in post-Cromwellian Ireland', Cosgrove, A., and McCartney, D. (eds), *Studies in Irish History: Presented to R. Dudley Edwards.* Dublin. 1979, pp. 118–36.

McDowell, R. B., 'Colonial nationalism and the winning of parliamentary independence', Moody, T. W., and Vaughan, W. E. (eds), *Eighteenth-century Ireland 1691–1800. A New History of Ireland*, Vol. 4. Oxford, 1986, pp. 196–235.

McDowell, R. B., *Ireland in the Age of Imperialism and Revolution 1760–1800.* Oxford, 1979.

McDowell, R. B., *Irish Public Opinion 1750–1800.* London, 1944.

Maguire, W. A., 'Lord Donegal and the Hearts of Steel', *Irish Historical Studies*, XXI (1979), pp. 351–76.

Mackrell, J. Q. C., *The Attack on 'Feudalism' in Eighteenth-century France.* London, 1973.

McLynn, F. J., '"Good behaviour": Irish Catholics and the Jacobite rising of 1745', *Éire–Ireland*, XVI (1981), pp. 43–58.

Madden, R. R., *The United Irishmen: Their lives and times...* 4 vols. Dublin and London, 1858–60.

Mahony, T. H. D., *Edmund Burke and Ireland*. Cambridge (Mass.) and London, 1960.

Mayer, A. J., *The Persistence of the Old Regime: Europe to the Great War*. London, 1981.

Meenan, J., and Clarke, D., 'The R. D. S. 1731–1981', Meenan, J. and Clarke, D. (eds), *RDS: the Royal Dublin Society 1731–1981*. Dublin, 1981, pp. 1–55.

Miller, D. W., 'Presbyterianism and "modernization" in Ulster', *Past and Present*, no. 80 (1978), pp. 66–90.

Monod, P. K., *Jacobitism and the English People, 1688–1788*. Cambridge, 1989.

Mousnier, R., *The Institutions of France under the Absolute Monarchy 1598–1789*. Translated by B. Pearce and A. Goldhammer. 2 vols. Chicago and London, 1979–84.

National Library of Ireland (comp.), *Manuscript Sources for the History of Irish Civilisation: First supplement 1965–75*. 3 vols. Boston (Mass.), 1979.

Norman, E. R., *The Catholic Church and Ireland in the Age of Rebellion, 1859–1873*. London, 1965.

O'Conor, C., 'The early life of Charles O'Conor of Belanagare and the beginning of the Catholic revival in Ireland in the 18th century', 1930, Dublin, National Library of Ireland, IR 92 o162.

O'Conor, C., 'George Faulkner and Lord Chesterfield', *Studies*, XXV (1936), pp. 292–304.

Ó Cuív, B., 'Irish language and literature, 1691–1845', Moody, T. W., and Vaughan, W. E. (eds), *Eighteenth-century Ireland 1691–1800*. A New History of Ireland, Vol. 4. Oxford, 1986, pp. 374–423.

O'Donovan, D., 'The money bill dispute of 1753', Bartlett, T., and Hayton, D. W. (eds), *Penal Era and Golden Age: Essays in Irish history, 1690–1800*. Belfast, 1979, p. 55–87.

O'Ferrall, F., *Catholic Emancipation: Daniel O'Connell and the birth of Irish democracy*. Dublin, 1985.

O'Flaherty, E., 'Ecclesiastical politics and the dismantling of the penal laws in Ireland, 1774–82', *Irish Historical Studies*, XXVI (1988), pp. 33–50.

O'Halloran, C., 'Irish re-creations of the Gaelic past: the challenge of Macpherson's Ossian', *Past and Present*, no. 124 (1989), pp. 69–95.

Olsen, V. N., *John Foxe and the Elizabethan Church*. Berkeley, Los Angeles and London, 1973.

O'Malley, L., 'Patrick Darcy, Galway lawyer and politician, 1598–1668', Ó Cearbhail, D. (ed.), *Galway: Town and gown 1484–1984*, Dublin, 1984, pp. 90–109 and 293–6.

O'Neill, T. P., 'Discoverers and discoveries: the penal laws and Dublin property', *Dublin Historical Record*, XXXVII (1983), pp. 2–13.

Ó Tuama, S. (ed.), *An duanaire 1600–1900: Poems of the dispossessed*. Translated by Thomas Kinsella. Mountrath (Co. Laois), 1981.

Palmer, R. R., *The Age of Democratic Revolution: A political history of Europe and America*, 1760–1800. Princeton (NJ), 1959.

Palmer, S. H., *Police and Protest in England and Ireland 1780–1850*. Cambridge, 1988.

Pattison, R., *The Great Dissent: John Henry Newman and the Liberal heresy*. Oxford, 1991.

Pocock, J. G. A., *The Machiavellian Moment: Florentine political thought and the Atlantic republican tradition*. Princeton (NJ) and London, 1975.

Pocock, J. G. A., '1660 and all that: whig-hunting, ideology and historiography in the work of Jonathan Clark', *Cambridge Review*, CVIII (1987), pp. 125–8.

Popkin, R. H., 'The crisis of polytheism and the answers of Vossius, Cudworth and Newton', Force, J. E., and Popkin, R. H., *Essays on the context, nature, and influence of Isaac Newton's theology*. Dordrecht, 1990, pp. 9–25.

Popkin, R. H., 'The spiritualistic cosmologies of Henry More and Anne Conway', Hutton, S. (ed.), *Henry More (1614–1687): Tercentenary studies*. Dordrecht, 1990, pp. 97–114.

Power, T. P., 'Converts', Power, T. P., and Whelan, K. (eds), *Endurance and Emergence: Catholics in Ireland in the eighteenth century*. Blackrock (Co. Dublin), 1990, pp. 101–27.

Pritchard, A., *Catholic Loyalism in Elizabethan England*. London, 1979.

Reid, J. S., *History of the Presbyterian Church in Ireland...* 2nd edn. 3 vols. Belfast, 1867.

Reynolds, J. A., *The Catholic Emancipation Crisis in Ireland, 1823–1829*. Westport (Conn.), 1954.

Richet, D., 'Autour des origines idéologiques lointains de la revolution français: élites et despotisme', *Annales*, XXIV (1969), pp. 1–23.

Robbins, C., *The Eighteenth-century Commonwealthman: Studies in the transmission, development and circumstance of English liberal thought from the restoration of Charles II until the war with the thirteen colonies*. Cambridge (Mass.), 1959.

Robertson, J., *The Scottish Enlightenment and the Militia issue*. Edinburgh, 1985.

Rogers, N., 'Aristocractic clientage, trade and independency: popular politics in pre-radical Westminster', *Past and Present*, no. 61 (1973), pp. 70–106.

Rogers, P., *The Irish Volunteers and Catholic Emancipation (1778–1793): A neglected phase of Ireland's history*. London, 1934.

Rupp, E. G., *Religion in England 1688–1791*. Oxford History of the Christian Church. Oxford, 1986.

Ryan, C., 'Religion and state in seventeenth-century Ireland', *Archivium Hibernicum*, XXXIII (1975), pp. 122–32.

Sagarra, E., 'Frederick II and his image in eighteenth-century Dublin', *Hermathena*, no. 142 (1987), pp. 50–58.

Sharratt, M., '"Excellent professors and exact discipline": aspects of Challoner's Douai', Duffy, E. (ed.), *Challoner and His church: A Catholic bishop in Georgian England*. London, 1981, pp. 112–25.

Sheldon, E. K., *Thomas Sheridan of Smock-alley: Recording his life as actor and theater manager in both Dublin and London...* Princeton (NJ), 1967.

Simms, J. G., 'The establishment of Protestant ascendancy, 1691–1714', Moody, T. W. and Vaughan, W. E. (eds), *Eighteenth-century Ireland 1691–1800*. A New History of Ireland, Vol. 4. Oxford, 1986, pp. 1–30.

Simms, J. G., 'The restoration, 1660–85', Moody, T. W., *et al.* (eds), *Early Modern Ireland 1534–1691*. A New History of Ireland, Vol. 3. Oxford, 1976, pp. 420–53.

Simms, J. G., *William Molyneux of Dublin 1665–1698*. Blackrock (Co. Dublin), 1982.

Skinner, Q., *The Foundations of Modern Political Thought*. 2 vols. Cambridge, 1978.

Stephen, L., and Lee, S. (eds), *Dictionary of National Biography*. 22 vols. London, 1885–1901.

Stromberg, R. N., *Religious Liberalism in Eighteenth-century England.* Oxford, 1954.

Sutherland, D. M. G., *France 1789–1815: Revolution and counterrevolution.* London, 1985.

Swift, J., *History of the Dublin Bakers and Others.* Dublin, [1949].

Sykes, N., *William Wake, Archbishop of Canterbury...* 2 vols. Cambridge 1957.

Thomas, P. D. G., 'Party politics in eighteenth-century Britain: some myths and a touch of reality', *British Journal for Eighteenth-century Studies*, X (1987), pp. 201–10.

Tuveson, E. L., *Millennium and Utopia: A study in the background of the idea of progress.* Berkeley and Los Angeles, 1949.

Viner, J., *The Role of Providence in the Social Order: An essay in intellectual history.* Memoirs of the American Philosophical Society, Vol. 90. Philadelphia (Pa), 1972.

Voogt, N. J. J. de, *De Doelistenbeweging te Amsterdam in 1748.* Utrecht, 1914.

Walker, A. K., *William Law: His life and thought.* London, 1973.

Wall, M., *Catholic Ireland in the Eighteenth Century: Collected essays of...* Dublin, 1989.

Ward, R. [E.] and C. C., 'The Catholic pamphlets of Charles O'Conor (1710–1791)', *Studies*, LXVIII (1979), pp. 259–64.

Ward, R. [E.] and C. C., 'The ordeal of O'Conor of Belanagare', *Eire–Ireland*, XIV (1979), pp. 6–14.

Webb, J. J., *The Guilds of Dublin.* Dublin, 1929.

Whelan, K., 'The Catholic church in County Tipperary 1700–1900', Nolan, W. F., and McGrath, T. G., *Tipperary: History and society: interdisciplinary essays on the history of an Irish county.* Dublin, 1985, pp. 215–55 and 454–56.

Whelan, K., 'The regional impact of Irish Catholicism 1700–1850', Smyth, W. J., and Whelan, K. (eds), *Common Ground: Essays on the historical geography of Ireland presented to T. Jones Hughes...* Cork, 1988, pp. 253–77.

Whelan, K., 'The Catholic community in eighteenth-century County Wexford', Power, T. P., and Whelan, K. (eds), *Endurance and Emergence: Catholics in Ireland in the eighteenth century.* Blackrock (Co. Dublin), 1990, pp. 129–70.

Wiener, C. Z., 'The beleaguered isle: a study of Elizabethan and early Jacobean anti–Catholicism', *Past and Present*, no. 51 (1971), pp. 27–62.

Woltjer, J. J., 'Dutch privileges, real and imaginary', Bromley, J. S., and Kossmann, E. S. (eds), *Britain and the Netherlands: Some political mythologies: papers delivered to the fifth Anglo–Dutch Historical Conference.* The Hague, 1975, pp. 19–35.

Wyse, T., *Historical Sketch of the Late Catholic Association of Ireland.* 2 vols. London, 1829.

VI. UNPUBLISHED DISSERTATIONS

Day, J. P., 'The Catholic question in the Irish parliament, 1760–82', University College, Dublin (1973).

Leighton, [C.]D. A., 'Theobald McKenna and the Catholic question', St Patrick's College, Maynooth (1985).

Murphy, S., 'The Lucas affair: a study of municipal and electoral politics in Dublin, 1742–9', University College, Dublin (1981).

O'Donoghue, P., 'The Catholic church and Ireland in the age of revolution and rebellion, 1782–1803', University College, Dublin (1975).

Sheehan, C., 'Charles O'Conor of Belangare [sic]: a survey of his literary activities', Fordham (1948).

Index